A WRITER PREPARES

A LAWRENCE BLOCK PRODUCTION

A Writer Prepares

LAWRENCE BLOCK

Foreword

March 3, 2020
Newberry, South Carolina

HELLO THERE.

I am at my desk in the second bedroom of a loft apartment a few blocks from the center of downtown Newberry. The town itself is about thirty-five miles northwest of Columbia, the state capital. Last August my wife and I came to Newberry so that I could spend a semester as writer-in-residence at Newberry College, where my friend Warren Moore has served as a professor of English for nearly twenty years.

I got here with the anticipation of one about to fulfill a longstanding fantasy. I had never graduated from college. While it could be argued that six decades as a self-employed professional writer ought to be credential enough, one generally required a doctorate to teach at a college or university—and the only diploma I'd ever earned was from Buffalo's Louis J. Bennett High School. Now Bennett was a good school, and in my four years there I'd earned a Jeweled Honor Pin and graduated as an officer of the class of 1955.

I was, as you'll read further on, the Class Poet.

And I had, if in a non-academic fashion, been a teacher of writing for a long time. From 1976 to 1990 I contributed a monthly column on the writing of fiction to *Writer's Digest,* and over the years published half a dozen instructional books on the subject. I conducted a week-long seminar at Antioch College in the late 1970s, and another a quarter-century later, at Writers' Week, the annual festival in Listowel, Co. Kerry.

And there was *Write For Your Life*. Inspired by my own exposure to facets of what for a while was called the Human Potential Movement, in the early 1980s I developed an experiential seminar for writers, and for a couple of years my wife and I hopscotched the country, presenting intense day-long interactional sessions with great success. (But that success was not financial. We earned, I eventually determined, something like 35¢ an hour for our troubles, and I've come to see that as a Good Thing; had WFYL paid off financially, we might have felt compelled to go on doing it, and a couple of years was enough. By the time we stopped, the whole business had begun to feel like a Guru Trip, and that was not a role I fancied for myself.)

So I was not entirely without teaching experience. And I had actually served as an adjunct professor at Hofstra University in 1982, riding the Long Island Rail Road to Hempstead once a week, presumably to teach a class in writing mystery fiction. I started with three students, and before long only one of them was showing up, and that's as much as I recall of the affair. Did he ever turn anything in? Did I have anything to say to him?

I've no idea. And I can only hope my student, whoever he may have been and whoever he may be now, has as little recollection of the whole business as I do. Some things are best forgotten.

SO. I CAME to Newberry, as you might imagine, with the mixed feelings likely to attend the fulfillment of a fantasy. I'd be offering two courses, a workshop for fiction writers and a literature survey course on crime fiction. Both classes would meet every Tuesday and Thursday from late

August until early December—and if I wasn't happy with the results, it was something I would never have to do again.

I thought I might enjoy it, and I did. I feared I might not know what the hell I was doing, and I didn't. I had, to one extent or another, all the hopes and fears you would expect, and probably a few more besides.

But what I honestly didn't anticipate was that I would fall in love with the school and the town. None of the scenarios that I'd entertained had me coming back in the fall of 2020 for another go at the Professor Block routine. (I'll be teaching two classes again, but they'll both be writing courses. One will be the workshop as it evolved last fall. The other will be Self-Realization Through Writing, a class for students with no interest in or aptitude for writing per se, and it's an apple that won't have fallen very far from the Write For Your Life tree.)

And so we've taken this apartment. We'll live here in the fall, when I'm teaching. We'll probably visit on other occasions, for a week or two at a time. And I can always catch the Silver Star at Penn Station and come down on my own, to hole up and get some work done.

As I'm doing now.

WHILE I WAS teaching last fall, I managed to fit in a lunch with Richard Layman, best known as the biographer of and leading authority on Dashiell Hammett. He drove over from Columbia, and over coffee invited me to a reception he and his wife were giving for James Ellroy, the self-styled Mad Dog of Crime Fiction, on the occasion of Ellroy's presenting the library of the University of South Carolina with his papers.

I hadn't seen Jim in at least twenty years, and welcomed the chance to touch base with him. And, while I was there, I mentioned to Richard that I was taking a more cavalier attitude toward my own papers, selling off some manuscripts to collectors and tossing out the rest.

The look on his face gave me pause.

And so I wound up saying that, if he could set it up with the appropriate people at the university, I'd be pleased to fill a few cartons with manuscripts and correspondence and contracts and, well, whatever else I had around.

And one thing led to another, and after a couple of phone conversations with USC Library's Elizabeth Sudduth, I was back in New York sifting through storage bins and rummaging through boxes and closets, and before I was done I'd sent more than thirty hefty cartons of material to Columbia.

What they'll make of it I have no idea. Nor do I very much care. Every scrap of paper I sent them is one less item my kids will have to throw out.

Nor is that all I've gained from the enterprise. I came across various manuscripts I'd written and set aside. A few unfinished short stories. The memoir of a career criminal turned confidential informant. A commissioned novel which had pleased the prospective publishers well enough; they'd paid me for it, but had then found themselves legally restrained from publishing it.

I might finish one or another of the short stories, though I have to say it seems unlikely. I might do something with either or both of the books, if the rights are clear and the material strikes me as worth publishing.

But there was a third book-length manuscript. *A Writer Prepares,* I'd called it, and it ran to a bit over fifty thousand words, and here I am in Newberry, sitting at a white parson-style desk that I bought from Walmart and put together, not without effort, all by myself, writing this introduction for it.

I DIDN'T OPEN a box, pull out the manuscript, and blurt out *Oh my God, I forgot all about this!* I hadn't forgotten about it, not for a moment, and when I started rooting around for material to send to USC I knew that *A Writer Prepares* was one of the manuscripts I could expect to find. I remembered writing it in the course of a positively feverish week at Ragdale, the Illinois art colony, and I remembered the utter exhaustion, physical and mental and emotional, that overwhelmed me by the time I'd brought it back to New York.

I figured I'd set it aside for a while. That *while* stretched to twenty-five years.

How'd that happen? I'm not sure, and can more readily explain *why* it happened, which is that I didn't want to endure any more of what I'd undergone at Ragdale. It had been exhilarating, that week-long plunge into the past, but it had drained me, while forcing me to look at parts of my history it was less than a joy to examine.

"When you gaze long into an abyss," Nietzsche told us, "the abyss also gazes into you." I'm not sure I know what that means, and I'm not entirely convinced that Nietzsche knew, either, but I liked the sound of it. And I was profoundly grateful for the week I'd spent gazing into my own particular abyss—but that didn't mean I was ready to scurry back for another long look.

Well, it's no mean trick for a writer to find a way to abandon a manuscript. One that's worked well for me over the years was to show the thing to my then-agent. Knox Burger, who as you'll read had bought my first crime novel during his tenure as editor-in-chief at Gold Medal, went on to become a literary agent, and in the course of time became *my* agent. On several occasions I got stuck on manuscripts and showed them to him, and in each case he obligingly suggested I do something else instead. If I wanted to abort a project, Knox could be counted on to hand me a coat hanger.

Not this time. He thought it was interesting, and worth finishing. It wasn't a candidate for a bestseller list, but it was certainly readable, and looked to be publishable.

And it was time for him to negotiate a new contract with William Morrow, who'd been publishing my Matthew Scudder novels and would want to go on doing so. He suggested offering them a package—two or three novels, plus *A Writer Prepares.* Toward that end, could I write some sort of introduction for what I'd brought home from Ragdale?

I could and did, hammering out half a dozen pages, which you'll see shortly. When you do, you'll note the following coda, bracketed and italicized:

[*NB: This intro will be finished after the book itself has been completed, and will very likely be substantially rewritten at that time.*]

Ya think?

KNOX MADE THE deal with Morrow. I don't remember the terms, but I believe it called for me to deliver three novels and the memoir over the course of the next three or four years. It was clear from the numbers that they were taking *A Writer Prepares* in order to get the novels. They'd be paying a respectable advance for the memoir, but the other three books were going to cost them a good deal more.

I recall the advance for the memoir as $35,000, and they'd have handed over half of that on signature, the balance to be paid on delivery and acceptance of the completed manuscript.

They never paid the balance, because I never delivered another word of the book. I wrote the requisite novels, even as I was writing Bernie Rhodenbarr mysteries for another publisher, but I never so much as thought to glance at *A Writer Prepares,* let alone resume work on it. No one at Morrow ever pressed me for the book, and somewhere along the way it was clear to me that the book was, at the very least, as dead as a doornail.

So I bought it back. I don't believe I wrote out a check. It seems more likely that I had them deduct what they'd initially paid me from what they owed me for a newly-completed novel.

Whatever form repayment took, it brought with it a sense of relief. I have always hated owing anything to anybody. It may not keep me up nights, but I'm a whole lot more comfortable when I'm free of obligations. For some years now, I've shaken off the usual pattern of making a deal before a book was completed. I'm much happier writing the book first, and then offering the finished product to a publisher.

My failure to finish *A Writer Prepares* had never given me much in the way of discomfort. It helped that I knew that no one at Morrow cared if I ever delivered the book. But it would come to mind now and again, and so it was a pleasure to close the books on it and forget the whole thing.

And so I did.

Oh, I knew it was there. In a manila envelope in the closet, just steps from the desk. I could fish it out and look it over anytime I wanted.

I never did.

UNTIL THIS PAST December, when I returned to New York and set about rounding up my papers for South Carolina. It turned up, as I knew it would, and for a few days I let it sit there, in its manila envelope, and then one day I took it out and had a look at it.

It had surfaced at the perfect time. A variety of factors had combined to make my months at Newberry remarkably productive. I wasn't doing any new writing to speak of, aside from introductions to two anthologies, one of them mine. But during that time I put an anthology together, set another one in motion, and astonished myself by taking a pair of long-dormant projects and saw them through to publication.

One was a collection of nonfiction pieces I'd written over the years— travel essays, love letters to New York City, a remembrance of my mother, a piece on collecting old subway cars, and no end of introductions to one thing or another. I'd already self-published with some success *The Crime of Our Lives,* a collection of what I'd written over the years on mystery fiction, and I'd always figured a non-mystery companion volume was in order. I had a desktop folder full of appropriate material, but somehow I never got around to doing anything about it.

Similarly, starting in the fall of 2009 I'd written 33 monthly columns on philatelic subjects for *Linn's Stamp News.* I'd published the first two dozen as an ebook, but never did much of anything with it, and for some time I'd known I ought to do a proper job of self-publishing the complete collection of columns, as both an ebook and a printed volume.

Somehow, by the time I caught the train for New York, both books were done. By the year's end, both were published and selling.

Amazing.

And when I had a look at the book I'd abandoned a quarter of a century earlier, I was predisposed to see its possibilities. Because I'd embraced the world of self-publishing, and done reasonably well with it, I didn't have to worry over what publishers to approach and how to fashion it for their approval. All I had to do was make the book into what I wanted it to be.

I started reading, and was pleased to discover that I liked what I read. I could see why Knox hadn't encouraged me to abandon the thing. What I couldn't see was why I'd never returned to it, and that wasn't attributable to the writing, but to the person who had written it.

I think he was the wrong age for it.

As I'd observed when I first imagined writing about those early years, the task called for someone young enough to remember and old enough not to care—about revealing too much, about other people's reactions. I was young enough, certainly, and what I see on the page now suggests that I wasn't much concerned with what readers might think. But something evidently did concern me, so that once the rush of furious creative energy abated, once I'd hammered out fifty thousand words and stopped to catch my breath, something within me evidently concluded that enough was enough.

Well, I'm older now.

AND NOW WHAT?

The simplest approach, and surely the easiest, would lie in publishing exactly what I wrote in 1994, neither more nor less. The problem is that there's no resolution; the account of my early days simply stops on one of those days, for no apparent reason beyond the fact that my stay at Ragdale had run its course. It was time to go home, and I could stroll a bit further down Memory Lane once I got there.

Except, of course, that I didn't.

One thinks of Samuel Taylor Coleridge, waking from an opium dream with a head full of poetry. He began writing and the words began to flow, and they went on flowing until he was famously interrupted by an otherwise unidentified person from Porlock.

And that was that. The words stopped their flow, and "Kubla Khan" never got any longer.

This is not to say that Ragdale was Xanadu, but there's something to the analogy. Coleridge wrote the poem in 1797 and didn't publish it until Byron talked him into it in 1816. That's almost twenty years, but "Kubla Khan" did not spend all that time in a manila envelope in the hall closet. Its author would trot it out from time to time and read it to groups of friends.

Few of them, I would suppose, hailed from Porlock.

Did he make little changes here and there? And did he tart it up some when he sold it to publisher John Murray?

Beyond fixing typos and tweaking the occasional infelicitous phrase, I've fought the temptation to improve on my original draft—not because it couldn't use it, but out of a disinclination to patch 1994's holes with a miracle fiber from 2020.

If that smacks of artistic integrity, well, my apologies.

SO WHAT WE have here, then, is a set of those Russian matryoshka dolls, each nesting within another. An 81-year-old man is groping for words, trying to introduce a man of 55, who'll tell you what he remembers about a fellow in his teens and early twenties.

A troika of unreliable narrators?

Perhaps. Nevertheless, the next fifty thousand words are the ones I brought home from Illinois. After you've read them, we'll see where we lead us.

Introduction

Spring 1994
New York City

I NEVER EXPECTED to be writing this.

IN NOVEMBER OF 1992, a fellow named Jim Seels came up to me at a signing in southern California to propose that he publish a bibliography of my work. I promised my cooperation. When the project was underway, I got a call from him. "What I need now," he said, "is a list of all your pen names, and the various books you wrote under them."

I explained that that was out of the question. I was perfectly willing to acknowledge three books I had written as Paul Kavanagh and four as Chip Harrison, and indeed had had those books reprinted under my own name. But my earlier pseudonymous work was something I did not want to talk about, for any number of reasons.

"Your fans want to know about these books," Seels said.

I quoted the Stones, something about not always getting what you want. That night I sat down and wrote a 1200-word essay on pen names, and why mine would remain unacknowledged. I explained how little I had thought of the books while I was writing them, how idiotic editing had made some of them even worse than they were when they left my typewriter, and how the publishers sometimes cavalierly placed my pen name on somebody else's book, or somebody else's pen name on mine. Furthermore, I had employed ghost writers over the years, so there were many books published under my pen names, and purposely crafted by their authors to resemble my work, which I had not written. Or even read.

I sent the essay to Seels. He liked it well enough, and agreed to run it in the bibliography. It was clear, though, that he'd have preferred my coming clean in print.

A FEW MONTHS later, Ernie Bulow came to town. Ernie, a writer, small publisher, and Indian trader based in Gallup, New Mexico, had done a fine book with Tony Hillerman called *Talking Mysteries*. He'd published a limited edition of the book, with University of New Mexico Press issuing a trade edition. The book sold well and got an Edgar nomination, and Ernie had agreed to do five similar volumes, one with me. We were to call it *After Hours*, and it would include several lengthy conversations of ours plus a couple of odd essays and my first published short story.

We sat down together and he set up the tape recorder. We weren't far into the first day's session when he brought up the subject of pseudonymous work. I gave him a short version of my essay for Seels, explaining why I didn't want to get into all that.

"But people want to know about all that," he said.

"People in hell want ice water," I said, quoting my mother-in-law.

"Look," he said, "there are a lot of people who already know the names you used. There's been quite a bit of research done." And he showed me an annotated list of my books from a paperback dealer named Lynn Munroe. It was over thirty pages long, and listed 200 items, some in a single line, some with lengthy paragraphs explaining why the author assumed the book in question was mine.

I explained my stance to Ernie. I refused to confirm or deny my authorship of pseudonymous books, would not sign them when they were presented to me, and certainly did not want to sit around and discuss them now. He did what he could to sway me from this position, failed, and gave in gracefully.

We talked widely on other topics for several hours. At the end I asked if I could borrow Lynn Munroe's list. He said he had a copy, and I was welcome to it.

IT KEPT ME up all night. There were books listed which I hadn't written, of course, but there were also books that I had written—but hadn't thought of in years. The effort that had gone into figuring out what I had or hadn't written was remarkable. Here's the entry for a 1960 title called *I Sell Love*, by Liz Crowley: "Monarch MB508 . . . this Human Behavior Series entry purports to be the true account of one prostitute's life. Actually it's a Block fiction. When Victor Berch ran his excellent Monarch pseudonyms checklist, he mentioned that two of the authors had asked him not to reveal their pen names. From my own interviews I knew that the only two of that gang who don't own up to their books are Block and Westlake. And Westlake's Monarch pseudonym . . . is immediately transparent to anyone reading the author profile. That left Block . . . . And so I visited the Library of Congress during my last trip to Washington, DC. Unlike the Nightstands and Midwoods, the Monarchs are all copyrighted. That's how we know that Lawrence Block wrote *I Sell Love*. By the way, Liz mentions the name of a movie she likes on p. 28: *A Sound of Distant Drums*. And on p. 46 she meets Honour Mercy, "Honey" from Kentucky, *A Girl Called Honey* from Lord & Marshall's Midwood 41."

Reading all of this stirred me up more than I ever would have imagined. I clucked at the flights of fancy some of these researchers were capable of, finding hidden meanings where none existed. I got a certain amount of satisfaction from the several pen names of mine that they'd missed. More than anything else, though, I simply felt overwhelmed by having been suddenly ambushed by my own past.

"Someday," I told my wife, "I ought to write about those years."

"You should," she agreed.

"But not yet," I said. "I'll have to wait until the time comes when I'm still young enough to remember it all, but old enough so I don't give a shit."

THAT ALL HAPPENED in April of 1993. In October I attended Bouchercon in Omaha, where a fellow named Martin Hawk was offering for sale his voluminous guide to pseudonyms. He had me in there, of course, with most but not all of the names I'd used, and several I hadn't. He told me he'd certainly appreciate it if I could help him make his list more accurate for the next edition. I told him it was already more accurate than I would have preferred.

"Someday I'll write about those days," I told a couple of people. "But not yet."

IN FEBRUARY OF '94 I went to Ragdale, a writers' colony in Lake Forest, Illinois. I had a book to write and went to work on it, getting almost half of it completed in the first two weeks of my four-week stay. Then, as sometimes happens, I realized I'd taken a wrong turn in the book. The first third of what I'd written was sound, but I was going to have to scrap the rest, replot, and do it over. And it was going to have to wait, because I wasn't ready to undertake that task yet.

So what would I do with the rest of my time there?

First thing I did was spend a couple of days writing a long short story ("Keller in Shining Armor"). Then, while contemplating my next move, I got a message from Otto Penzler; he would need an introduction for the hardcover edition he was going to publish of *The Canceled Czech*, a book

I had written in 1966. There was no rush, he said, but I figured it was something I could get out of the way while I decided what to do next.

I had more trouble with it than I'd expected. I found myself reminiscing in the intro about what my life had been like when I wrote the early Tanner books, of which *The Canceled Czech* was the second. With the introduction about two-thirds completed, I realized that I was ready for a longer stroll down Memory Lane—that I was in fact ready to write that memoir about the early years.

I couldn't get to sleep that night. My mind was racing all over the place. I woke up the next day and got to work as soon as I'd had my breakfast, and I literally could not stop working. I broke for meals, then kept going back to it. I didn't stop until midnight, by which time I'd written 8000 words. Even then I couldn't get my mind to quit, and I had a hell of a time getting to sleep.

The next morning I went right to it again. In a little more than a week, I would write 50,000 words.

AROUND THE TIME I was getting ready to be a writer, Erskine Caldwell published *Call It Experience*. It was his autobiography, and he began by explaining that it concerned only his life as a writer. That was all he felt inclined to write about, he said, and probably all that anyone would be interested in reading about, anyway.

That made sense to me, and it still does. I'd rather not burden you with too much in the way of personal details. Nor am I inclined to let this book be an invasion of anyone's privacy, least of all my own.

But writing, as I've remarked elsewhere, is a holistic pursuit; it is done with the entire self, not just the tips of the fingers. And so this book, too, inevitably reports on the whole self.

It is as honest and forthright as I am capable of being at the moment. I could not have written it a year ago. Had I postponed writing it another year, I might have been inclined to open myself up even more; on the other hand, I might have thought better about the whole enterprise.

[*NB: This intro will be finished after the book itself has been completed, and will very likely be substantially rewritten at that time.*]

1

February, 1994
Lake Forest, Illinois

IN AUGUST OF 1956 I got off a train at Grand Central Station. Seven hours earlier I had boarded that train in Buffalo, where I had lived all my life until I'd gone off to college the previous fall. The college was Antioch, in Yellow Springs, Ohio. Antioch had—and still has—as a distinguishing feature a program of cooperative education. The year was split into four semesters, two of them devoted to academic pursuits on the Yellow Springs campus, the other two spent at a job obtained through the school's Co-op department. While some students did manage to save a portion of their earnings, that wasn't the point; the jobs were supposed to provide real-world vocational experience, with the twin goals of enabling you to make an informed career choice and giving you a head start on other eager beavers.

The school encouraged freshman students to spend their whole first year on campus. I did so, and, when the academic year ended in June, I joined my parents and sister, Betsy, on a trip to Miami Beach. We drove down and back in my father's '56 Chevrolet. It was blue, and he had only recently traded in a brown '54 Chevrolet for it. I think he may have regretted the move. "I never had a dime's worth of trouble with that car," he said more than once. The new car had its baptism of fire on the trip north. Somewhere in the Carolinas I threw a cigarette out the window, and it blew back in and wound up underneath the pillow I was sitting on. We kept smelling smoke, and scanned the horizon for signs of a forest fire. At last we pulled over and discovered that the fire was in our car, and that I was sitting on it.

My father, I must say, took this remarkably well, although I'm sure it must have deepened his regret at having parted with the other car.

PAUL GRILLO MET me at Grand Central. He was several years older than I, and had been one of my hall advisors the previous year. Now we were going to room together for three months in New York. Paul was from Elkhart, Indiana, but he had lived in New York before as an Antioch co-op, and was reasonably familiar with the city. He had decided that we ought to live in Greenwich Village, and, arriving before me, had found us a large furnished room at 147 West 14th Street. He told me how to get there and pointed me toward the subway.

I had been in New York twice before, the first time in December of 1948, when I was ten and a half years old. My Dad had grown up in the city. He went to Cornell, where he met and married my mother, a Buffalo girl. They'd lived very briefly in New York after graduation, then moved to Buffalo and remained there ever after. He wanted to show me New York, and it seems to me that we went everywhere and did everything in what must have been a frenzied weekend. We stayed at the Commodore Hotel. We saw the Statue of Liberty on Bedloes Island, we went to the top of the Empire State Building, we rode the Third Avenue El, we saw Ray Bolger on Broadway in *Where's Charley?* and were in the studio audience at *Toast of the Town*, the Ed Sullivan show. This last was a little hard for me to grasp, because I didn't know what television was. I suppose they must have had TV in Buffalo by then, but I didn't know anybody who had a set.

Several years later, we'd made another trip to the city. This time my mother and sister came as well. We stayed at the Commodore again and saw *South Pacific* and *The King and I*. I remember two things from that trip. At *South Pacific*, Betsy, five years younger than I, thought Bloody Mary was snarling "Stingy basket!" at Marines who aroused her displeasure. The rest of us found this amusing, and for a while the phrase became a family joke. And one afternoon my father and I went for a walk and, in a Times Square novelty shop, I came upon a group of mildly obscene photos. I can only recall one of them—I may very well have only seen one of them. It was a trick photo, and showed a woman with three breasts. The caption read, "Wanted—a man with three hands!"

I HAD A job waiting for me in New York. I was to be a mail boy at Pines Publications, at 110 East 40th Street. The company was owned by a man named Ned Pines, and was run, as far as I could tell, by another man named Frank Lualdi. Mr. Lualdi ordered his lunch every day, not from an ordinary coffee shop, but from an upscale place called the Brass Rail. For years afterward I would think of him whenever I walked past the Brass Rail—which, if I remember correctly, was on the east side of Fifth Avenue between 42nd and 43rd. I never went in, because I figured I didn't belong there. It was for important people like Mr. Lualdi.

Pines was a diversified operation, publishing a movie fan magazine, a few die-hard pulps including *Ranch Romances*, a *Readers Digest* imitator, a handful of comic books, and a solid paperback line, Popular Library. My work consisted largely of distributing the mail and interoffice memoranda and running errands. For this I received $40 a week, of which I took home $34. (Toward the very end of my employment, I and the two non-Antioch mail boys received an unsolicited raise to $45.)

The job wasn't much of a challenge, nor was there much you could learn there. I'd chosen it because it was in publishing, which seemed at least peripherally related to writing, and because it was in New York, which was where you went if you wanted to be a writer. I suppose I spent sixty or sixty-five days at Pines, but I don't remember much of what I did there. Everyone, as I recall, was remarkably nice to me. And, although the position was not designed to be A Job With A Future, it became one, at least for a moment.

A little more than halfway through my term there, the head of the promotion department called me over as I was depositing his mail on his desk. I think his name was Victor Robinson, and he informed me that his assistant, whose name was Jules Shapiro, was going to be leaving at the end of the month. Would I be interested in the position?

I might be, I said, but I was an Antioch student on a co-op job, and I was sort of scheduled to go back to school the end of October, but—

"For God's sake, go back to college," he said. "You don't want to drop out of school for something like this."

That was the end of that. Looking back, I suppose he was right. But the fact of the matter was that I did want to drop out of school. I never seriously considered it, not after he'd made it so clear what he thought of the idea, but I'd have loved to do just that. It wasn't that I didn't like school. I felt entirely at home at Antioch, and, while I didn't care much about studying, I liked the hanging out well enough. I didn't want to drop out in order to get away from it all. I wanted to drop out in order to get on with it.

I PROBABLY LEARNED more than I knew at Pines Publications. But the job there wasn't the point.

New York was the point.

The first day, after I'd lugged my suitcase up three flights of stairs and settled in on 14th Street, I walked all over the Village. That very night I managed to wander onto Barrow Street. At 15 Barrow was a jazz club called Café Bohemia. I'd heard of it; my freshman roommate, Steve

Schwerner, who'd introduced me to jazz, had talked of listening to Charlie Parker at the Bohemia. (Steve came to Antioch determined to become a jazz disc jockey, and had a program his first year on WYSO, the campus station. He had already decided that his professional name would be Steve Charles, and was concerned that his listeners at Antioch might lose track of him years hence. Thus he started things off each week by welcoming his audience to the Steve Charles Show, "with your host, Steve Schwerner." Steve wound up getting a doctorate in education, heading the guidance department at Queens College, and returning to Antioch as Dean of Students, where they gave him a weekly program on WYSO. He plays some of the same music he played then, but he doesn't call it the Steve Charles Show this time around.)

I'd missed my chance to hear Charlie Parker—he'd died before I knew what jazz was—but that first night at the Bohemia I bought a bottle of beer for fifty cents and stood at the bar and listened to Al Cohn and Zoot Sims. For the rest of my stay I bounced all over the Village—the bars, the coffee houses, the park. I played bridge in the owner's private game in the back room of Caricatures, a tiny Macdougal Street coffee house next door to the old Kettle of Fish saloon. There was a hand-written poem of Maxwell Bodenheim's in the window, and Joe Gould was across the street at Minetta's, and Café Rienzi was just up the block, and every single day I saw and heard things I had never seen or heard before.

On Sundays I joined the crowd singing folk songs around the circle in Washington Square Park. Guys in dark suits came and took our pictures every week, and the conventional wisdom held that they were FBI agents. I can't imagine who else would have wanted our photographs. I suppose I have a file somewhere, and under the Freedom of Information Act I'm entitled to see what's in it, but thanks to the Freedom of Apathy Act I don't have to bother. So the hell with it.

Paul and I stayed at 147 West 14th for two weeks, along with Fred

Anliot, another Antioch co-op. Fred had pulled strings to get a job on the railroad and was a fireman on a diesel train. Union featherbedding was responsible for the position—there's no fire on a diesel, so what do you need a fireman for?—and he was making union wages, which came to about two and a half times what I was making. I don't know what Paul was earning. It seems to me he was unemployed for much of our three-month stint.

We left the place on 14th Street because someone decided it cost too much. It set us back $24 a week, which doesn't seem that burdensome split three ways, but we decided we could do better. We moved to a much smaller room on the ground floor at 108 West 12th Street. There was a single bed with a box spring and mattress. We put the mattress on the floor and rotated; one of us took the box spring, another the mattress, and the third slept on the floor. That room was only $12 a week, but it was unendurable. We were there for two weeks, and then Paul—it must have been Paul—found us a first-floor front apartment at 54 Barrow Street. It was a three-room railroad flat with a living room and a kitchen and a bedroom, and it was in the heart of the most desirable part of the Village and right around the corner from the Sheridan Square subway stop. Fred returned to Antioch in September, and Paul and I stayed put until we went back to school at the beginning of November.

Shortly after the move to Barrow Street, the Sunday afternoon sessions in Washington Square took on a new dimension. The police chased everybody away from the fountain at six, and on one such occasion Paul and I invited those who wanted to keep the party going to come back to Barrow Street with us. This immediately became a part of the ritual, and we had a houseful of noisy strangers every Sunday for a little over a month. At that point the crowd was too large, and somebody had a house—a whole house!—on Spring Street, and from that day on everybody went from the Circle to Spring Street, and our days as hosts were over.

I was too busy discovering the world and falling in and out of love to do any writing. But sometime that October, on a Saturday or Sunday afternoon, I was alone at the Barrow Street apartment. I decided to try writing something. I set up my Royal portable on the table in the kitchen and went to work. The first sentence was "Anyone who starves in this country deserves it," which now seems to me rather lacking in compassion. The narrator was a young man who lived by his wits, stealing from his employer, then moving up to mail fraud. He sneered and boasted for six or seven pages, then ran out of steam and shut up.

I showed the story to a few people, and they found nice things to say about it. Then I set it aside, and at the end of the month I stuck it in my suitcase and went back to Antioch.

One course in which I enrolled upon my return was a writing workshop led by Nolan Miller. Nolan had published several novels during the forties, and had sold some short stories years ago to the slick magazines. His workshop met once a week, and the format was not unusual. He would read something one of us had handed in, and we would discuss it. I suppose one could say of this approach what Churchill said of democracy: It's an utterly terrible system, but every other system is worse.

I wrote a story almost every week for the workshop. This was fairly remarkable, in that most of the other members wrote next to nothing, although some of what they did write was, as I recall, rather good. I cannot for the life of me remember anything about any of the stories or sketches I turned in.

Did I try to sell them anywhere? I think not, but I couldn't swear to it. During my freshman year I had been a passionate submitter of my work. I wrote two- and three-page short stories, dopey little vignettes after Salinger, witless fables in which the survivors of a global holocaust turn out to be Adam and Eve—the same kind of juvenile crap everybody writes at that age. I wrote poems, too, and I came to prefer poems to short stories for a couple of excellent reasons. First of all, they were shorter. They didn't take as long. Just as important, it was a lot harder to tell if they were any good or not.

I sent my work to all the best magazines in the field. I collected rejection slips from *The Atlantic* and *Harper's* and *Poetry* and *The New Yorker*. I sent things out expecting them to come back, and come back they did, as well they might have done. Each returned with a rejection slip attached, and I treasured these rejection slips and pinned them up on my bulletin board. On one, from *Farm Journal* (and I have no idea what poems I sent to *Farm Journal*, or why) there was a personal note typed at the bottom of the form slip. "We would have printed your poems," it said, "but felt they would have gone over the heads of our readers. Sorry!" My friends were impressed. I don't know why; couldn't they guess who'd typed it?

Back at school, I wrote stories for Nolan's workshop but mostly submitted poems to magazines. One little magazine, a respectable journal called *Accent*, sent everything back just as everyone else, but I was getting handwritten comments on just about everything I sent them. I found this encouraging. Toward the end of the academic year, a magazine called *Poet Lore* accepted two of my contributions. They paid in contributor's copies, which I eventually received and subsequently misplaced.

Another poem of mine made it into the student literary magazine. The most noteworthy thing about it, to my mind, is that I had them leave the K off my last name. *"Johnny Appleseed"*, *by Lawrence Bloc*. I thought it would look more distinctive and interesting that way. Then, when the magazine came out, I realize that what it looked like was a typographical error.

What a towering urge I had to be published! There are some writers who start out knowing what they want to write; indeed, it is the message that cries out for the medium. They have something they want to say to the world, some story that demands to be told.

I was very different. If I had anything to say, surely I hadn't a clue what it might be. I just knew, as I had known since I was fifteen, that I wanted to be a writer, and that I wanted things I had written to be in print, for all the world to see. I wanted to get paid for what I wrote, and to earn my living that way. I suppose I wanted to be rich or famous, but I didn't really regard wealth or renown as attainable. I have since read James Michener's observation that in America one can make a fortune writing, but that one cannot make a living. I didn't know that anybody could make a fortune at it, and I did think I could make a living.

I knew I didn't want to do any of the things writers did to make a living. I didn't want to be a newspaper reporter, and I certainly didn't want to teach. I didn't think in terms of creating some other kind of career for myself, something to do while I struggled to make it as a writer. I must have figured I'd find a way.

Meanwhile, I made my first sale to a magazine, though not for something I wrote. *Ranch Romances*, one of Pines Publications' last remaining Western pulps, used to pay $2 for clippings they could run as fillers. I found a newspaper item that struck me as right up their street (or down their long trail, perhaps) and sent it off to Helen Tono, the editor, reminding her how I used to bring her mail every morning. I got a nice note by return mail, along with a check for two bucks.

THE FALL SEMESTERS at Antioch were just two months long. In January it was time to go to work again. My father had thought that I might like to come home for three months. I wouldn't have rent to pay or meals to buy, and could save most of my salary. And he could get me a job. He'd served as a Republican committeeman, and could pull a string and get me on at the Erie County Comptroller's Office.

God, what a dopey job! What I mostly did was audit the expense accounts of various county workers. They got seven or eight cents a mile for the driving they did on the job, and would submit these very specific records of where they went and the miles they'd accrued. I sat at my desk with a street map of the county spread out in front of me, and a little pencil-like stick with a tiny wheel at the end of it. I would run the wheel along the map and a gauge would tell me how much mileage I'd covered. I was supposed to check each entry on each expense account and knock off eight cents here, eight cents there . . .

After I'd done this for eight hours, I'd go home and have dinner. All my Buffalo friends were away at college. All my Antioch friends were either at Antioch or working at more interesting jobs than mine in more interesting spots than Buffalo. My New York friends were, logically enough, in New York.

That's where I wanted to be, and I went there one weekend in the middle of my career as a petty bureaucrat. I stayed at the Nunnery, an enormous loft at 14 Cooper Square shared by four young women. One was my friend Joan Weiss, from Antioch, and another was her girlhood friend Heather Merryman. Heather came from a family of crazy rich people in Connecticut, and during this period in her life she was paying a fourth of the rent at the Nunnery, which came to $15 a month. She was in psychoanalysis five days a week, for which her parents paid $400 a month. I remember thinking that, if she could arrange things so as to pay $15 a month for analysis and $400 for rent, she would wind up considerably happier and better adjusted.

I spent a weekend at the Nunnery, with Joan and Heather and Dave Van Ronk and some people whose names I never did get. There was a never-ending pot of paella on the stove. People would drop by, stopping first to buy an eel or something of the sort at the market on First Avenue. Everything went into the paella.

I should have stayed there until it was time to go back to school. God knows I wanted to. There wasn't an hour of that weekend that wasn't more interesting than the whole three months in Buffalo. But I couldn't stay. My poor father had cashed in a favor to get me this fucking job, and I had to stay until it was done. No one at the office would have cared if I didn't come back, I don't think they would have noticed, but no matter. I had to go back.

Once I got there, I sat down and made my first real sale to a magazine. One evening Heather and I had wandered into the Salvation Army Mission on the Bowery, just down the street from the Nunnery. There we got sophomorically incensed at the way they made the derelicts sit through a sermon in order to get a bowl of soup. I was especially struck by one speaker who announced that he was "glad there was a Bowery, and glad there were men like you, so that I can carry Christ's message."

Back in Buffalo, I turned it into an article. But the experience gained something in the telling. I wrote how "my fiancée and I" had gone slumming and dropped in on the service. But the sermon worked its magic, I reported. "We came to scoff," I said, "and remained to pray." I nattered on for 700 words, titled the thing "We Found God on the Bowery," and sent it off to *The War Cry*, the official magazine of the Salvation Army. They bought it, paid a cent a word for it, and sent along their check for $7, along with an invitation to get more involved with their organization. I limited my involvement to cashing the check.

IN APRIL I turned in my odometer, or whatever you called it, and went back to Antioch. One of the first things I did was dig out that story I'd written on Barrow Street. Somewhere or other, probably in a writers' magazine, I came upon a listing for a magazine called *Manhunt*.

I had never read an issue of *Manhunt*, but I knew of the magazine. A year before I'd picked up a paperback collection of Evan Hunter's stories, published in the wake of his bestseller, *The Blackboard Jungle*. The stories were mostly about juvenile delinquents, as we used to call the little bastards, and reading them was a sort of epiphany for me. I thought they were good stories, and I could imagine myself writing them, or something similar. I didn't much identify with the kids in the stories, but I found myself identifying with the writer. I could see myself doing what he had done.

Most of the stories, I had noticed, had been originally published in *Manhunt*. You might think that would have moved me to go out and hunt down a copy of the magazine, but it didn't. However, when I saw *Manhunt*'s address and editorial requirements listed, I thought of my story and sent it to them.

And got it back with a one-paragraph note from the editor, one Francis X. Lewis. "This almost works," he wrote. But what it lacked was an ending, some kind of twist that would make it dramatically effective. If I could come up with a good ending for it, he'd like another look at it.

Well, I thought, I'll be a son of a bitch.

So I chased around Yellow Springs until I found a copy of *Manhunt*. I bought it and took it back to the dorm and read every story in it. I thought some of them were good and I thought some of them were so-so, and right away I saw how I could change the ending and make it work. I had this con artist bragging about how he was going to be able to give up all of this petty stuff, because he had invested his ill-gotten gains in this uranium stock that was sure to make him rich. But *we* know the con man's been conned.

I typed it up and sent it out, and I suppose if nothing else it proved that I'd read O. Henry, because that was how he'd wound things up in a classic story called "The Man at the Top." It came back right away, as well it might have, with another note from Mr. Lewis, saying thanks but no thanks, this ending was a little too pat and predictable, but I should try them again some time when I had a story that might work for them.

Oh, well.

I finished out the term, and returned to Buffalo around the end of June. My father had found a car for me, a '53 Buick. I had looked at the available jobs and decided to go "own plans" this time. I'd drive out to Cape Cod for the summer, find some sort of seasonal work, and try to get some serious writing done.

The night before I drove to the Cape, I couldn't fall asleep. I had a burst of creative insomnia, the sort where the mind keeps coming up with terrific ideas. In this instance, what came to me was the right way to revise that story for *Manhunt*. I couldn't wait to get out to Cape Cod and set up my typewriter and do it.

I drove to Hyannis, stayed the first night in a tourist home, then found a room for rent in an unfinished attic over a barber shop right on the main street. It was $8 a week, and the only thing wrong with it was that it had a pitched roof. Over and over again I picked the wrong time to stand up, and *wham!* I brained myself on a rafter.

Aside from that it was Paradise.

I revised the story for *Manhunt*, splicing in the new ending I'd thought up; the smartass narrator tells the reader that he's welcome to take over his old scams, because he himself is on to bigger and better things. A fellow has offered him big money—I forget how much—and all he has to do for it is kill a guy. "I start tonight," it concludes.

Retelling it just now, I have to admit it doesn't sound like something designed to make Chekhov eat his heart out. But I just knew it was the kind of snapper ending that Mr. Lewis wanted. I mailed it off, wished it well, and went out and got a job at Mildred's Chowder House. I worked from four to midnight taking hot dishes out of a dishwasher and stacking them. At midnight they gave me something to eat and the boss told me he'd see me at eight the next morning.

I told him I thought I was supposed to work four to midnight.

"You work when we need you," he explained. "Today, four to midnight. Tomorrow, eight to four."

"Oh," I said.

I went back to my attic and sat up for three or four hours reading. Then I started to set my alarm and decided no, I'd give it a sporting chance. If I happened to wake up in time, I'd go to Mildred's. If not, the hell with it.

Predictably enough, I slept to noon. I never did go back and ask for my pay, although I'd certainly earned it. I think I must have been scared to go back. I figured they'd yell at me.

I SPENT THE next two weeks living in the attic and writing stories. I wrote damn close to a story a day and mailed them all off to different magazines. During the first week I got a note from *Manhunt*. It was signed by some other guy, not Mr. Lewis, and said that Mr. Lewis was on vacation, but that others in the office had read the story and were almost certain that Mr. Lewis would want to buy it. If I didn't mind, he said, they'd like to hold the story until Mr. Lewis returned.

I was on the verge of ecstasy. It certainly sounded as though I was going to sell the thing, but it hadn't quite happened yet, so it was no time to celebrate. But boy, did I have plans! I already had it figured that I could write a story for *Manhunt* every month, and I was trying to calculate what that would come to in dollars and cents.

Meanwhile I was living on peanut butter sandwiches and 15¢-a-can Maine sardines. That's not as bad a diet as it sounds, but then how could it be?

Two weeks of this was as much as I could handle. Although my expenses could hardly have been lower, I was nevertheless running out of money. Even if *Manhunt* took the story, God knew when I'd get paid for it. And none of the other stories were eliciting enthusiasm from other editors. And I wasn't having that easy a time coming up with fresh ideas.

So I broke down and took a job as Assistant Salad Maker at East Bay Lodge in Osterville, gave up my cozy attic, and moved into the staff quarters. They gave me a bed there, and my meals, and $110 a month. All I had to do in return was work eleven hours a day, seven days a week. And I had to work a split shift, with two and a half hours off in the afternoon, so that meant my time was spoken for from seven in the morning until eight-thirty at night.

THE JOB MIGHT have been interesting if it hadn't been unendurable. The chef was an instructor at the New Haven Culinary Institute, and the other four cooks were his favorite pupils. We who worked in the kitchen ate well. (That put us well ahead of the bellhops and waitresses, who quit that sweatshop at an impressive rate. Every couple of days another bellhop would tie his uniform to the tree in the front yard and leave. That seemed to be the local tradition.)

I couldn't stand it. Obviously, I couldn't do any writing. I had no time, no energy, and no privacy. The owner, a tight-assed old fart named Leghorn, liked to see people working. There were kitchen jobs I could do more efficiently sitting on a stool, but I had to stand up because he didn't like to see his help sitting down while they worked.

I quit after ten days. This time I asked for my pay, but as I recall I didn't get any. There'd been a commission paid to the employment agency that got me this winner of a job, and Leghorn deducted that from what I'd earned and figured out that I owed him money. I hope he's not still waiting for it, the stingy basket.

I decided to go back to Buffalo and start over. On the way, though, I hit the brakes too late, or they locked, or some goddam thing, and I plowed into the rear end of a station wagon full of children.

NOBODY WAS HURT, thank God, and the only car that sustained any real damage was the Buick. I got it fixed and limped on home and gave it to my Dad to sell. Then I got on a bus or a train—who remembers which?—and went to New York.

I found a room at 105 East 19th Street, a decent enough rooming house that years later went co-op, and at one point housed the offices of Mystery Writers of America. When I lived there, it housed the kind of people who could come up with $12 a week for rent. That was about what I could afford, but not unless I found work. I wanted to get a job, but I didn't know what the hell I could do. I made the rounds of employment agencies, and they offered me a variety of clerk-typist jobs for $50–55 a week. I could probably get by on that, but the work sounded tedious and I couldn't see what I'd learn from the experience.

Heather was still at the Nunnery, and her brother Phil was in town with his wife, Carmen. (You'll note that there's no comma between "brother" and "Phil." That's because Heather had more than one brother. There is, however, a comma between "wife" and "Carmen," because Phil did not have more than one wife. It's crap like this that makes me want to get down on the floor and chew the leg off the chair. Would you really think Philip Merryman was a bigamist if I left out that stupid comma?)

Phil, a brilliant mathematician, had heard about my pursuit of a job and opened up a copy of the *Times*. "Here," he said. "Dozens upon dozens of ads. Administrative assistant, $5500 a year to start. Management trainee, $110 per week. Here."

"They're all for college graduates," I pointed out.

"You're tall," he said. I asked what that had to do with it. "You look large enough to have graduated from college," he explained. "You're certainly bright enough. What do you suppose they'd teach you in the next two years?" I must have looked dubious. "If they check," he said, "by the time they find out you never graduated, you'll be ready to go back to school anyway. But they probably won't check. Look, if you don't want to lie, just lower your head shyly and mumble something about a Master's. You'll actually be saying, 'I don't have a Master's, either,' but they won't be able to hear that."

WHILE I WAS looking, I turned down Time-Life.

My father had been in Alpha Epsilon Pi at Cornell, and remained friendly all his life with some of the men he had known there. One was Morton Tolleris, long a New York City Criminal Courts judge. Morty's brother Ralph was married to a woman named Beedie, who did something at *Time*. I spoke to her, and learned that she could get me on as a copy boy at the magazine.

There were two drawbacks. *Time* copy boys worked a five-day week, but their off days were Monday and Tuesday, not Saturday and Sunday. And the salary was only $55 a week.

"I sort of decided that I wouldn't work for less than $60," I told her.

She probably thought I was crazy. I was going back to school in twelve or thirteen weeks, so how far apart were we, $65 before taxes? But I don't really think the money had anything much to do with it, and working weekends certainly wouldn't have bothered me.

But what I didn't want was to get a job *through* anyone, and thus be stuck with it. I could still remember how much fun I'd had at the Erie County Comptroller's Office.

I've never doubted that I made the right decision. But I have to admit that if a kid of mine turned down a shot at *Time Magazine* because he thought he might be able to make five bucks a week more typing invoices for some bra and girdle manufacturer, I'd throw something at him.

THERE WERE SOME ads that I found appealing. *Young Man Wanted to Assist Detective*—that sounded promising. I went to the agency and filled out a form, but I don't think I ever heard back. *Assistant Editor for Literary Agency*—that sent me trotting to Qualified Employment Agency, on West 42nd Street, where a fellow quizzed me on my reading habits and my literary ambitions. He asked me if I read any magazines regularly, and I mentioned *Manhunt*. He seemed amused by that, and asked what *Manhunt* authors I particularly liked. I mentioned Evan Hunter and a couple of others. His amusement persisted.

The job, he explained, was a good one. The base pay was $60 a week, but you could earn more than that if you were productive. First, though, I had to take a test to see if I could handle the work. He wrote out an address for me: Scott Meredith Literary Agency, 580 Fifth Avenue.

"Oh, I know them," I said. "Actually, they wrote me once. To express interest in my material."

Damned if he didn't look more amused than ever.

2

IN 1957, SCOTT MEREDITH'S offices were on the 18th floor at 580 Fifth. The building was (and still is) around 35 stories tall, and the 18th floor was the first stop on the express elevator. When you walked in the door, you were in a narrow reception area with a door at the end and a sliding window midway along the wall on your right. The reception area was decorated with the framed photos and letters of some of Scott's more prominent clients. Arthur C. Clarke was on the wall, as was Mickey Spillane. (Scott had represented Spillane briefly. They had parted quite a while ago, and not without acrimony, but you'd never have guessed this from Scott's promotional material.) Evan Hunter was on the wall, too, and I realized why the guy at Qualified had looked so amused.

The little window opened onto the bullpen, where all of the employees worked. There were five editors (or editorial associates, or whatever the hell we were) and a secretary-receptionist. The editors were all male. The secretary-receptionist was a middle-aged Englishwoman named Joan, and it was she who opened the window when I rang, determined who I was, and bade me have a seat. Moments later a fellow in his late thirties appeared and introduced himself as Sidney Meredith. He seemed pleasant enough, although his features suggested that his totem animal was the rat. He escorted me into the bullpen, seated me at an empty desk with a Remington standard typewriter on it, and explained what I had to do. There was a story that had been submitted to the agency by a prospective client. I was to read it and write a letter in response. I could do one of three things: I could accept the story, and tell the author we were going to market it aggressively, I could state that the story needed revisions in order to be salable and explain what they were, or I could return the story as unsalable and point out what was wrong with it.

He handed me "Rattlesnake Cave" and left me to have at it.

I wonder how many writers and editors once read "Rattlesnake Cave." There was a time, certainly, when half the publishing world seemed to have worked for Scott Meredith at one time or another, and dozens of pre-screened hopefuls took the test for every one that was hired.

I don't remember the details of the story—I only read it once—but it was a remarkable tour de force. Although the byline read "Ray D. Lester," the story had been written to order by Lester Del Rey to contain the greatest possible number of structural flaws. Specifically, it was designed to be the antithesis of Scott's plot skeleton.

The plot skeleton was explained in considerable detail in Scott's book, *Writing to Sell*. Briefly, the plot skeleton was a recipe for successful fiction. A strong and sympathetic lead character is confronted with a problem which he must solve, and he finally does so. Scott Meredith did not dream this up all by himself, it's a formulation that goes back to Aristotle, but he certainly got a lot of mileage out of it; the last I heard, the damned thing was still in print.

I didn't know from the plot skeleton, but I knew a lousy story when I read one. I also knew that nobody bright enough to button a shirt would give you a test story that didn't have a lot wrong with it. So I wrote a letter politely declining to represent "Rattlesnake Cave," and explaining where the author had gone wrong. The frame device made the story less compelling, the lead character was about as decisive as Ethelred the Unready, and what a letdown it was when the cave turned out not to have any snakes in it after all.

I batted this out on the typewriter—a nice solid typewriter, too—and handed it in to Sid. He explained that they would be in touch if I passed the test. "If you don't hear from us," he said, "it means you didn't get the job."

I'd turned nineteen two months ago, and this was a dream job. I figured I'd done okay on the test, but I didn't have high hopes.

COUPLE OF DAYS later, I checked the mail at my rooming house. There was a postcard from one of the employment agencies I'd gone to. "Please report to employment agency," I read.

I made a face and tossed it aside. There was a very nice fellow at one of the agencies, and he kept sending me notes about $50-a-week jobs, and I kept turning him down or telling him I wanted to think about it. I figured this was more of the same.

An hour later a muted bell rang. I went over and had another look at the postcard, which I hadn't gotten around to throwing away yet. I read it again. "Please report to literary agency," it said this time.

I got the job.

MONTHS LATER, I found out two things. First of all, they'd been trying to fill that position for several months. A couple of hundred people had taken the test. All had failed miserably. It often took a while to hire somebody, but it had never taken this long before.

The other thing was that I had done so well on the test they thought I'd been coached. My letter was pure plot skeleton, and I'd managed to nail just about every last one of Lester Del Rey's booby traps.

On top of that, I'd written the letter in decent English. You didn't have to be Shakespeare to work there, but you had to be able to write a sentence. Your job, after all, was writing letters, and the letters you wrote would go out over Scott Meredith's signature. He wouldn't actually sign them, his brother Sid would sign them, but he'd sign Scott's name. So the letters had to be pretty good.

IF MY PERFORMANCE on the test was impressive, my first week on the job was astounding.

Sid explained how it worked. The agency represented two kinds of writers, professional clients and fee clients. Pros were just that, writers who produced salable professional prose and were represented by the agency on a straight commission basis—10% on US sales, 15% on Canadian, 20% on foreign. Fee clients, on the other hand, were writers who paid a reading fee to have their work considered. If it was salable, it would be marketed on the same terms as the pro clients. If it could be made salable with further work, the writer would be advised to redo the script, and would be charged no further fee when he resubmitted it. If it was unsalable, he'd receive a lengthy letter explaining just what was wrong and how to avoid making the same mistakes in the future.

There was, I was given to understand, an unwritten subtext to all of this. First of all, a minuscule proportion of the scripts I was going to read would be salable. Maybe one or two percent tops. Second, I was never to advise anyone to rewrite a script, because there was nothing in it for us. It would still be unsalable, and I wouldn't be getting a fee to read it.

Finally, a letter telling a writer that his story didn't cut the mustard had to do so in a particular way. I was supposed to stress that it was a flawed plot that kept the writer from sitting on the same shelf with Hemingway and Faulkner. "Always give 'em the plot skeleton," Sid told me. "Especially the first-timers. 'As I point out in my book, *Writing to Sell . . .*' and then you give 'em the plot skeleton."

Meanwhile, you told them what good writers they were, awarding them high points for prose and dialogue and characterization. In point of fact, I was to learn, most of the people who sent us stories could not write their names in the dirt with a stick. Their sentences were lousy. Their words were ill-chosen. Some of them belonged in a remedial-English class. Others belonged in a back ward.

Didn't matter. While I might choose to point out some correctable weakness in the prose or dialogue, that wasn't my job. I had to nail the plot and nail it good, and I had to wind up by stating, reluctantly but forcefully, that the flaws were intrinsic to the story in such a way that it could not be successfully revised. Far better to try again with a brand-new story, which I'd really be looking forward to seeing soon. With, it went without saying, another reading fee.

The fees were pretty reasonable, so much so that the poor bastards were unlikely to realize they were getting screwed. Short stories and articles cost the writer a dollar per thousand words, with a minimum fee of $5 a story. Book-length manuscripts under 150,000 words ran $25; over that length they cost $50.

For my base salary of $60, I was expected to process manuscripts worth forty credits. A $5 story was worth one credit, a $25 book five credits. Thus, for replying to submissions with reading fees totaling $200, I would be paid sixty bucks.

The more I did, the more I would earn, at the rate of a dollar a credit over my base. If I read stories with reading fees adding up to $250, say, I'd take home $70 that week. And so on.

The length of your report also varied with the fee. A Scott Meredith fee report was about as flexible a form as the villanelle. It began "Dear Mr. Smith," unless he'd been submitting stories long enough to be on a first name basis. It ended "All best wishes." Then you skipped two spaces, indented to the middle of the page, and typed "Sincerely," and then you skipped four more spaces and, under the "Sincerely," you typed SCOTT MEREDITH. Then you skipped two more spaces, didn't indent, and typed

SM:uck. (The SM stood for our Fearless Leader. The other two or three letters were your initials. I used lrb.)

Larry Harris (later Laurence M. Janifer) had written a poem about particular language of the fee report, in a rather elegant French form known as a rondeau. A client and former employee of Scott's, he recited it to me while I was working there, and I have never succeeded in forgetting it. Here it is:

> *Unlike the Ainu or the Manx*
> *We hide the fact that we are vicious,*
> *Starting our letters off with Thanks,*
> *Ending each one with All best wishes.*
> *Further evolved than bugs and fishes*
> *We are polite to nuts and cranks*
> *Starting our letters off with thanks*
> *Ending each one—O Nature's pranks!*
> *Ending each one with All best wishes.*

In between Thanks and All best wishes, a fee report took the form of a business letter, with narrow margins all around, no-indent single-spaced paragraphs, and double spacing between the paragraphs. The author, having been thanked for sending us the story, was then praised for its excellence before the sad news about the flawed plot was broken to him. For a $5-for-under-5000-words story, the analysis of strengths and weaknesses went on to fill half of the first page and all of the second, for a total of about 700 words. For a $25 novel, the report would be proportionally longer, running to the bottom of the fourth page. (If, God forbid, some joker paid fifty bucks and sent in a novel more than 150,000 words long, the report went on even longer, to the bottom of page six or seven.)

Submissions streamed into that office. Sid opened all the mail, set aside the checks for deposit, and placed the manuscripts, each in a file folder, in a cabinet in the big office. If the manuscript was an initial submission, it was in a folder all by itself. If this author had a history with us, the manuscript would be accompanied by copies of all the correspondence to and from him over the months or years. Each manuscript was tagged with a date two weeks after that on which it had landed on Sid's desk. That was the date our reply would bear, because every submission was reported on precisely two weeks after receipt. We didn't want to keep our clients waiting, but at the same time wanted to make sure they knew that Scott (who presumably read each submission and wrote each report himself) had had time to give their effort thoughtful consideration.

When I went to work there, one other fellow was writing fee reports. His name was John Dobbin and he was a mild-mannered fellow in his late thirties, a former merchant seamen who had had a novel, *Flesh and the Sea*, published by Avon Books in 1955. Each morning John and I would take a handful of file folders from the front of the drawer and go to work, returning for more when we were done.

Around us, the rest of the staff performed their various tasks. Jim Bohan was the pro man, making submissions and handling correspondence relating to those clients whom Scott represented on a straight commission basis. Ivan Lyons wore two hats, servicing Scott's Personal Collaboration clients and acting as the entire faculty of Scott's writing school. (The school was called Workshop for Writers, or something like that, and nothing in its promotional material indicated that it had anything to do with SMLA, or we with it. Its mailing address was 1 West 47th Street, which was the side door of 580 Fifth. The signatures on the letters that accompanied each of the course's ten lessons were those of John Van Praag, Roy Carroll, and a third chap whose name I have forgotten. All three of these guys were published writers, having been pen names of Scott Meredith himself back when he wrote pulp stories. And all three of them were now Ivan Lyons, who got a little wistful sometimes when he read the Writers Digest ads of a competing correspondence school for writers, with pictures of their more successful graduates and reports of their sales. As far as anybody knew, no graduate of Scott's course had ever sold anything to anybody.)

The school was never a great success as a profit center, either, and because it was licensed as a school it had to give proportional refunds to students who dropped out. The idea of ever giving money back to anyone did not sit well with Scott, and within the year the school went out of business.

Scott's personal collaboration service, on the other hand, was quite lucrative. It was also unquestionably felonious.

Here's how it worked. As an up-and-coming writer, you could elect to collaborate with the great Scott Meredith. For a modest fee ($25 for a short story, $75 for a group of three stories, $100 for a novel, is the fee schedule I remember) Scott would lead you through the process of outline, first draft, and revision, guiding you at every step along the way. Then, when you had polished the final version to Scott's specifications, a final letter assured you that Scott was taking your baby out to market, and hoped to have good news for you shortly.

Not bad, huh? Except, sad to say, virtually all of the PC stories were at least as awful as most of the fee scripts, and no amount of suggestions from Ivan or anyone else would have rendered them salable. Scott was not fool enough to send them around. They went in a file, and when their authors inquired, they got a letter from Scott. He still had faith in the material, he assured them, and he wanted to keep representing it. If they did finally ask for the stories back, they got them with an appended list of the markets to which they had presumably been submitted.

In fairness, I should mention the one great success of the Personal

Collaboration service. John Farris, now a rather well-known writer of horror and dark suspense, was one of Scott's professional clients, and something of a boy wonder. The agency had made several good sales for him, and Farris decided he wanted to write a big novel about a high school, and that he wanted Scott's help on it. He proposed paying a hundred bucks for Scott's personal collaboration.

This was patently ridiculous. Farris may have been a kid, but he was a pro. But what could Scott do, tell him that PC was a con game? Besides, who was to say that Scott's presence might not provide a set of psychological training wheels?

And what the hell, a hundred bucks was a hundred bucks.

So Ivan, as Scott Meredith, sat back and provided words of encouragement while Farris sent in first an outline and then one chapter after another of his book. There wasn't much for Ivan to do, although he made a small suggestion from time to time. Farris, it was clear, was perfectly capable of writing the book himself, and that's essentially what he did. Once it was complete, Scott—the real Scott, not Ivan—went out and sold it to a hardcover house. Rinehart, I think. The book was *Harrison High*, and it earned a lot of money for Farris and a nice commission for Scott. And, for at least the next decade, Scott's promotional pitches for his PC service pointed to *Harrison High* as the kind of success available to Personal Collaboration clients.

So that's what Ivan did. At the time, though, I didn't know just what it was he was up to. I certainly didn't have a clue I'd be sitting at his desk someday myself, muttering under my breath and stringing the suckers along.

Another desk was occupied by Henry Morrison, who handled foreign rights for Scott, and functioned in addition as a sort of utility infielder. Henry had been employed for less than a year, and was only a year or so older than I. He was, I later learned, roundly delighted when they hired someone even younger than he. And it was Henry, looking for a little amusement, who brought up *Manhunt*.

But I'm getting ahead of myself. There was one other desk, Joan's. Her Mayfair accent on the telephone was worth her salary all by itself, but she performed other functions as well. Scott, who didn't much care if people lived or died but couldn't bear to fire them himself, occasionally talked her into giving an unsatisfactory employee the bad news. And, when she had a spare moment, she would type out some Recents.

What was a Recent? It was a note from Scott. "One of your recent magazine submissions was close," it said. "This is to express interest in your material." And it was clipped to one of the brochures which explained the agency's services and the fees charged for them, along with an impressive list of pro clients and recent sales.

I had received one of these back in the spring. Shortly after my first note from Francis X. Lewis at *Manhunt*, I got a note and brochure from Scott. I had no reason to doubt its veracity; my recent *Manhunt* submission had indeed been close, and I wondered how Scott Meredith knew that. I would have loved to become an SMLA client, but I certainly wasn't going to pay a reading fee for the privilege. I didn't think it was a scam. I just didn't figure I could afford it.

Now I learned that Recents were not all that thin on the ground. There were two different magazines that furnished Scott Meredith with the envelopes in which unsolicited manuscripts had been submitted to them. Joan copied all of the return addresses onto envelopes, and out went the Recents.

And back came the checks. I don't know what the rate of response was, but it must have been wonderful. In two sentences, Scott managed to let a wannabe writer know that (a) he was getting noticed by editors, and (b) this guy Meredith really had his finger on the pulse of things.

When I learned about the Recents, I was damn glad I hadn't sent in a story and a five-dollar check. But now I thought I understood why the fellow at Qualified Employment had looked so amused. "Scott Meredith wrote me once," I'd said, looking to impress him. "To express interest in my material." So that's why he'd smiled.

I still didn't know the half of it.

ON MY FIRST day on the fee desk, I got five stories read and five reports written. I took them all to Sid. He read them all and had me make a slight change in one of them. The rest were fine.

The following day I got seven reports out, the third day eight. That brought me up to speed; I was, you may recall, supposed to turn out forty credits a week.

I figured I was probably doing all right. What I didn't realize was that my performance was downright phenomenal. Typically, a new man would struggle to get a handful of reports out each day for the first week or two, and most of what he did got sent back to him for revision. So I was really doing great, and I was younger than springtime, and Henry saw me as a likely source of innocent amusement.

One afternoon, perhaps my sixth or seventh on the job, he and Jim and Ivan began talking about *Manhunt*, joking about what an ill-conceived and poorly edited magazine it was. I was deep in my fee reports, but they kept at it until they managed to get my attention, and finally I felt moved to join in.

"Don't knock *Manhunt* too much," I said. "They're about to buy a story of mine." This news seemed to have more impact than I would have expected, and Henry pressed for details. "The editor was out of town," I said, "but his assistant said he was pretty sure Mr. Lewis would like it, and he asked to hold it until Lewis comes back. Actually, I should be hearing from him pretty soon."

Henry leaped from his chair, a look of utter delight on his face, and disappeared into the back office. When he returned, his delight had given way to astonishment. "He's telling the truth," he told the others. "The story's in inventory."

I didn't know what the hell he was talking about. Whose story? It couldn't be my story. And what inventory?

He went into the other room again. Moments later Sid came out and took me aside. "Well," he said, "it seems you've sold a story to *Manhunt*."

"It's not official yet," I told him, "but it looks as though I'm going to have a sale. Mr. Lewis is on vacation, but—"

"There's no Mr. Lewis," he said.

He went on to explain that Scott Meredith was the editor of *Manhunt*. Lest others in the industry perceive this as a conflict of interest, he used the name Francis X. Lewis, and his actual identity was a closely guarded secret. (The previous editor of *Manhunt* was a fellow named John McCloud, and he had something in common with Francis X. Lewis. He didn't exist, either. He, too, was really Scott Meredith.)

"All of this is a secret," Sid explained. "You're gonna learn a lot of secrets working here, and this is one of them. You must not ever tell anybody that we edit *Manhunt* here in this office." I swore I'd never say a word.

"And if you do," he said, "we'll deny it."

Nor had Lewis, which is to say Scott, been out of town when my revised story arrived early the previous month. He'd been there, he'd read it, and he'd decided to buy it. Indeed, he'd placed it in inventory. But *Manhunt*, owned by Michael St. John's Flying Eagle Publications, was having cash-flow problems at the moment. Thus Scott had wanted to stall on paying for the story, and had written me the note from the nonexistent Mr. Lewis's equally nonexistent assistant. Scott was, coincidentally, out of town now, he wouldn't be back for another week or so, and that was when he'd intended to let me know he was buying the story. Or maybe he would stall a little longer, for cash-flow reasons. But in either case he'd already made his decision, and I'd made my first sale.

"Your story's two thousand words long," Sid said. "*Manhunt* pays 2¢ a word, so you'd be getting forty dollars for your story."

"That's great," I said. Gee, I thought. Forty bucks. Great.

"But our clients get more," Sid went on. "A client of ours would get a hundred dollars for the same story. You want to be a client?"

Of course I wanted to be a client.

He just happened to have a contract with him. It was only a couple of paragraphs long, listing commission rates and committing both parties to the author-agent relationship for a period of one year, the agreement to renew automatically every year unless canceled in writing by either party.

"It's a good deal," he said. "You write stories, we'll represent you. And sometimes assignments come in, some editor has a hole in an issue and he needs something quick. You're right here in the office, plus you're a client, you'll get some of those assignments."

Great, I thought.

"Sign here," he said.

I signed.

"Now you'll get a hundred dollars," he said. "But don't ask me when." He turned to go, then stopped to correct himself. "Actually," he said, "you'll get ninety dollars. We get ten."

3

IT WAS QUITE remarkable. I had a great job. I had sold my first story. I had an agent. I hadn't actually met him yet, but I had a signed contract.

I was to learn that most agents did not bother with contracts, in the belief that the nature of the relationship required continuing good will between the parties, and that either party ought to be able to end the relationship at will. I have had three agents since, and with each of them I had no contract more formal than a handshake. (With one, Gerald Kelly of Kelly, Bramhall & Ford, I did not even have a handshake; we never met.)

Even if I'd known this, I'd have been no less eager to sign the contract Sid handed me. When I'd written my name and handed it back to him, it was official. I was a writer.

I WAS FIFTEEN and in my junior year of high school when I learned that I wanted to be a writer. I remember exactly when the idea came to me.

I was in Miss May Jepson's English class. She assigned a lot of compositions, which was fine with me; I'd never had trouble writing. On one occasion, we were to write a couple of pages on our vocational plans. I knew I'd be going to college, that was pretty much a given, but I had no idea what I wanted to do afterward. My father was an attorney who had only sporadically practiced law over the years; at other times he'd been a partner in a liquor store, sold insurance, owned a toy store, built houses in a development, and made various other unsuccessful attempts to get rich.

I didn't think I wanted to follow in any of those footsteps. He'd have liked me to become a doctor, but I didn't think I wanted to do that, either. I didn't know what I wanted to do, and I made that uncertainty the theme of my composition, enumerating the possible vocations that had suggested themselves to me since early childhood, when I'd wanted to become a garbage man until my mother told me they all got chapped hands.

The piece was light throughout, and I remember how I ended it. "On reading over this composition," I wrote, "one thing becomes clear. I can never be a writer."

Miss Jepson gave me an A. More to the point, in the margin beside my last sentence she wrote, "I wouldn't be too sure of that!"

I read her comment and made my decision. I was going to become a writer.

I'd already given some evidence of, if not talent, at least a facility with words. In the eighth grade, we'd been required to provide an essay for the annual contest sponsored jointly by the Buffalo Evening News and the local chapter of the American Legion. That year the topic was "What is Americanism?" Schools throughout Erie County participated, and a dozen winners were chosen, from high schools and grammar schools in three categories, City, Suburban, and Parochial. I was one of them.

I don't remember much about my essay. Just as Calvin Coolidge's minister was against sin, I was all in favor of Americanism. I remember that much. I remember, too, that my mother looked my essay over before I turned it in and suggested a minor change or two, just a word here and there. Mrs. Johnson, my English teacher, picked two essays, mine and Lorraine Huber's, to represent PS 66. She didn't change anything in the essay, but she did alter my pen name.

That's right, pen name. All essays were submitted under pseudonyms, so that the judges couldn't be influenced by recognizing an essay as the work of a friend's kid, or predisposed favorably or unfavorably by ethnicity. So I had to pick my first pen name, and I decided to match the spirit of the contest by concocting one from the names of three presidents. I selected Rutherford Delano Quincy, using parts of Rutherford Birchard Hayes, Franklin Delano Roosevelt, and John Quincy Adams.

(I knew the names of all the presidents, and could—and still can—recite them in order. I hadn't made a point of memorizing this data, but was a stamp collector, and the regular-issue stamps in circulation at the time bore the likenesses of the presidents, with each on the denomination corresponding to his chronological ranking. Rutherford B. Hayes, our 19th president, was on the 19¢ stamp. John Quincy Adams was on the 6¢ stamp. FDR wasn't on a stamp in that series; it had been issued in 1938, and he was alive and in office at the time. No living person can be portrayed on a United States postage stamp, with the singular exception of Elvis Presley.)

So I decided to be Rutherford Delano Quincy, but Mrs. Johnson decided otherwise. Rutherford was too long, she decided, so she reduced it to Ford. And Delano might put off some diehard Roosevelt-haters, so she changed that to Delaney. Quincy she left alone.

Ford Delaney Quincy. It struck me at the time as a pretty dopey name, but maybe Mrs. Johnson knew something. God knows she had the touch that year. I won, and, remarkably enough, so did Lorry Huber.

This had never happened before. I don't know how many public grammar schools there were in Buffalo at the time, but the numbers they bore ran into the eighties. Mrs. Johnson came off looking like a grade-school Maxwell Perkins, and Lorry and I had our essays printed in the paper and joined the other ten winners on a Christmas-vacation trip to Washington.

You'd think that would have been enough to make me entertain the idea of writing for a living. I mean, look at the payoff. One 200-word essay had brought me recognition and travel. God knows I would write a lot more for a lot less in the years to come.

But it never occurred to me. I don't suppose I thought of writing as something that people did. I read books, and I knew that they had authors, but I didn't take it any further. Anyway, that essay of mine wasn't writing. It was giving them what they wanted.

BY THE TIME Miss Jepson put the idea of a writing career in my head, I was ready to entertain it. For one thing, I was reading, and on a more sophisticated level than I had done earlier. Somewhere along the way I'd discovered 20th Century American realistic fiction, and I was reading my way through it with delight. I read everything I could get hold of by James T. Farrell, John Steinbeck, Ernest Hemingway, Erskine Caldwell, John O'Hara, and Thomas Wolfe. I'm sure much of what I read sailed over my head, but a lot didn't, and the books were terrifically real for me.

Be a writer? I thought it would be a wonderful thing to be. And Miss Jepson actually thought I might be able to do it? Well, why not?

So I made my decision, and whenever anyone asked me what I was going to do after college, I said I was going to be a writer. A lot of people assumed this meant I would go to work on a newspaper, and indeed the blurb beside my yearbook photo listed "journalism" as my career choice. I knew I didn't want to do that. Go up to strangers and ask them questions about subjects that were clearly none of my business? How could I possibly do that? And why would I want to?

No, I knew what I would do. I would write poems and stories and novels, and they would be published, and people would read them, and everybody would tell me how great I was.

FROM THAT POINT on, most of my writing was designed to get people to tell me how great I was.

I started with Miss Jepson, since she'd already shown evidence of leaning toward that opinion. I knocked myself out on my compositions, and turned in other bits of writing as well, poems and such. Verse came easily to me, and I suspect I came by the facility honestly. My mother had long been an versifier of no mean ability, turning out occasional poems to accompany birthday presents and bridal-shower gifts. Here's an example, turned out to grace some Tupperware given to my cousin, Fay-Anne Lippman, at a kitchen shower prior to her marriage to Philip Bernis:

> *They tell me that they send you home*
> *If you bring a present without a poem.*
> *We've racked our brains until we're frantic*
> *But it's tough with a gift so unromantic.*
> *These plastics come with our best wishes*
> *So "Phil" them up with your "Fay"-vorite dishes.*
> *What can we say? Now, umbeshrien,*
> *You and Phil have a pot to pee in.*
> *Or, if you prefer it, Happy Kitchen!*
> *Now you and Phil have a pot to pish in!*

Now I don't want to suggest that this effort would have had Ogden Nash chewing up his pencil in envy, but there are two points worth noting. First, the meter is faultless and the rhymes are not bad, with *umbeshrien* and *pee in* positively inspired. (*Kitchen* and *pish in* is off by a hair, but, as we used to say, close enough for folk music. *Home* and *poem* rhyme in Buffalo. Trust me.)

Moreover, my mother went on to use the opening couplet dozens of times in the ensuing years. While she never gave any thought to the idea of writing professionally, she displayed a professional attitude. When you've got something good, she knew, you get all the mileage you can out of it.

In the remaining years of high school, I too produced poems for all occasions. I wrote poems for the ads my fraternity placed in other fraternities' dance programs. I wrote a love poem for my friend Mel Hurwitz to present to the girl he was then dating. (I charged him a dollar, and it was the first actual cash I ever earned writing. Don't ask me what I did with the dollar. Don't ask Mel what he did with the girl, either.)

During my last semester in high school, someone decided to hold a contest to select a Class Poem. The winning entry would be printed in the yearbook, the *Bennett Beacon*, and the author would be designated Class Poet, and would have his picture with the rest of the class officers.

I submitted two entries, one in stately iambic pentameter ("Four years have passed since first we called you Home . . .") and the other in a sort of impressionistic free verse. These were submitted in such a way as to keep the judges unaware of the contestants' identities until after a winner had been selected. We didn't use pseudonyms, although I had old Ford Delaney Q. on hand if he was needed.

My blank verse epic, extolling the virtues of a place I couldn't wait to get away from, was selected as Class Poem. "I knew it was yours," Miss Jepson confided. "I knew the other was yours, too. The one in free verse. It came in second."

I NEVER WENT back to see Miss Jepson after I graduated.

I never went back to see any of my teachers, and I had some terrific ones. Miss Daly, whose three years of Latin did me more lasting good than anything else I ever studied anywhere. Miss Sherman, who taught me Spanish I my junior year, and who found out I'd managed to avoid signing up for a study hall and had the last period of the day free. "You're now assigned to an unofficial study hall at the back of my Spanish II class," she informed me—and I wound up learning two years of Spanish in one.

And Mr. Raikin, whom I had for World History my sophomore year. He would walk up and down the aisles as he lectured, and early on he caught me doodling in my notebook when I was supposed to be taking notes. "Larry," he said, without missing a beat, "see me after class." When I did, he told me not to doodle in my notebook, and I agreed that I wouldn't. The next day the same thing happened—"Larry, see me after class." I did, and assured him it wouldn't happen again. At the end of the week he gave us a snap quiz, and Monday morning he returned our graded papers to us. "Larry, see me after class," he said, and handed me my paper, on which I'd gotten 100. After class he said, "Larry, a notebook's only a crutch. If you want to doodle in it, go right ahead."

That impressed the hell out of me, and I'll tell you something, it still does. Mr. Raikin was a magnificent teacher, and the system rewarded him with a handsome promotion. They made him a school principal, thus depriving generations of students of the chance to have him as a classroom teacher.

I never went back to Bennett, or to 66, either. So I never saw Mrs. Johnson again. Or Mr. Green, a deliciously witty man and a fine history teacher. Or Mrs. Goldfus, my fifth grade teacher, who talked my parents and the school administration into letting me skip the sixth grade, thus guaranteeing me six years as a social outcast. She was a superb teacher, was Mrs. Goldfus, and who's to say that my adolescent maladjustment didn't provide the outsider's perspective so essential to a writer of fiction? I didn't come from a dysfunctional family, I wasn't beaten or interfered with, and if I hadn't skipped sixth grade maybe I would have grown up normal, and been a doctor or a lawyer or a businessman.

I never saw any of them again, those excellent teachers of mine, and I wish I had. But I especially wish I'd gone back to see Miss Jepson while I had the chance. In the late seventies I wrote my first book on writing and mentioned her in the dedication. I tried to send her a copy, but no one was able to provide her address. She'd long since retired to California. I suppose she must be gone now. I wonder if she ever learned that I'd become a writer. I wonder if she ever had any idea what she started.

I wish I could have thanked her.

IT WAS DURING my high school years that I first used a pen name and saw it in print. I'd grown fond of the Letters to the Editor section in the evening paper, finding it a great source of unintentional humor. For some reason I decided to write a letter of my own, and did so after seeing the Hallmark Hall of Fame presentation of *Macbeth* on television. My letter decried the program for its violence, and offered a plot summary. ("First they kill the King . . .") I ended on a ringing note ("Let's all get together and clean up television!") and signed the thing "Allor Bryck," an anagram, albeit an uninspired one, for Larry Block.

Looking back, I marvel at the satisfaction it gave me to see that letter in print, a feeling greatly enhanced when the paper printed indignant responses from some resolute defenders of the Bard. It was heartening to see so many lunkheads taking me seriously. I don't know if Steve Allen took Allor Bryck seriously or not, but he read the letter aloud on the *Tonight* show, to show his audience what kind of nuts there were out there in the world.

I wished I could have seen the program, but it was satisfying enough just knowing about it.

YEARS LATER, IN the mid-eighties, I developed a seminar for writers and called it *Write For Your Life*. (I wish to God I'd called it something else. People thought I was saying "Right For Life", and that the seminar was either for or against abortion. A couple of hotels wouldn't let us book space because they wanted to steer clear of controversy. "Controversy?" I found myself screaming. "We're helping people write better. What the hell's controversial about that?" "Now I'm sure there's much to be said on both sides," they'd reply.)

Write For Your Life grew out of some est-like seminars Lynne and I had taken, and was designed to address the inner game of writing. (Jesus, *that's* what I should have called it.) One of its key sections dealt with primal negative beliefs about oneself and their effect on one's writing. In the course of leading the seminar all over the country, I found that certain specific negative beliefs have wide currency among writers. One such belief is, "It's not safe to let people know who I am."

This conviction, coupled with an urgent and apparently conflicting wish to be known, seems to impel a great many fiction writers. I came to see that it was very much a part of my own emotional makeup.

On the one hand, I yearned to be seen and known and admired. On the other, I was certain that, if people really knew me, they wouldn't like me a bit. Thus it was essential that I hide my real self. To appreciate the extent of this belief, consider this. For years I harbored the worry that someday I would have to have an operation, that I would be given general anesthesia, and that, when the anesthetic was wearing off, I would talk. What on earth was I afraid I would tell? I hadn't done anything, for God's sake. But I might let people know me, and that was dangerous.

Writing fiction was the perfect answer. "Look!" my stories could cry. "This is me! But don't take this the wrong way, because it's not *really* me. It's just a story."

Pen names would assist this process no end. A pen name, screening me from the possible adverse judgment of others, was enormously liberating; it allowed me to write anything without worrying lest I reveal too much of myself. Most readers wouldn't know who really wrote the piece, while my friends would know I didn't take it seriously enough to put my own name on it.

In addition, a pen name allowed me to play a role. I played roles all the time writing fiction, slipping out of my skin and into that of a character. Eventually, when my pen names developed personae of their own, I would be wearing masks within masks, pretending to be a writer who was pretending to be a character. A couple of my pen names wound up with listings in reference works like *Contemporary Authors*. Two of them, Jill Emerson and John Warren Wells, kept dedicating their books to each other, and I found myself scheming to marry them off and get their wedding announcement printed in the *Times*.

But all of that was yet to come. For now I was working night and day writing fiction. The stories I wrote at night, when I managed to sell them, were printed under my own name. The fiction I wrote by day was in letter form, and my pseudonym was Scott Meredith.

4

ONCE I'D SETTLED in at Scott Meredith, I moved from the rooming house on East 19th Street. It was clean and reasonably priced, if cramped and lacking in charm, but the immediate neighborhood was non-residential, and that made it no place to be at night or on the weekend. You had to walk several blocks to get something to eat or drink.

Even so, I might still be there if a friend hadn't proposed finding an apartment together. He was Bob Aronson, who'd that June finished his fifth year at Antioch. I don't recall what sort of work he was doing, but it wasn't terribly fascinating, and he regarded it as a stopgap until he either returned to Yellow Springs to pick up the few credits he needed for his degree or got summoned by his draft board.

I didn't know him well, but found him an affable fellow. We looked at a few places in the West Seventies, and then he led the way to the Alexandria, a residential hotel at 250 West 103rd Street. There we were able to rent a large one-bedroom apartment for $120 a month. Thus for slightly less than $15 a week for each of us, we got a sizable bedroom, an enormous living room, a Pullman kitchen and our own bathroom. The place was completely furnished and linens were provided, with maid service once a week. We had no light bill to pay, no lease to sign, no deposit to hand over, and there was even a phone, with the hotel switchboard functioning as a free answering service.

The neighborhood would not have been my first choice, but it turned out to be fine. The IRT Broadway local stopped at the corner of 103rd, half a block from our door. The Red Chimney, a coffee shop on the same corner, served the best hamburgers I've ever had anywhere, with a thick slice of Bermuda onion on the plate, along with a tiny packet of Chiclets. There were other places to eat all along Broadway, including Broderick's and the Great Shanghai.

There were plenty of bars there, too, although the only one I remember frequenting was the Ekim, on the east side of Broadway. The name is Mike spelled backwards, but I don't know that that's how they came up with it. I remember Bob and I were there once and he prepared Depth Charges by ordering a shot of bar whiskey and a glass of beer and dropping the shot, glass and all, into the beer. I'm not sure what the point of it was, but I was willing to try it. It was at the Ekim, I remember, that I got a first look at Allen Ginsberg's *Howl*. Someone had picked up a copy, and we squinted at it in the dim light. I don't think that was the same night as the Depth Charges.

The Hotel Marseilles was a block away at Broadway and 102nd, and it had a reputation as a whorehouse. I don't know if it deserved it. I do know that Cornell Woolrich lived for a time at the Marseilles, though I don't know if he was there at the same time that I was at the Alexandria.

The Alexandria's still standing, but it's an apartment house now, and I suppose it went co-op or condo. New York used to have a lot of residential hotels like the Alexandria, decent and affordable, easy to move into, easy to live in, easy to leave. They're gone now, and it's too bad. The city's a less welcoming place without them.

I HADN'T SAID anything about going back to Antioch when I made the rounds of employment agencies, or after I'd knocked off "Rattlesnake Cave." I wasn't that stupid. It was hard enough getting a job without letting them know I was going to leave it in three months.

According to form, I'd be returning to Antioch at the end of October.

By the time I'd put in a week at Scott Meredith, I already knew I wasn't going back. I'd gone to school in the first place to prepare myself for a writing career, and it was immediately evident that I could do this much more effectively at 580 Fifth Avenue.

I certainly knew it by the time I moved uptown to the Alexandria. I wouldn't have bothered moving if there was any chance I'd be moving again in a month or two. It took me a while to broach the subject to my parents, but when I did they offered surprisingly little resistance to the idea. They both supported my choice of a writing career wholeheartedly, were suitably delighted that I'd sold a story, and saw my job at SMLA as the opportunity it was. I suspect, too, that my father may have welcomed the prospect of not having to pay my tuition for the coming year. In any case, I duly informed the college that I wouldn't be back, and scarcely gave the place another thought after that.

I had enough other things to think about. I don't think it's much of an exaggeration to say that every day in that office was the equivalent of a semester in practical education. This came not from Scott, who was a remote, Oz-like presence behind the door of his private office, but from the constant buzz of schmoozing and shop talk in the big office.

Later generations of SMLA missed out on this. Two years after I left, Scott moved to a much larger suite of offices on the seventh floor. There the guys writing fee reports and conning PC clients were off by themselves, and couldn't overhear what the pro men were saying. It was probably still good experience, but they didn't get the education I got, and they couldn't have had nearly as much fun.

SMLA provided a moral education as well. Every letter we wrote was designed to manipulate, and was dashed off with a cavalier disregard for the truth. My fee reports applauded the talent of writers who showed no talent, condemned the plots of stories with perfectly satisfactory plots, and were written with the singular goal of getting the poor mooch to submit another story and pony up another fee. The same ethical standard prevailed at higher levels. The professional clients were handled almost as cynically, as were editors and publishers.

To the best of my recollection, none of this bothered me a bit. I had been properly brought up, and was not at all disposed to lie or cheat or steal, yet once I'd cleared the hurdle of "Rattlesnake Cave" I accepted everything that went on in that office with the tractability of a Good German. The saps with their fee scripts were *Untermenschen*, placed on the planet to be exploited. *Der Führer* was always right.

The agency's moral atmosphere had a far more obvious impact upon Henry Morrison. It seems to me that he was at once unsettled and fascinated by it. A Gemini, he had in full measure that sign's ambivalent relationship with truth. (This, I should point out, is a latter-day perception; when I was 19, I didn't know what a Gemini was.) I remember his announcement that he intended to write a trilogy about a literary agency. He was frequently declaring his intention of writing one thing or another, and as far as I know never wrote anything. He had the title for his agency trilogy, however. He was going to call it *We Lie Like Hell*.

WHILE I DIDN'T miss much of the conversation that bubbled on around me, I couldn't have spent all that much time sitting around and kibitzing. I was too busy working.

Here was a typical daily routine: I would get up around 8:30 and get to the office by nine. I don't think I ever woke up in time to have breakfast before I left, and more often than not I buttoned my shirt on the way out the door and knotted my tie on the IRT. (We wore ties and jackets to work. I don't know why. None of us ever had to meet the public. My shirt was generally white—this was 1957, when men wore white shirts unless they were going to be on television. Once, however, late in my term at SMLA, I bought a black button-down shirt and wore it with a white tie to set it off. I guess Scott must have seen it on one of his rare visits to our office, and shortly thereafter Henry took me aside. "Larry," he said, "Scott never heard of Mark Hellinger, and he'd rather you didn't wear a black shirt and a white tie to the office." The next day, perversely, I showed up in the black shirt again, but with a black tie. Nobody ever said a word.)

I'd be at my desk at nine, or not too long thereafter, and I'd go to the file cabinet to select a handful of folders. Sid loaded them in from the back, and we were supposed to take the ones in front, but in actual practice a certain amount of selection went on. There was an advantage, for one thing, in getting as many first-timers as possible, because you could just about write a report on an initial submission without looking at the story.

This was literally true, and I did so on many occasions. Having read enough of the first page to know it was lousy, I would roll a sheet of paper into my typewriter, type the date and the author's name and address, skip four lines, and get to it. I would thank him for sending us his story, tell him I could see he was no stranger to his typewriter—a most felicitous phrase which I'd found in a copy of a predecessor's fee report, and which I used whenever I had the chance, never without wondering what people thought I meant by it. I would praise the story for virtues I was quite certain it lacked, and then I would talk about the importance of plotting and explain the sacred plot skeleton. "As I point out in my book, *Writing to Sell*," I would begin, and I'd launch into a lengthy paragraph that scarcely varied from one report to the next.

By the time I was done with the plot skeleton, I was halfway down the second page. "Now let's look at your story," I would write. Whereupon I would indeed look at his story, scanning it for the names of the characters and a few specifics from the plot. Then I would turn back to the typewriter and criticize his plot in terms of the plot skeleton. A final paragraph softened the blow, urging him to get right back to that typewriter to which he was clearly no stranger. I would, I assured him, be looking forward to seeing more of his work soon. All best wishes, sucker.

When a writer came back for more and sent in a second story—or a third, or a tenth, or a twentieth—I had to be more creative in filling the space, and this meant reading the story more carefully so that I could be more specific. I might comment more on individual characters whom I'd found well-drawn, might even cite a happy turn of phrase if I could find one. Inevitably, however, I found something wrong with the plot.

"I know you've heard this before," I might write, "but let me go over the Plot Skeleton with you one more time . . ."

I never had to redo a letter for lack of a way to pad it out to the bottom of the second page. But it was easier with first-time submissions, and I grabbed as many of those as I dared. Every other fee man soon reached the same conclusion, so nobody could hog the first-timers. Still, I made sure I got my share.

Another way to get ahead of the game was to grab up the books. A book, you recall, was worth five credits, a story but one. Since a book typically ran a minimum of 200 pages, while the stories averaged between five and ten, it would appear a book would take ten or twenty times as long to read. Thus a fee man, struggling to reach his quota or greedy to exceed it, would be better off with stories. Right?

Wrong. The reading was the least of it. It was the writing that took up your time. The fee report for a short story ran, as I've said, somewhere in the neighborhood of 750 words. The four-page report that the author of a book got for his $25 ran around 1750. For a tad more than twice the writing, you'd get five times the compensation.

And what, after all, did the reading time amount to? Before long I learned to read a book-length manuscript in 15 or 20 minutes. I would focus on the center of the page, and my eyes would not move as I turned the pages. By the time I was done, I would have absorbed enough of the sense of the story to write my report. I wouldn't retain what I'd read, and would have forgotten everything about it an hour after I'd written my report, but I considered that a definite plus. Who wanted to remember this crap?

This is not to say that I read every book this way. Often I wanted to take things a little easier and just sit back and read the thing. You worked hard writing fee reports, but the place wasn't a sweatshop. If you could do the work in the first place, you could probably hit your quota every week without killing yourself.

And, every now and then, something came in that I could enjoy reading. This didn't necessarily mean it was going to turn out to be salable. But I could still read it with a certain amount of enjoyment, even if I ultimately had to reject it.

After all these years, I can assure you that little of what I read at my desk has stayed with me. But there are a couple of writers whose work I recall with affection, if not quite with pleasure.

One was a husband and wife team who wrote novels. His name was Royce and hers was Nancy. I don't recall the surname. They plotted the books together, he wrote them, and she wrote letters to Scott when she submitted them. (That at least is how they presented themselves. It would not have surprised me to learn that one of them existed as a figment of the other's imagination.)

I got their first effort, and made sure I got the ones that followed it. I would have read them for free. I would have paid to read them.

The writing was smooth and lively, but that was the least of it. The books were positively incendiary, far more sexually provocative than anything available this side of Paris. This made them unpublishable, sad to say, even as it made me breathlessly eager to read more. I didn't just want to read the books, either. I wanted to meet them, and I wanted to shoot Royce and run off with Nancy.

There was no point in telling them to tone down the sex, either, because without it there was nothing much left. Anyway, I didn't want them to tone it down. I wanted them to heat it up.

Interestingly enough, Royce and Nancy were just a little bit ahead of their time. By the summer of '58, Harry Shorten was getting ready to launch a line of sex novels at Midwood Tower. Less than a year later, Bill Hamling had Nightstand Books in gear. Royce and Nancy, saucy and prolific, would have been naturals. It would have been a piece of cake for them to turn out a book a month for one or the other of those houses.

I was out of SMLA by then, and writing sex novels of my own, but I've wondered over the years if anybody at the agency ever thought to recruit Royce and Nancy as pornographers-in-training. I hope so. God knows they had a calling.

THEN THERE WAS Caswell Oden.

His story's fresh in my mind, because I thought of him when I was putting *Write For Your Life* together, and I told his tale every single time I gave the seminar. It was instructive. And it never failed to bring down the house.

Mr. Oden had retired at a relatively early age after having made a pile in the oil business. He lived in Shreveport, Louisiana, and he dreamed of selling a story to a national publication. But he knew this would never happen, because he knew full well that New York editors had it in for him. They would never buy a story from him and that was that.

But this didn't mean he was going to quit trying.

I don't remember anything about his first story except that it was, alas, unsalable, and we bounced it back to him in timely fashion with the usual fee report attached. His next letter, attached to another story, lamented the fact that nobody would buy a story from him, and ended with a proposition. Scott represented a lot of big-time professional writers, guys who sold stories at will to the best markets. Suppose he got one of those guys to write a story and put Oden's name on it? The magazine would buy it, the pro would get the money, Scott would get his commission, and Oden would pay a little more besides, all for the satisfaction of seeing his name in a major national publication.

Can't do it, I told him. Wouldn't be ethical. And I went on to explain that his latest story, while once again chockful of talent, just didn't quite make the grade.

He came back with another proposition. His first idea was no good anyway, he said, because as soon as an editor saw his name, that would be the end of it—because the bastards had it in for him, and no editor would ever buy something he'd written, even if somebody else wrote it. So how about if we did it the other way around? He'd write the story, and we'd get one of our top writers to agree to put his name on it instead of Oden's, and that way the magazine would take it. He wouldn't have his name in the magazine, but he'd have his story in it, and that was even better; he'd know who'd written it, and it would be a nice private joke on the damn editors. How did that strike us? And, meanwhile, here's another story.

We all shook our heads over that one, and then it was my job to tell him no, that wouldn't be ethical either, and why didn't he stop looking for short cuts and simply write a story we could sell to a good market? Oh, and by the way, this latest one wasn't it.

His next communication was a letter, with no story enclosed. He thought my idea was a great one, but maybe he was going about it wrong, because his stories sure kept missing the mark. Was there some kind of story that was easier to sell than others, some market that might be particularly open to new talent? If so, we should just tell him what it was and he'd go for it. He didn't care what it was, either, just so he could write for it with some reasonable hope of success.

We talked it over and agreed on the proper response. Confessions, we told him. That was the ticket. You wouldn't find great literature in the confession magazines, and you'd never have the thrill of seeing your name in print, because confession stories didn't carry bylines. The presumption was that the stories were all true, and that they'd been written by the persons who'd lived them. (Did the readers really believe this? I've often wondered.)

The confession market was a strong one, we explained, and had always been receptive to new talent. Although there were solid pros who sold every word they wrote to the top markets, there was no such thing as a big name, since no names appeared. If all he cared about was writing something and selling it, confessions looked like the way to go. And I went on to suggest that he pick up copies of all the major confession magazines, read their stories carefully, analyze their contents, and, if he felt so inclined, have a go at it.

He replied by return mail. He'd already dashed out and bought up every confession magazine available in Shreveport, and he was going through the stories like the Wehrmacht through Belgium. He was getting a good sense of the formula, and he wanted us to know he was going to follow it exactly. The story he produced might not be terribly inspired, but it would be right on target, exactly the thing they were looking for. And he felt really good about this, and we'd hear from him soon.

And we did.

In less than a week we received a manuscript from him. This was his right-down-the-middle formula story.

It was 15,000 words long.

The confession magazines of the day had very precise length requirements. The great majority of their stories ran 5–6000 words. In addition, most of them included one or perhaps two novelettes in an issue, running 10–12,000 words.

None of them ever ran anything 15,000 words long.

That was Strike One.

His story was told from a male viewpoint. The intended audience for confession magazines was exclusively female (and, I always thought, not terribly bright). While no one in the business cared who wrote the stuff, the protagonists of the stories were also almost invariably female (and, again, not terribly bright). Some of the magazines occasionally included a story with a male narrator, while other magazines had a policy against ever doing so.

None of the magazines, as far as anyone knew, had ever published a male-viewpoint novelette. Yet our Mr. Oden had produced an excessively long male-viewpoint novelette as his according-to-formula effort.

Strike Two.

But hey, that was nothing. We didn't have to look at the word count to know this was not going to go down in history as Caswell Oden's first sale. We didn't have to determine the narrator's gender. All we had to do was read the title.

First, though, I should prepare you by explaining that the confession magazines of the day were a prissy lot. The last I heard, they'd turned racy, much in the manner of soap operas and daytime talk shows and, indeed, the whole damned culture. But in the late fifties they were the farthest thing from racy.

The time-honored formula was Sin, Suffer and Repent. While the suffering was dire and the repentance profound, the sinning itself was off-stage and vague. There was no titillation in it, and you might well have had trouble figuring out just what it was that the protagonist did, or had done to her. There was never an off-color word, never a graphic scene, nothing you couldn't have read aloud in church.

Here's his title: "I Diddled My Wife's Sister."

In *Write For Your Life*, I used Caswell Oden's saga to illustrate the way a strong negative belief manifests in one's life. One harbors an irresistible urge to prove that it's true. Our Man in Shreveport believed that no editor would ever buy a story from him, and while he would have told you he was struggling to overcome that reality, he was in fact doing everything he could to demonstrate its truth. He studied the confession market, he sat down at his typewriter and went to work, and he couldn't have done a better job of writing a story that no editor would ever buy—from him or from anyone else.

"We all have our negative thoughts," I would say. "We all struggle against them while making sure we prove them true. One way or another, every last one of us is diddling his wife's sister."

WHEN I REACHED into the file cabinet, besides looking for first-timers and possible sources of titillation, I was always hoping to find something we could sell. The obvious motive was not hard to spot. When we accepted a story, I wrote a three-line response instead of hammering out two full pages.

Such an incentive might have led us to recommend everything, but we knew where that would get us. As it stood, the agency never took on a story simply on the basis of a fee man's recommendation. All I could do, if I liked a piece of writing and thought it salable, was pass it on to the pro man—Jim Bohan at the onset, and Henry after a couple of months when Jim moved on to other things. (I've no idea what other things he may have moved on to. His departure was more a matter of moving away from something—i.e., Scott Meredith. I think the place was driving him crazy.)

If the pro man liked the story I passed on to him, we took it on—and I got to write my three-sentence note. If not, he frowned and gave it back to me. Since he was also reading and making marketing decisions about my own work, I had every reason to avoid making him frown. My job, after all, was not to look for diamonds in the gutter. My job was to get rid of the garbage.

Even so, now and then I read something terrific, and it would contrast so brilliantly with the sewage I'd been wading through that I could hardly let it go unrecommended. In my stint at SMLA, I actually did discover several writers who went on to have professional careers. Most were short stories that we sold to secondary markets, but I also found a first novel by a fellow named Charles Runyon; I liked it, the pro man liked it, and it was snapped up by Gold Medal, the first house we showed it to. Runyon, whom I met briefly at a Mystery Writers of America dinner many years later, went on to publish quite a few books of crime and science fiction.

I didn't know much about the confession market, although I did know enough not to diddle my wife's sister. One day the pile on my desk yielded a confession story from a first-timer named Barbara Bonham. I could tell it was good. Henry agreed, and I wrote her we were taking it on. She sent in another story by return mail, and the same day that I read it and prepared to try it on Henry, the editor to whom we'd sent the first story called up and said he was buying it. Her second story was just as good, and we sent her a contract. She made a nice living writing confessions, and I believe she went on to do quite well writing romance novels.

Another favorite of mine was a fellow named Grover Brinkman, who lived, if I remember correctly, somewhere in downstate Illinois. I didn't discover Grover—he'd been a fee client for years, but unlike most of them he was damned good, and sent us stories we could sell. I didn't take on everything he sent, but probably passed every other story to Henry, who more often than not agreed with my judgment. Most of his stories sold to the lesser crime-fiction magazines for $30 or $40 a pop, but Harold Straubing at *True Men's Stories* liked the way Brinkman wrote, and bought a 3000-word short story from him now and then for $200.

Every now and then Brinkman would inquire hopefully about the possibility of being taken on as a professional client, and by all rights he should have been, but we always turned him down. I guess Scott felt there was no percentage in it. Since Brinkman seemed willing to continue as a fee client, why give up the $5-a-story he was paying?

I've often wondered what happened to Grover Brinkman, an unassuming fellow who earned his living operating a movie house and sat up late writing stories. He was a much better writer than I was that year, and with the right agent he could have made a decent living at it.

THERE ARE, IT seems to me, a lot of side roads and detours on Memory Lane. I set out to take you through my daily routine, and I haven't even had breakfast yet.

Around ten o'clock, when I'd already knocked off my first fee report of the day, Joan would phone the coffee shop across the street and order something for all of us. This coffee break was a perk—Scott picked up the tab—and it was a welcome one. I usually had an order of rye toast and a cup of hot chocolate.

We took an hour for lunch, and more often than not I'd have something quick across the street at Shelley's. There were a lot of choices, especially on 47th Street between Sixth and Seventh, where you could eat well and inexpensively at Fundador, Gus & Andy's, or the Alamo Chili House, which charged 15¢ extra for any dish ordered without beans. There was a lunch counter on Sixth Avenue called the Handy Kitchen that gave you a great bowl of stew for 95¢, and had hamburgers almost as good as the Red Chimney.

Sometimes several of us lunched together, often at the Hoy Yuen, a Chinese restaurant on West 48th. Henry couldn't get over the fact that I always ordered the hot turkey sandwich, and for years afterward nothing could shake him from the conviction that I didn't like Chinese food. As a matter of fact I liked Chinese food very much, and ate regularly at the Great Shanghai around the corner from the Alexandria. But I didn't like Chinese food the way they prepared it in Hoy Yuen's uninspired kitchen. On the other hand, they made a very respectable hot turkey sandwich.

AFTER LUNCH I'D return to the office for more of the same. I'd keep at it until five, although I might stay a few extra minutes to finish off a fee report.

I certainly didn't keep records, but it seems to me that I generally exceeded my weekly quota by fifteen or twenty credits, and consequently earned $75 or $80 a week before taxes. (After I'd been there a few months, I decided to see how much I could make in a week if I put my mind to it. I took work home every night—there was a glut of manuscripts at the time and we were freely encouraged to do this. I somehow managed to grind out 110 credits that week, and earn $130. It was quite an accomplishment, and one I never sought to duplicate.) Every Friday morning we would tell Sid what our tally would be by the end of the day. (If we estimated high or low, the difference would carry over to the following week.) Armed with this data, he would send Murray to the bank, and later in the day we would receive our pay envelopes. We got paid in cash, and didn't have to stand in line at the bank—another perk.

Now that I've mentioned Murray, I suppose I really ought to say something about him. Murray Weller was a thoroughly unappealing little man who functioned as a sort of Head Gopher, fetching the mail from the Post Office in the morning, posting the outgoing mail at night, and riding herd on the messengers.

(Sid hired the messengers, and was very proud of the method he'd devised for screening them. He asked them if they knew where Vanderbilt Avenue was. This was his "Rattlesnake Cave," and he had complete faith in it. On one occasion he was busy with something, and asked me to check out a fellow who'd come looking for a job as messenger. "Be sure and ask him where Vanderbilt Avenue is," he told me. The guy was a middle-aged fellow down on his luck, and he obviously needed the job more than the spaced-out kids who usually quit after a couple of weeks. He seemed fine until I asked him where Vanderbilt Avenue was. Poor bastard didn't have a clue. "He seems okay to me," I reported to Sid. "Nice fellow, sure to be a hard worker." "How'd he do on Vanderbilt Avenue?" "He's sure he could find it," I said. "Anybody can *find* it," Sid said. "You just ask somebody until they point you in the right direction. That's not the point. We never have anything going to Vanderbilt Avenue anyway, there's no publishers there. But if a man knows Vanderbilt Avenue, he knows Midtown. This guy doesn't know Vanderbilt Avenue, we don't want to hire him." I had to go back and tell the poor schmuck we couldn't use him. I wish I'd had the sense to lie to Sid. I was lying to everybody else, it was part of my job description. What the hell was the matter with me?)

Murray was awful—coarse, vulgar, slovenly and stupid. He wasn't exactly nasty, but he was certainly brutish and short. He must have had an early prototype of the razor Don Johnson used in *Miami Vice,* because he always had a three-day growth of beard. I could never figure out how he managed it. He was constantly propositioning Joan, who would have cheerfully killed him if she could have done so without touching him. He often had dirty pictures to show you, and on one unforgettable occasion he proudly passed around a disheartening snapshot of a small child holding her skirt up over her head. It was, God help us all, his daughter.

While Murray was fiercely loyal to his employers, this alone was not enough to explain his presence there. How did he keep his job? How had he ever contrived to get hired in the first place? It was one of the true mysteries at SMLA, and no one could come up with a decent explanation.

Some years later, the word got around. The little wretch was Scott's brother-in-law.

I LEARNED AN incalculable amount writing fee reports for Scott Meredith. I learned from what I heard and what I saw, but I also learned from the actual work I did, from reading all those dreary stories.

It's not uncommon in writing classes to study great works of fiction, to take them apart and see how they're made, even to transcribe them verbatim as a way of absorbing the essence of a master's style. I'm not disposed to label all of that as valueless, but I'm convinced you can learn far more, and far more easily, from bad work than from good. The very best writing is seamless; you can see that it's good, but you can't tell why, or what the author did to make it work so well. It's easier by far to see what's wrong with bad writing, and how it got that way.

After only a couple of months at SMLA, I was struck by the way so many of our fee clients combed the thesaurus for synonyms for "said," and compounded the felony by tacking on an adverbial modifier. It weakened their dialogue considerably. I pointed this out occasionally in fee reports, and I had the temerity to write an instructional article on the subject. "Gloomily Asserted Smith" I called it, and Henry liked it enough to send it off to *Author & Journalist*, and they bought it.

So I began writing about writing almost before I'd done any writing of my own. But I was doing plenty of that as well.

5

I'D MADE A sale to *Manhunt*. So I set out to make a place for myself in the world of crime fiction.

Since then I've occasionally observed that, had I sold my first story to *Calling All Girls*, I might have spent the rest of my life writing about strong, sympathetic lead characters with braces on their teeth. There's some truth in that—I was certainly inclined to respond positively to signs of encouragement. But it's clear to me that I haven't spent over 35 years writing mysteries just because I sold one. Before *Manhunt*, you will recall, I sent "We Found God on the Bowery" to *The War Cry*, and got an acceptance and a check by return mail. I never again tried to write anything for *The War Cry*, or any other religious publication. While at SMLA, I wrote a science fiction short-short called "Make A Prison." It worked its way all the way down to the very bottom of the S-F food chain, finally selling to Bob Lowndes at *Original Science Fiction Stories* for a half cent a word, then wound up in Judith Merril's prestigious annual anthology. I was elated—but I never wrote another piece of science fiction.

I'd always enjoyed mysteries. My parents often had them around the house, and in my early teens I read quite a few. I went through a slew of Erle Stanley Gardner's Perry Mason novels, and remember reading books by Agatha Christie, Rex Stout, and Peter Cheyney, among others. When I discovered capital-L Literature I pretty much abandoned mysteries, but by the time I got to college I'd concluded that some mystery writers were doing interesting things. I remember, for instance, that Steve Schwerner and I developed a passionate enthusiasm for the work of Fredric Brown, who wrote equally engagingly in the fields of mystery and science fiction.

I already knew that I enjoyed reading crime fiction, and my sale to *Manhunt* seemed to indicate that I could write it. At Scott Meredith, I found myself in an office full of knowledgeable people who considered crime fiction eminently respectable, and regarded the better writers in the field as artistically superior to the authors of most mainstream commercial fiction, and not vastly inferior to the folks writing capital-L Literature.

So that's what I decided to write. As a first step, I set out to read it. All of it.

I SPENT NINE months in all working for Scott Meredith, and I know I did not live the life of a monk. I had friends in the city—friends I'd made when I lived in the Village and worked at Pines, friends from Antioch who landed in the city on co-op jobs for three months at a time, even a couple of friends from high school who were attending college in or around New York. I saw them, and I went out on dates with girls from Antioch, or girls someone introduced me to.

On Fridays after work John Dobbin and I would stop at a rancid little bar on Sixth Avenue and have a couple of pops. On evenings and weekends I went down to the Village and hung around the bars and coffee houses. I saw *West Side Story* at the Winter Garden, and I saw Tom Paisley and Gail Garnett at the Sullivan Street Playhouse, and I must have seen other shows, and no end of movies.

I hung out with the folk music crowd, and wrote a few songs. "The Ballad of the IRT," about a heroic homeward-bound Brooklyn shipping clerk beheaded by a closing subway door, wound up on Dave Van Ronk's second Folkways album. A batch of political parodies were included in the Bosses' Songbook. (A few of these were true products of the folk process. I remember sitting around one night drinking with Van Ronk and Lee Hoffman, the three of us hammering out "The Twelve Days of Marxmas" and "I Don't Want Your Union, Mister." Lee, who later published a couple of my songs in a folk-music fanzine called *Caravan*, was married at the time to Larry T. Shaw, then the editor of *Infinity Science Fiction*. Later she began writing Westerns as good as any I've ever read. Her readers, of course, never had a clue she was a woman.)

But when I think back on those months it seems to me that all I did was read and write.

What did I read? I read everything.

I started with magazines. There was a secondhand bookstore on Eighth Avenue just above 42nd Street that had a wonderful stock of back number crime fiction magazines. (All of the bookshops in the Times Square area sold pornography, of course, but back then they had to carry other merchandise as well; there just wasn't enough erotic material on the market to sustain them.) The magazines went for the same price as secondhand paperback books—two for a quarter. As meager as my discretionary income may have been, at that price I could buy all I wanted.

I bought every copy of *Manhunt* I could find, and sought out its imitators as well, digest-sized magazines with titles like *Trapped, Guilty, Pursuit, Murder, Keyhole, Off-Beat,* and *Web.* All of these others were *Manhunt* imitators, even as *Manhunt* itself was a sort of spiritual descendant of the legendary *Black Mask*, and the covers and contents of the others duplicated *Manhunt* as closely as possible. (*Manhunt*, meanwhile, had undergone a format change a year or so previously and was no longer digest-sized; like *Alfred Hitchcock's Mystery Magazine*, it had switched to a page size like that of *True*, or *Mademoiselle*. This was not ultimately a success, and within a couple of years both *Manhunt* and *AHMM* switched back to digest size.)

Before long I was carrying around checklists, so I wouldn't buy the same magazine twice. I put together a near-complete run of *Manhunt*, along with dozens of copies of its fellows. And I read my way through just about every story.

I read rapidly, of course, though I didn't fly through the stuff the way I did with fee scripts. I don't know how much I consciously retained of what I read, but what difference did it make? I wasn't taking a college course, and wouldn't be called upon to pass an exam. I wanted to know how these guys did it, and it seemed to me that this was the way to find out.

It seemed to work. I was not studying the markets quite the way beginning writers are often advised to do. I was not reading analytically, taking stories apart piece by piece to see what made them tick. Rather, I was saturating myself in the material, enjoying some of it and suffering through the rest, until I somehow internalized a sense of what a crime-fiction story was and was not. I didn't learn all this intellectually, but digested and absorbed what I'd read so that my own imagination began to produce viable story ideas, and when I sat down to write them up I knew how to do it.

Or at least I could muddle through. I've since looked at some of those very early efforts, and they weren't very good. The prose and dialogue was nothing to be embarrassed about, but there was a great deal I didn't know about getting a story started, and getting in and out of a scene. One story I wrote on the kitchen table at the Alexandria was called "Ride a White Horse," and it was one of my successes; Scott wound up selecting it for *Manhunt*. (Of the couple of dozen crime shorts I wrote while I was working there, only two followed my first sale into *Manhunt*. First was "A Fire at Night," narrated by a pyromaniac who, we discover at the end, is also a fireman. Second was "Ride a White Horse." All the others sold to secondary markets, except for a few that wound up in a landfill.)

"Ride a White Horse" concerned a fellow who meets a girl in a bar and falls in love with her. She's a junkie, and by the end, tantalized by what she finds in heroin and wanting to be in the same place she is, he's ready to tie off and shoot up himself. What struck me when I read it years later was that it took about five hundred words before he even laid eyes on the woman. I was on the third page of the story before I was *into* the story.

I think I know what must have happened. I think I very likely sat down at the typewriter determined to write a story but lacking an idea. I started writing, created a character, had him come home from work and decide he felt like having a drink, sent him around the corner to a saloon, and kept at it until he was involved in something. That's not a bad way to drum up a story idea, but you have to go back afterward and clean up your mess. The story should have opened with him meeting the girl. I'm surprised nobody made me redo the opening. I guess the plot gimmick was strong enough to make up for the sluggish beginning.

I DON'T KNOW how many stories I wrote, but it seems to me that it was a rare week when I didn't turn one out. Most of them were written at my kitchen table on 103rd Street, but once in a while an idea grabbed hold of me while I was at the office, and I'd shove the stack of fee manuscripts aside and take a whack at it. This was acceptable, incidentally; as long as I was hitting my quota, I didn't have to be devoting every moment of the work day to agency business.

Typically, I wrote a story at one sitting. They were short, rarely exceeding 4000 words, and, while I might not have known what I was doing, I knew how to do it quickly. When I'd finished a story—I didn't do a second draft—I gave it to Henry. Once in a while he gave it back, explaining that it didn't work, that the plot premise really wasn't worth developing. Every now and then he'd have a change to suggest, and I'd take it home and revise it accordingly. Most of the time he marketed it, and sooner or later it sold.

If it was better than average, and if Scott didn't grab it for *Manhunt*, it would be given a shot at the top books in the field, *Hitchcock* and *Ellery Queen*. (With no success, I must say. It was another four or five years before I sold anything to *AHMM*, and *Ellery Queen* didn't take a story of mine until 1975.) Some of my stories were submitted to Harold Straubing at *True Men's Stories*, but he never bought one. Then they made their way down the ladder.

The best of the secondary markets was a pair of alternating bi-monthlies, *Trapped* and *Guilty*. (By having two different titles, a publisher could double his exposure time; a bi-monthly stayed on the newsstand for two months instead of one. *Guilty*, incidentally, consistently outsold *Trapped*, irrespective of the covers and contents, which as far as anyone could tell were identical. I guess it was just a better title.)

W. W. Scott edited both magazines, and he bought a lot of stories from me. He got first look because his rates were better than his competition. He paid a cent and a half a word.

I never met W. W. Scott, nor did it ever occur to me to wonder what the initials stood for. He edited other magazines beside *Trapped* and *Guilty*, including a sort of medical-confession hybrid called either *True Medic Stories* or *Real Medic Stories*, I can't remember which. (Both titles stick in my mind, and it's not unlikely that there were in fact two magazines, alternating bi-monthlies like *Trapped* and *Guilty*.) I suppose the audience was composed largely of nurses, or girls who dreamed of becoming nurses. At one point he mentioned to Henry that his inventory was low, and Henry suggested I read an issue of the magazine and try something for them. The rates were attractive—4¢ a word, with the ideal story coming in at around 4000 words. And Mr. Scott liked the way I wrote, so he'd be receptive to a piece with my name on it.

I read enough to figure out what kind of story I could write for him— an arrogant surgeon (if you can imagine such a character) is performing an operation, and something goes dramatically wrong because of the narrowness of his vision, and by the time things work out he's learned a valuable lesson.

That was great, except I barely had enough medical knowledge to change a Band-Aid. So I sat down with my friend Duck Buchanan and we worked it out together.

I knew Duck from Antioch. His name was Richard George Torrence Buchanan III, and his mother was a longtime editor at *Parents Magazine*. His nickname, which he eventually grew to dislike, came to him on a summer job during high school, when he'd emptied latrines or drained cesspools, something romantic like that. Duck was colorful. He drove a green Austin-Healey 3000 and a motorcycle, lived a perfect *Playboy* lifestyle, and seemed only to go out with women named Susan, Carol or Barbara. I don't know if he was officially a pre-med student at the time— Antiochians changed their majors almost as often as they changed their underwear—but he certainly knew a lot about medicine. On a recent co-op job he'd assisted someone who was developing artificial heart valves, and he'd done such exotic things as scrub at operations.

So we collaborated. We batted it back and forth and decided our arrogant hero would be performing a sigmoid resection when, so to speak, the shit hit the fan. Duck fed me all the details of the operation and I went home and wrote the story. I still remember the opening sentences:

"My name is Brad Havilland. I'm 42 years old, and I'm the best bowel surgeon in the state."

Now who could possibly stop reading after that?

In private, we called the story "Pain in the Ass." I had the wit to title it something else, and W. W. Scott thought it was the cat's pajamas. The story ran 4000 words, the payment was $160, and Duck got a fourth of that, or $36 after commission. We were both elated.

So was W. W. Scott, who wanted more. Duck and I were all for it, but we had a hell of a time coming up with a plot. Eventually we worked up one that we referred to as "Heartburn." It had something to do with cardiac surgery, I guess, but I don't remember anything more than that. W. W. Scott didn't think it was nearly as good as "Pain in the Ass," but he took it anyway.

IF W. W. SCOTT PASSED on a story, the next stop was Pontiac Publications. They paid a penny a word, and got out a batch of identical magazines whose titles kept changing. *Two-Fisted Detective Stories, Off-Beat Detective Stories, Web Detective Stories*—I'm sure there were others, but those are the titles I remember.

There was one sure way to spot one of their books on the newsstand. The title of every story was followed by an exclamation point. A lot of comic strips are like that, with every line of dialogue ending with either an exclamation point or a question, and for some reason it seems to work in comics. It certainly doesn't work anywhere else, and Pontiac's contents pages were pretty silly. I always wanted to sell them a story with an unutterably prosaic title. "One Dull Day!", say. Or maybe "Bored Speechless!"

Another Pontiac quirk was to make up pen names for authors. When the same writer had two stories in an issue, it was standard procedure to run one of them under another name. Most editors checked with the agent to see if the writer had a second name he liked to use. Some editors, too rushed or lazy to bother, used house names, generic pen names which could appear on anybody's material. Pontiac took your name and inverted it to create a pen name. Thus Al James became James Allen, and another SMLA client, Dan Sontup, was imaginatively transformed into Topson Daniels.

This happened to me a couple of times. Pontiac rechristened me as B. L. Lawrence.

*   *   *

I REMEMBER ONE story of mine that wound up at Pontiac. I seem to recall writing it at my desk in the office, but I can't be sure of that. It concerned a woman given to prowling around the downtown bars, very conscious of the lecherous glances men sent her way, very much aware of their eyes. She rejects one man, then picks up another and goes home with him; at the critical moment, she draws a knife and stabs him to death.

Here was the final sentence: "Afterward, in her own apartment, she put his eyes in the box with the others."

Henry informed me that the story was stomach-churning, but that didn't stop him from sending it out, and Pontiac paid their standard rate for it. I suppose I got something like $25 bucks for my troubles.

Twenty years later I was thinking about that story. My friend Cheryl Morrison had sold a couple of articles to Bruce Fitzgerald, who was editing a magazine called *For Women Only*. The title was stunningly inaccurate, in that the magazine's readership must have been 98% male. The book was composed of nude photos of male models, the overstock from another gay men's magazine called *Blueboy*. By cleverly billing itself as a woman's magazine, *For Women Only* could get on newsstands that wouldn't have touched *Blueboy* with a ten-inch pole.

To render all of this a tad more credible, the prose content of the magazine was devoted to stories and articles that would presumably appeal to women. They didn't really have to appeal to anybody, since few women would be moved to pick up a magazine full of pouting butch numbers because they wanted to read an article on estrogen-replacement therapy. But if they looked as though they were *trying* to appeal to a female audience, the magazine got better distribution.

Cheryl knew I had a piece sitting around that I'd written for *Cosmopolitan* on the special problems involved in dating a divorced father. I'd taken a kill fee and was free to place it elsewhere, but no one seemed to want it. She thought Bruce might like it, so I sent it to him and he bought it right away and paid a nice price. He wrote that he also published fiction. Did I have anything suitable?

I had a story in the files that I'd never been able to sell. It was called "Leo Youngdahl, R.I.P." and was the fictional retelling of an incident that had happened at my father's funeral. For some reason I'd used a female narrator, perhaps to distance myself from the original event. I sent it to Florida and Bruce liked it.

Later, I tried to think of something else to sell him. I found myself remembering the story about the eyes. I was uncommonly fond of that last line, and I wondered if I could possibly use it again. The original story had appeared twenty years ago. I didn't know the name of the magazine in which it had been published, and wasn't sure I'd ever even seen a copy. I'd forgotten my original title, and all I knew about the magazine's title was that it had an exclamation point at the end of it. And all I really recalled of the story was the way it ended.

Suppose I wrote it again. I was confident I could do a much better job of it, building up far more effectively to the final line I liked so much. It seemed to me that it was legal. I could hardly sue myself for plagiarism. But was it ethical? More to the point, would anybody notice?

I went ahead and wrote it, called it "Hot Eyes, Cold Eyes," and sent it to Bruce in Florida. I didn't have to wait long for a response. He liked the story very much, he wrote, but it was a little savage for the *For Women Only* audience. He'd really like to buy it, but only if he could make a slight editorial change, and he wasn't sure how I'd feel about it. But would it be all right if he left off the last line?

BACK IN 1957, A fellow named Ted Hecht was editing a group of men's magazines at an outfit called Stanley Publications. Just as *Dude, Gent, Escapade, Nugget, Bachelor, Swank* and others had blossomed in imitation of *Playboy*, so had any number of secondary magazines sprung up in the wake of *Argosy* and *True*. Hecht's books were way down the ladder. They had titles like *Real Men* and *All Man*, and they had three proto-typical stories: "Reinhard Heydrich, Blond Beast of the SS," "Grovers Corners—Sin City on the Wabash," and "Migrating Lemmings Ate My Feet." (Larry Harris once observed that a writer could go on writing for the male-adventure market as long as he could keep coming up with new animals to be eaten by.)

Hecht would call up periodically, short of inventory and in need of material to meet a deadline. He had some article ideas and wanted some-one to write them. The pay was $75, the piece was to run around 2500 words, and time was always of the essence.

I don't know how many articles I wrote for Hecht. Eight or ten, I'd guess. The first one was actually entitled "Reinhard Heydrich, Blond Beast of the SS." I can't remember whether Heydrich was Hecht's partic-ular notion or if he just wanted something about a Nazi. I caught the as-signment on the first hop ("Sure, Henry, I can do that"), spent two hours on a Saturday at the library, and brought the article to the office Monday morning. I used some nuggets from a piece of British propaganda (Hey-drich, as a young officer in the Kaiser's navy, knocked up his captain's daughter, then refused to marry her because she wasn't a virgin). I made up others, like having Heydrich single out a comely young concentration camp inmate and torture her for hours with a cigarette lighter. (How could you do that? Wouldn't you run out of lighter fluid?)

Another piece Hecht requested was on the Morro Castle disaster, the cruise ship that burned in Havana harbor. I wonder why he picked that. Maybe he had access to free artwork. Once again I went to the li-brary and got the piece written. But I much preferred the kind of article where you didn't have to do any research, and wrote a few on spec that Hecht bought. "She Doesn't Want *You*" was one of them; it advanced the startling possibility that the prostitute the reader lusted after was herself a lesbian, and not interested in men at all. (I only got $50 for that one, because I'd done it on spec. Hecht evidently assessed a penalty if you provided the idea as well as the text.)

While I was by no means ashamed to write this crap, I knew I didn't want to put my own name on it. Instead I used Sheldon Lord.

Sheldon Lord. I had selected the name early on, but didn't get to use it much. One time W. W. Scott had two of my stories in one of his magazines; he phoned up to find out which one I wanted a pen name on, and what name I wanted to use. That was Sheldon Lord's first byline. (Pontiac, as I've mentioned, never bothered to ask, probably figuring the author didn't give a rat's ass—which was probably true more often than not.)

I don't know where the name came from. Not from Sterling Lord, certainly; had I been aware that there was a prominent agent named Sterling Lord, I very likely would have looked elsewhere for a pen name. At Antioch the previous year I'd dated a young woman named Marcia Lord, and that's probably where I got the Lord part. I didn't know any Sheldons, but I thought it was a classy name, tough but respectable. The sort of guy you could trust when he took you aside and told you the lowdown truth about that shitheel Reinhard Heydrich.

As I've said, I wasn't ashamed of writing these pieces, and drew a certain amount of satisfaction from them. Not the least valuable thing they did was confirm for me that I would much rather write fiction.

And, during the second half of my sojourn at SMLA, I got a little extra mileage out of them.

I took them uptown to Columbia, and gave them to my professor.

6

WHEN I LOOK back on those years, one thing I have a tough time understanding is the importance I attached to avoiding military service.

Remember the time period. This was the late fifties, the era of the peacetime army. Korea was history, Vietnam not even a blip on the radar screen. Unless you were sufficiently intrepid to join the Marines, and thus risk drowning at boot camp on Parris Island, the only way you were going to get hurt was if you got drunk and fell out of a Jeep. What the hell was I scared of?

Wasting time, maybe. If they drafted you, you gave them two years of your life. If you enlisted, you stood a good chance of going someplace interesting, like Europe. But then you gave them *three* years of your life. Even if you opted for one of those six-month enlistments, you were still stuck with giving them one evening a week and two weeks every summer for years on end.

It never occurred to me that anything interesting or worthwhile might come along during a hitch in the Service. I figured it would be arduous, unpleasant, humiliating and boring. That's what everybody said, and I figured they were probably right.

I probably would have stood it just fine. They wouldn't have had me jumping out of airplanes. After six weeks of basic training, which would very likely have been not much worse than an exponential version of everything I didn't like about Boy Scout camp, they would have almost certainly made me a clerk-typist and sent me to Fort Hood, Texas, or Fort

Polk, Louisiana, or some other garden spot. And I would have spent my time typing up the Army equivalent of fee reports, not working nearly as hard, and doing a lot more drinking and whoring during my off hours.

Would I have been bored? Well, of course I would have been bored. So what? Wasn't I a fellow who had endured three solid months at the Erie County Comptroller's Office? What could Uncle Sam think up that could be more boring than that? And what duty could touch running a pedometer over an Erie County street map in the realm of pure-dee chickenshit?

Ah, hindsight. All I knew about the Service in 1957 was that I wanted to stay the hell out of it.

So I went to Columbia instead.

HERE'S HOW IT happened. In December, after I'd been at the agency for three months or so, I realized that I could get drafted. By withdrawing from Antioch, I'd given up my deferred status. If my draft board called me, I was screwed. I'd be wearing khaki before I knew it.

There was a way to insure against this eventuality. If I were a matriculated student at a college or university, they wouldn't take me. I didn't want to be a student, I didn't want to study anything, I barely had enough hours in the day for the things I was doing already—but I didn't want to get drafted, either.

So I applied to Columbia's School of General Studies, and of course I was accepted. GS was Columbia's adult education program, and most of the people who attended did not matriculate. They took courses for the sheer pleasure of learning, or to acquire skills that would be valuable in their careers, or to get out of the house and keep from dying of boredom. They paid considerably less per credit than if they were enrolled as matriculated students—and, since they were mostly women over fifty, the prospect of getting drafted was of relatively little concern to them.

Since draft avoidance was the only reason I was going, the sheer pleasure of learning didn't enter into it. My object, in selecting a course of study, was to pick courses that would interfere as little as possible with my real interest, which was writing.

So I signed up for three writing courses.

All I can say is that it made sense to me at the time. I figured I was going to be writing anyway, so I'd make my writing do double-duty, submitting one copy to a professor and giving the other to Henry to sell. There was a novel-writing workshop, and I knew I really wanted to get a novel underway, so I signed up for that. There was a course called Advanced Non-Fiction, and I was doing some articles anyway, so I enrolled. And there was a course on writing for radio and television, which was emphatically not something that interested me, but it fit into my schedule neatly enough. I took it.

I must have been out of my mind.

I was able to enroll for the classes I wanted, and I got my schedule. All of my classes were at the same time of day—7 to 9, I think, or maybe 8 to 10. I had my novel-writing workshop on Monday, the non-fiction class on Tuesday, and radio-TV on Wednesday.

On a January Monday I came home from work, had something to eat, and trotted off to my first class. The instructor, a rather theatrical gentleman, told us how we would proceed. We would each be working on a novel, and each week he would read what a couple of us had brought in, and we'd discuss it. Did anyone have a novel already underway? Wonderful! And had anyone brought in something to be read?

Someone had. I sat and listened, and two things began to become clear to me. First, I was going to have to write a novel, and I didn't have a clue how to do that. Secondly, I was stuck here in this goddam chair listening to him read the very same kind of amateur crap I had to read all day long, and I wasn't getting paid for it.

The following day I showed up for Advanced Non-Fiction. The professor was a very decent older gentleman named Vernon Loggins. He'd published several scholarly biographies of composers with Louisiana State University Press, and he too favored the workshop approach, with a student's work read and discussed at each session. Once again I got to listen to material not much removed from the stuff Sid kept cramming into the file cabinet.

Then it was Wednesday, and I was at my radio and TV class, where we were to spend the semester writing an original teleplay. The instructor showed us the format we were to use, with the page divided in half vertically, the audio on one side, the video on the other. I didn't know much about script writing, but I knew that format had gone out of use with "Kukla, Fran and Ollie." By the end of class I realized that the dude teaching it knew less about the subject than I did, and that I wasn't going back.

I spent the weekend trying to get a novel going, and brought in a chapter Monday evening. I'd entitled the thing *The Diamond Whore*, and he praised that as catchy and provocative. He said lots of encouraging things about the first chapter, too, but I knew better. I knew it was a pale imitation of Fredric Brown's wonderful first novel, *The Fabulous Clipjoint*. I knew, too, that what I'd written was awful, and that I had nowhere to go with it.

Then the fellow who'd read a horribly boring chapter the previous week read the horribly boring chapter that followed it. I realized I was going to get to hear chunks of that dreary novel for the next three months.

The hell I was.

From that point on I had Monday and Wednesday nights to myself. I never again attended either class, nor did I formally withdraw. At the end of the semester the Monday night man gave me an Incomplete, while the TV guy gave me an F.

But I got a B in Advanced Non-Fiction.

It was a curious class. There were probably twelve to fifteen people signed up for it, but, as usually happens in a writing workshop, half of them never brought anything in, and the others always did. Of the latter group, almost everything they were working on related to Asia.

Only one person was actually Asian. He was Chinese, with relatives who'd played an important role in Chiang's Kuomintang government, and he was writing a doctoral thesis in history on some aspect of Nationalist China. He was taking this course not because he wanted to be a writer but with the aim of improving his writing for the thesis itself. He wasn't that confident of his facility with written English, and wanted to improve it. So every Tuesday he came to class, and intermittently we'd hear some more of his thesis.

I wonder if the class did him any good at all. It seemed to me that he was the best writer in the class. His sentences and paragraphs flowed smoothly and his material was lucid and well-organized. It wasn't interesting, it was far too specialized and academic to be interesting, but you couldn't fault him for that. It wasn't supposed to be interesting.

Another woman, a retired schoolteacher, had spent a year in Japan on a Fulbright scholarship. She was writing a book on her experiences, and every week we got to hear another chapter. *Chapter Three—I Eat Raw Fish! Chapter Four—We Visit the Public Baths!*

Another woman was a committed feminist, and was writing a book to be composed of a dozen or so biographical sketches. The topic? Women of Asia.

Yet another woman had recently retired from the Marine Corps and wanted to do magazine articles on various topics, some military, some historical, some neither. Thank God for her. I don't remember whether she was good or bad, but at least she wasn't coming in with another installment of the same damned thing every week. Anything's bearable, I found out, if it's no more than 3000 words long and you only have to hear it once and then you're done with it.

There were some other students I've forgotten. And there were the ones who never brought in a thing, or at least never read what they'd written.

And there was me.

I didn't attend every single week, though I certainly showed up more often than not. At a guess, I'd say I got to two classes out of three. And, when I did show up, I almost always brought in an article.

Where did I get them? That was easy. I handed in the ones I was writing for Ted Hecht.

WELL, WHAT THE hell else was I supposed to do? I had to turn in something. I suppose I might have written something special for the class, something with an Asian slant to it, so to speak. "Yashimoto, Blond Beast of the Co-Prosperity Sphere." That sort of thing.

Instead, I brought in carbons of my articles for *Real Man* and its fellows. I know I submitted my Morro Castle epic, and a few others I can't remember. I left "She Doesn't Want *You*" at home, but, I blush to admit, among the articles I brought in was the one about nasty old Reinhard Heydrich.

I wasn't prepared for the reception I got.

I didn't figure Loggins would like the stuff. I thought he might grudgingly acknowledge it as professional while lamenting the fact that I was wasting my talent on such swill. And I'd have had no quarrel with that.

Instead, he expressed great admiration for the pieces I submitted, but said he didn't see how I could expect to sell them. While they were at once interesting and well-written, it didn't seem to him as though they had much chance in the marketplace. They were excellent, he felt, but they weren't commercial.

I knew better. They weren't excellent—they weren't even good—but you couldn't tell me they weren't commercial. Because I don't think I ever showed him an article that I hadn't already sold.

"This is fine work," he would say. "But where could you possibly place it?" Perhaps one of the men's magazines, I suggested. But would it really fit their requirements? I allowed as how I thought it might.

One time, unable to find my carbon of a particular article, I handed in tear sheets. He still worried that the piece, while praiseworthy, would very likely prove unpublishable.

LATER, WHEN I ultimately left Scott's employ and returned to Antioch, I might have attempted to get academic credit for my time in Vernon Loggins's classroom. I'd earned a B in the course, and I'm fairly sure the credits would have been transferable.

I never even considered trying. I was perfectly happy to pretend as though the whole semester had never happened, and to forget about that B, and the F and the Incomplete as well.

Why, I wonder? Perhaps because I felt less than proud of my performance. Perhaps my reason was the same unstated one that had kept me from going back to claim my day's pay from Mildred's Chowderhouse. Perhaps I felt the small gain wasn't worth the embarrassment.

7

JUST BECAUSE I never went back to my Monday-night class, that didn't mean I'd given up on the idea of writing a novel. I was quick to give up on *The Diamond Whore*, title and all, but I remained entirely certain that I wanted to sit down and turn out what Randall Jarrell defined as "a prose narrative of some length that has something wrong with it." (I wish I'd been familiar with that definition at the time. It might have made the whole business a little less terrifying.)

Real writers, I knew, wrote novels. That was where the money was, and the glory, and the satisfaction. That's what I most enjoyed reading, and that's what I wanted to write.

I couldn't figure out how to do it.

I was certainly *reading* my share of novels. Even as I filled my apartment with back copies of *Manhunt* and its fellows, I was buying up secondhand paperback crime novels at the same mad pace, and reading them as fast as I was buying them. When I liked a writer's short stories, I went in search of his novels. A *Manhunt* short story by David Alexander led me to try one of his books, and before long I'd read his complete works. (Alexander, a writer for the *Morning Telegraph*, had as his series character a Broadway press agent named Bart Hardin, who lived on West 42nd Street upstairs of Hubert's Flea Circus, wore brightly-colored vests, drank Irish whisky, and never took a drink before 4 pm or turned one down after that hour. I read somewhere that Alexander wrote each of his first drafts in the first person, then carefully rewrote them in the third person. Why, I have long wondered, would anyone do that more than once?)

I rushed headlong through the complete works of everybody I could find who wrote crime fiction that I admired. For a very small fee I joined the Mercantile Library, just a block from the office. They had a great selection of popular fiction and never got rid of a book, which made them a fine source of out-of-print work. I read Hammett and Chandler and Ross Macdonald, Fredric Brown and Ellery Queen, Rex Stout and Cornell Woolrich. I read everybody.

I should stress that I didn't do this out of sheer professional dedication. I read the stuff because I enjoyed it. And I've always believed that it helped me internalize a sense of what a novel was. But I couldn't access the knowledge. I couldn't even figure out how to begin.

John Dobbin, who'd been published by Avon, had written his novel with the guidance of a book on the subject by Manuel Komroff, and he made me a loan of it. I got about a third of the way into Komroff's book and my head was spinning. According to him, the first thing you did when you wanted to write a novel was buy yourself stacks of three-by-five index cards in three colors. The white cards were your character cards and the blue cards were your incident cards, or maybe it was the other way around. I forget what the pink cards were. By the time you'd filled up all the cards and arranged them in the proper order, you were ready to write your book, and perfectly organized, too.

I was awash in despair. I was perfectly willing to believe that this was the way to do it, and I'm sure it worked superbly for Komroff, who wrote elaborately plotted historical novels that spanned generations and had hundreds of characters. But I knew I couldn't write anything that way. I couldn't even bring myself to buy the cards.

I read somewhere that Fredric Brown used to ride buses all night before he wrote a book. That was how he worked out his plots. It sounded better to me than index cards, so one night I decided to stay up and ride the subway until dawn. I got on the uptown IRT, rode it all the way to Riverdale, then stayed on it for its return run and rode clear out to New Lots Avenue in Brooklyn and back again. I didn't think of a single plot. All I could think of was how tired I was, and when the train got back to 103rd Street I got off and went to bed.

LARRY HARRIS HELPED me edge a little closer to writing a novel. He got me a gig writing *The Strange Sisterhood of Madam Adista*.

Larry was 26 at the time. He too had worked for Scott at a tender age, preceding Henry on the foreign rights desk. (How they hated each other. I was never sure exactly why. Maybe it was karmic. One time Larry said something nasty about Henry, and someone else offered that you had to understand Henry. "There is a time for understanding," Larry said, "and there is a time for hate.")

I thought Larry was remarkably exotic. He was Jewish, and married a Jewish girl named Sylvia. The two of them converted to Catholicism together. They lived out in Brooklyn. Larry wrote various stuff, crime fiction, science fiction, and had once been called upon to complete a magazine serial for Craig Rice, who'd gone on a drunk and never delivered the last installment. Rice had since died, and Larry had a profitable sideline turning out "recently discovered stories by the late Craig Rice." Scott had done well representing Craig Rice during her lifetime, and saw no reason why the woman had to stop writing just because she was dead. (Evan Hunter completed a novel Craig had left unfinished at her death, and it was published as *The April Robin Murders*, with a joint byline, Craig Rice and Ed McBain. And Larry later wrote *The Pickled Poodles*; originally conceived of as another recent discovery, it was instead presented as a novel by Larry M. Harris, based on characters created by Craig Rice.)

Larry was intimately acquainted with the Times Square porno scene, and wrote an article about it. At his request, Henry sent it to *Playboy*; when they passed, it was immediately submitted to Ted Hecht, who snapped it up for a hot fifty bucks. (Boy, did those two hate each other.)

One day Larry showed me a booklet. I don't remember the title, but it was a cheaply printed affair, maybe 48 pages long, staple bound, with a cover showing a woman in what I would later learn was dominatrix drag—high heels, domino mask, long gloves, etc. He explained that it was an example of over-the-counter flag porn. (Flag, short for flagellation, was a generic label for any sort of S&M pornography.)

The boys on 42nd Street, Larry explained, had done very well with this little number, and, since the author was unavailable, one of them had commissioned him to produce a sequel. "But I can't," he said. "You do it."

I asked him why he didn't want to do it himself.

"I told you," he said. "I can't. But you could. Ten thousand words, and they'll pay a hundred dollars."

Not a fortune, but not bad for a guaranteed sale. I agreed to read it, and after I did I got in touch with him. "I thought it would be dirty," I said.

"No," he said. "It can't be dirty. They sell this out in the open, not under the counter. If it was dirty, they could get arrested."

"Nothing happens," I said.

"No," he agreed. "Nothing happens. Nothing has to happen in the sequel, either. They want to call it *The Strange Sisterhood of Madam Adista*. And the name to put on it is Larry G. Streater."

Who, I wondered, was Larry G. Streater?

"I guess they think that's my name," he said. "I guess I told them it was."

"Ah," I said. "What happens in the book?"

"Madam Adista returns," he said, "and has a strange sisterhood, and initiates some sweet young thing into it." Was there a lesbian element?

"There's the implication of lesbianism," he said. "There's a lesbian aura. If there were actual lesbianism, they could get arrested." And what about punishment and torture? Was there any of that? "There's the threat of punishment," he said. "Maybe she takes her down to a dungeon and shows her whips and chains and instruments of torture, and the sweet young thing is horrified. But there's no actual torture, because—" They could get arrested? Right, he said.

I said I figured I could probably do it. I could use the $100, and this would be the longest piece of writing I'd done. Maybe it would be a good warm-up exercise for the novel. And, I said, I wouldn't have to pay Scott a commission on this, would I?

"You won't have to pay *Scott* a commission," he said.

At the time there was something on Broadway north of 42nd Street called Ripley's Believe It or Not Odditorium, with a museum full of the kind of oddities you might expect on the first floor. Down a flight, they had their Chamber of Horrors, filled with replicas of devices to gladden the heart of Torquemada. There was an iron maiden, there was a rack, there was a broad axe and a chopping block, and some of the scariest-looking people on the planet used to spend hours down there, just staring at all of this weird shit. I based Madam Adista's dungeon on what I'd seen down there, and it was a great success. I wrote the book over the weekend, and Larry took it to 42nd Street and brought back $90 for me.

The Strange Sisterhood of Madam Adista was a hot ticket on Times Square for years. All the bookshops carried it, openly displayed but wrapped in cellophane to discourage browsers. The book bore the pen name "Rodney Canewell" as a clue to its contents. They charged ten bucks for it on 42nd Street, and must have reprinted it many times.

They wanted more of the same, too, and somewhere along the way I wrote *The Wrath of Aunt Lorna*, which Larry dutifully agented for me. I don't remember what that was about, and I can't recall ever seeing it offered for sale. Maybe they called it something else. I remember that I wrote it, and I remember that I got paid.

Were these books good warm-up exercises for my first novel? I suppose they must have been. The simple feat of sustaining the flow of a fictional narrative for 10,000 words was an accomplishment. I was going to have to string 60,000 words together in order to write a novel, and the task seemed less Herculean with Madam Adista safely behind me.

And, of course, it prepared me in ways I never would have anticipated. A year later, when I was the toast of 42nd Street, I could look back on Madam Adista as having launched me on my career as a pornographer.

IF I'D HAD EVEN a short-range crystal ball, I'd have been a lot more sanguine about the prospect of writing a novel. In the spring of '58 I saw the whole business as unimaginably difficult. Within a year, I'd have written and sold four of them, and shortly thereafter I was turning out one a month.

Lacking this certainty, I looked around for something to write about. I read something, I don't know what, about the 1916 Easter Rising in Ireland and the Troubles that followed over the next decade, and I thought that would be a wonderful subject for a novel. Unfortunately I didn't know anything about it, and I felt I ought to do the necessary research. I hit the bookstores on Fourth Avenue—it was still Bookseller's Row, though the rise of the paperback was beginning to have an impact. I bought everything I could find in the way of Irish history, and did a little reading at odd moments. I hadn't read much before it struck me that I ought to know something about English history in order to understand Irish history, and so I began assembling a library on the subject. One of the first things I bought was Sir Charles Oman's six-volume history of England before the Norman Conquest.

Now that's preparation. I wanted to write a thriller set in Ireland in the 1920s, and I started out by studying about pre-Roman Britain. Only a man who was utterly terrified of writing a novel would think that was a sensible approach.

I never wrote the first sentence of a novel of the Irish Troubles, and find it incomprehensible that I ever thought I ought to. But for a couple of years I continued to tell myself it was something I would get around to sooner or later, and I went on reading English and Irish history well into the early '70s. I amassed quite a library on the subject. It all went in '75, when I sold off most of my books after my marriage ended.

In the early '80s I led a once-a-week Mystery Writers of America short-story workshop, and for the first time in ages I had occasion to think of my Irish novel and the research I'd undertaken on its behalf. There was a woman in the class, a pretty good writer, and she was planning to set a short story in Jerusalem. So she was studying guidebooks, and trying to get a good street map of the city, and otherwise preparing to research the thing to death. If she were setting the same story in New York, I said, would she bother to name the streets? She agreed that she probably would not, and was able to see that her research was a guilt-free form of procrastination, a way to avoid plunging in and writing a story that scared her.

THE IRISH NOVEL, I soon saw, was something that would have to wait until I was ready. Anyway, it was far too ambitious for a first book.

So I decided to write a lesbian novel instead.

GOD KNOWS I'D read enough of them.

In the late fifties, lesbian fiction was an extremely popular paperback category. Two kinds of readers were drawn to the books—gay women who could identify with the characters, and men who were turned on by the idea of female homosexuality. Several publishers worked to meet the demand, most notably Crest. Fawcett originally established the Crest imprint as a reprint line, since Gold Medal published paperback originals exclusively. Crest added originals as well, especially lesbian novels.

I read them all, books by Ann Bannon and Valerie Taylor and everybody else who came down the pike. I read and reread Ann Aldrich's lesbian nonfiction, with loads of detail on the lesbian psyche and lifestyle. (Years later I would learn that Ann Aldrich was one of the innumerable pen names of Marijane Meaker, who also wrote tough psychologically-oriented suspense novels for Gold Medal as Vin Packer and kid's books as M. E. Kerr.) Some of these books were quite good and some of them were not so good and some of them were lousy. Didn't matter. I read 'em all.

Why, I wonder? I found them arousing, but that seems insufficient explanation for the fascination. I was nineteen years old, for God's sake. I found *everything* arousing. And the books themselves were a far cry from pornographic, and barely erotic. They never told you what the women were doing, let alone described it. (I knew what they were doing, as a matter of fact, but I understand that some men, equally devoted to lesbian fiction, didn't have a clue. They read the books anyway.)

After years of thought, and after having heard and read all the usual explanations, I've concluded that I can't explain why I felt such a strong identification with gay women. If I had to come up with an explanation, I suppose I'd have to attribute it to a carryover from a past life. I realize this will dumbfound those readers who are only willing to believe in one life at the most, but I can't help that. There are other elements in my personality that only make sense to me in past-life terms, the most obvious being my similar (if utterly nonsexual) fascination with Ireland.

I was drawn to Ireland and things Irish long before I ever thought of setting a novel there. One of my earliest memories is of hearing someone sing "Toora Loora" on a Sunday morning radio program for kids. I must have been four or five. I never got the song out of my head. When I was nine years old I learned other Irish songs from the *Book of Knowledge*, and I still remember all the words to "The Wearin' of the Green." (It wasn't until years later that I found out the tune. I'd made up my own tune for it, something reminiscent of "McNamara's Band.") And when I finally got off the plane at Shannon in 1965, I felt immediately at home. It seems undeniable to me that I lived several past lives there.

HOW STRANGE TO be writing this all down, putting it out for the world to see. I never in my life expected to be doing this.

READING THOSE LESBIAN novels, I experienced something besides identification and titillation. I had a strong sense that I could do this, that I could write one of these books. And I suppose a novel began to take shape somewhere in my unconscious mind.

Then one day I went down to the Village after work and got drunk.

More accurately, I got drunk on the way down there. I don't know why, but for some reason when I left work it occurred to me to pass up the subway and walk downtown. This was not such a strange idea, as it was a beautiful spring day. What was unusual was that I decided to stop and have a glass of beer at every bar along the way. I don't know that I managed to hit them all, but I got to enough of them to render me positively shitfaced by the time I crossed 14th Street.

And that's about as much as I remember of the evening, and probably as much as anyone in his right mind would care to remember. Somewhere in the course of the evening I ran into Paul Eiden, and he put me into a cab and sent me home.

(Paul was a new fee man at SMLA, probably thirty-five or forty, and the kind of sometime-writer you found all over the Village in those days. He'd tended bar at a batch of downtown saloons, picked up the odd day's work at a moving and storage company, and wrote a good sentence. He was particularly good at knocking out men's magazine articles, and the pen name he insisted on using was Matthew Shipwreck.)

I woke up the next day with the worst hangover I had ever had in my life. In the years to follow I endured some that might have been worse, but not by much. Everything hurt, but that was the least of it. It was the kind of hangover in which every minute on the clock takes roughly an hour and a half of subjective time. It was shaping up as the worst day of my life, and it was going to last forever.

Going to the office was completely out of the question. Fortunately I didn't have to. This would have been in late April or early May of '58, and by that time I no longer had a desk at the office. Like John Dobbin before me, I had achieved the status of an Old Reliable and could come in once or twice a week, pick up a stack of fee manuscripts, and do them at home, scheduling my time however I wished.

I didn't have a roommate anymore, either. A couple of months earlier, Bob Aronson had bitten the rifle bullet and gone for one of those six-month enlistments. After he marched off to basic training, I had the management of the Alexandria switch me to a single room on another floor. (My rent stayed the same, $60 a month.)

So there I was, all alone, with nothing I had to do. And, sometime in the early afternoon, I sat down at my typewriter and proceeded to bat out a detailed chapter-by-chapter outline of a lesbian novel.

I DON'T KNOW how to account for it. God knows I got drunk enough times thereafter, and had my fair share of hangovers. None of them ever unleashed such a burst of creativity. Post-alcoholic remorse, yes. Despair, indeed, and plenty of it. But no creative energy. Years later I would write a book called *After the First Death*, in the first chapter of which the narrator wakes up after a drunk and there's a dead prostitute sprawled on the carpet. In none of my own dead-whore-on-the-floor mornings, I assure you, did I leap out of bed and outline a novel.

I can only guess that the plot was all there, tucked away out of sight in some part of my mind I didn't know about. Maybe it would have emerged hangover or no. Maybe not. But there it was, right there on two single-spaced pages.

As soon as I got home to Buffalo, I was going to write it.

8

I'D ALREADY GIVEN notice. Earlier that spring I'd realized that, if I was not interested in a career as a literary agent or another job in publishing, it was time to move on. I wasn't learning much at the job now, and I'd read so much bad writing that it all seemed the same to me.

I decided to go back to college.

My folks may have suggested it, after I'd mentioned that the job had lost its edge. Wherever the idea came from, it made sense to me. I was obviously not going to maintain my draft-exempt status by going to Columbia nights, and it still seemed important for me to stay out of the army.

More important, there wasn't any reason *not* to go back to Antioch. I had left for a reason, and a good one—to keep the job at Scott Meredith. If I were to leave the job, why not return to Yellow Springs? What else was there for me to do?

Did I even consider writing full-time? I think not. I probably could have made a living that way, between the crime fiction magazines and the other markets I'd cracked. But I don't remember giving it much thought. It seems to me that I have tended all my life to perceive only two alternatives in situations which actually have held many more options than that. Here the alternatives I saw were staying on the job or returning to college. I never really looked for a third way.

*   *   *

I TOLD THE college I wanted to come back, and they told me that was fine. Shortly thereafter I had to make a trip out to Ohio; two factions were vying to make some point in campus politics, and one wanted me to edit the college newspaper for a semester on my return. I agreed to present myself as a candidate, and went out there to interview with Pub Board, the committee that made those decisions. A couple of friends coached me on how to approach the interview—all I recall is that I professed myself to be a fan of functional modern typography, whatever the hell that is—and I got the job.

Back in the city, I told Sid of my intention to leave. He thought it was wise of me to complete my formal education—other people always think college is a good idea, just so they don't have to go there themselves. Nor was he upset to lose me. It was rare for anybody to stay on the fee desk for much more than a year. If you were capable enough to get and hold the job, you were good enough to go on to something better, and it usually didn't take too long until you did.

The college had given me a form so that I could obtain co-op credit for the term of my employment. I showed it to Sid and asked him if he would fill it out, verifying my employment, providing a description of my duties, and evaluating my performance. He looked it over. "Sure," he said. "Why not?" Then he looked at it again, frowned and handed it to me. "I'll tell you what," he said. "You fill it out, okay?"

So I filled it out, gave myself an excellent rating, and took it in to him. And he signed Scott's name to it.

HOW CAN I have written this much without having said much of anything about Scott Meredith?

He deserves a whole book to himself, and now that he's gone he may get it. (No one would have dared write about him while he was alive.)

I know a fellow who's started a book about Scott, and I hope he sees it through to the end.

Like everyone else who had any contact, I have some stories about the man. But I won't tell them here. They're other people's stories, not mine. And I haven't got many stories of my own, because I never knew the man.

I don't mean I never knew the *real* Scott Meredith, never got beneath the slick surface, never probed the secrets of his soul. I never even knew the slick surface. I worked there for nine months, and I barely met the fellow.

Scott stayed in his large private office in the back, and rarely passed through our office when he left it. We didn't see him much. Henry was running in there all the time, and Bob Grindell, who took over foreign rights when Henry replaced Jim as pro man, was also in there a fair amount. Scott never had any reason to talk to any of the rest of us, and didn't.

I was only in his office once. It happened when I switched from fee scripts to Personal Collaboration.

After Ivan left, there was a rapid turnover on the PC desk. One fellow stood it for three days, then went out to lunch and never came back. I ran into him a week later in the Village and asked him what had happened. "I just couldn't stand another minute of it," he said. "They were decent about it, they mailed me my check." He asked who'd replaced him, and I said that a chap named Henry Chin was now doing PC. "Ah, the wily Oriental mind," he said. "Perhaps he'll prove better equipped to cope." Henry Chin coped, but not for long, and PC men continued to come and go. And at one point I took it over. I don't know whether Sid offered it to me or I volunteered.

I guess I thought it would make a change, and that it would be good experience. There was certainly no financial incentive for making the move. On PC I earned a straight $65 a week, which was only five dollars more than my base and ten or fifteen bucks less than I usually wound up earning. Whatever my reasoning, I took it, and I hated it.

It was hard not to. Instead of just writing a fee report and being done with it, the PC man had to take each piece of crap and help the author polish it. This didn't make it good. It didn't even necessarily make it better. Finally, after the victim had been led through outline and first draft and rewrite, the PC man wrote this glowing letter about how eagerly we would be marketing the book or story or whatever the hell it was. Then it went in a box and stayed there, and the PC man tried to jolly the sucker into repeating the process.

I not only hated it, I was also lousy at it. This did not escape unnoticed, and one day Scott called me in. I believe it was the only time I was ever in his office.

"Larry," he said, "what the hell are you doing on PC? You were doing great writing fee reports and you were making a lot more money. Wouldn't you rather go back to it?"

"Sure," I said.

"That's settled, then," he said, and I went into the other office and changed desks.

MEMORY'S A CURIOUS THING.

Part of our family lore during my childhood was the story of a time a friend of my mother's explained how she'd slammed a finger in the car door. "Oh, God, that's terrible," my mother said. "That happened to me once and it was just excruciating. The pain was the worst I've ever experienced, and the nail turned black and fell off, and it took ages to grow back. The whole business was absolutely awful and I'll never forget it." Then she stopped abruptly and frowned. "Wait a minute," she said. "Was it me? Or did it happen to my brother Hi?"

I HAVE A Scott Meredith story that's like that. One morning either Bob Grindell told me a dream he'd had, or I made up a dream and told it to him.

Let's say it was Bob's dream. It always makes a better story if you can give the good lines to the other person.

So here's what happened. During the coffee break one morning Bob Grindell said to me, "I had the damnedest dream last night. Scott called me into his office and he was really upset. 'Bob,' he said, 'Helen's left me.'

"I said, 'Helen Nielson?'" (Helen Nielson was a client, a fine writer of mystery fiction.) "And he said, 'God forbid. No, not Helen Nielson. Helen, my wife.'

"'That's really terrible,' I said. 'I'm awfully sorry.' 'I know,' he said. 'It's very upsetting. Now here's what I want you to do. I want you to write her a letter over my signature. Make it warm and sincere . . .'"

Who's dream was it, Bob's or mine? Or was it my brother Hi?

DURING MY ABSENCE, Antioch had changed its calendar. They did this every once in a while, just to keep you on your toes. It wasn't enough that the damned school had you picking up and moving halfway across the country every three months. They had to keep tinkering with the system, tweaking the schedule, changing the core curriculum, teaching you to adjust rapidly to new realities.

The new calendar called for three academic quarters, October – December, January – March, and April – June. Starting in October, I would be in Yellow Springs for nine straight months. I'd be taking classes the first semester, editing the school paper in the middle quarter, and taking another load of courses in the spring. Because I'd be getting co-op credit for my hitch at SMLA, and because I'd spent my whole freshman year on campus, I would be able to graduate on schedule in June of 1960.

Although I wouldn't be starting school until the fall, I wrote my last fee report sometime in late May or early June. I'd been in touch with Steve Schwerner, my freshman roommate, and we'd made plans to spend the summer in Mexico. First I'd go home to Buffalo, then back to New York to meet up with Steve at his parents' house in Pelham. Then we'd fly to Mexico, and contrive to get home sometime around Labor Day, well before it was time to get to Yellow Springs.

RIGHT BEFORE I left, I had another drunken evening in the Village. According to Van Ronk, at one point I staggered into the Figaro and announced in a loud voice that I was leaving the city. "The hell with New York," I shouted. "I'm going back to Buffalo. I'm going to write a fucking lesbian novel!"

BACK IN BUFFALO, I carried my suitcases into my bedroom and un-packed. On the second or third day I set up my typewriter on the little maple desk I'd had since grade school. I had a book to write, and I didn't have time to waste.

I wrote my lesbian novel. The outline that had poured out of me during that endless hangover was a sound one, and I was ready get crack-ing on the book. I don't know how long it took me, but I'm sure it was no more than three weeks. My birthday's June 24th, and I finished a day or two before that. While I hadn't been racing a deadline, it pleased me to have completed a novel before I turned twenty.

It was a great experience writing that novel. While I never confused it in my mind with *War and Peace*, while I knew nobody was likely to compare it with *Moby-Dick*, I was able to take it seriously. The characters were very real to me. I wrote it as well as I knew how, and I felt equal to the task. While the book didn't write itself, neither did I get stuck along the way.

I'm sure it would embarrass me to read the book today. I must have read it through when it was published, but I doubt that I've looked at it since. I'm sure I'd find something to wince at in every chapter. The writing, I suspect, would cause me less pain than the awful callowness of the author.

Shall I tell you the plot? Jan, fresh out of a midwestern college and confused about her sexuality after a wretched heterosexual experience, comes to New York and settles in Greenwich Village. There she meets Mike—I think his name was Mike—a young folksinger trying to make it on his own in the big city. On Macdougal Street, at the approximate location of the old Swing Rendezvous, is a lesbian bar called the Shadows, and there she meets up with the darkly attractive Laura, who's been living on Minetta Lane, as I recall, with her lover, Peggy.

Triangle time. Mike and Laura both want Jan. Jan and Peggy both want Laura. Shit happens. Jan has an affair with Laura, Peggy wanders off and gets drunk and is raped by some local toughs, Jan realizes that she's not really gay, and she winds up with Mike. The End.

The structure, as I think back on it, was fairly sophisticated for such a youthful effort. I wrote the book in the third person, with Jan the viewpoint character. Every third chapter, however, was told from the point of view of one of the subordinate characters, and included that individual's back story as well as advancing the ongoing narrative. I had evidently been paying attention when I read my way through Fredric Brown and Evan Hunter.

It was surprisingly easy to write from a female point of view. But I made mistakes I wouldn't become aware of for years. Jan never carried a handbag, for example. She was always digging in her pocket for her keys or her money. No one ever noticed, including the woman who edited the book. Maybe people just figured it was a lesbian thing, not carrying a purse, jamming your keys in your pocket. Butch as all get out.

*   *   *

I CALLED THE book *Shadows*. That was the name of the bar, but the title came first. It seems to me I had the title in mind before I got drunk and woke up and wrote the outline. I remember asking Larry Harris what he thought of the title.

"I don't know," he said. "Maybe *In the Shadows* would be better."

"*In the Shadows?*"

"Yeah, that would work," he said. "Victor McLaglen, Barry Fitzgerald, desperate men with handkerchiefs over their faces—"

I asked him what the hell he was talking about.

"Your Irish novel," he said. "What did you think we were talking about?"

"Oh, I won't be ready to write that for a while yet," I said. "I was thinking of doing a lesbian novel."

"Oh," he said. "Well, for a lesbian novel, just plain *Shadows* would be fine."

I called it just plain *Shadows*, and I sent it off to Henry in New York. I knew the book had to have a female pen name on it, because who would want to read a lesbian novel by a man? I used the name Rhoda Moore. Who knows why.

Before I left for Mexico, Henry reported that he'd read the book and it looked okay. He was going to start the marketing process. I went to Moe Cheplove, our family doctor, and got the shots I'd need in Mexico, along with a prescription for penicillin, to be taken in case I suspected I'd caught something nasty from a Mexican toilet seat.

I met up with Steve in New York, stayed for a night or two with his folks in Pelham, then took a night flight to Houston, arriving there around dawn. We spent a long day hitching down to Laredo, checked into a hotel a few blocks from the border, and walked on across into the Mexican border town of Nueva Laredo.

We found our way to the public square. Immediately a cab driver rushed up to us and offered us girls. We asked if he could get us some marijuana. He backed away, shaking his head. "No, no, señores," he said. "Marijuana is illegal in Mexico." We started on around the square, walked maybe thirty yards, and another cabbie made the same offer, got the same response from us, and turned us down with the same words. "I guess my information was wrong," Steve said, and we continued walking around the square.

When we'd gotten halfway around it, a Mexican walked up to us. "My name's Ernesto," he said in unaccented English. "I understand you boys are looking to buy a little pot."

We bought a couple of joints and took them across the border to our hotel. We smoked them the following afternoon. It was my first experience with marijuana. Steve had smoked before, but only once or twice, and never with particularly good dope. We got wonderfully, gloriously high, and just lay on our backs looking at the stains on the ceiling and thinking deep thoughts. While I never became a heavy user of marijuana, I smoked many times over the next fifteen years, less toward the end because the drug so often made me anxious and paranoid.

But I never had a high that could match that first time in Laredo.

WE SPENT THREE days in Laredo, visiting the whores in the Boys' Town cribs. Then we took a bus to Mexico City, where my friend Peter Hochstein was visiting his Antioch roommate, Rafael Davidson. Steve and I got a hotel room and looked up a fellow named Bob, a Korean War vet who was attending Mexico City College on the GI Bill. The school had been established specifically to serve the needs of American vets. Classes were all in English, and tuition was cheap, as was the cost of living in Mexico. A vet on the GI Bill could take a few courses, attend class if and when he felt like it, rent a decent apartment, eat at restaurants, and still be able to afford to spend his nights drinking and whoring.

That's what we did for about a week. Bob took us to an establishment at 9 Medellín that was like a social club; you could drink Dos Equis all night, and no one seemed to care if you went upstairs with a girl or not. We met Alonzo Perry there, a black ballplayer from Alabama who'd moved down to play in the Mexican League, and we met other vets and hangers-on. Bob himself was an authentic Beat, and the perfect host. I've often wondered what became of him.

IF WE'D HAD any sense we'd have stayed in Mexico City until it was time to go back to college. We'd met some interesting people, had found some amusing ways to pass the time, and were living well in a beautiful and exciting city. (It had only a fraction of its present population, and was not the polluted sinkhole it has since become.)

But no, we had to move on, had to see the real Mexico, the Mexico the tourist never discovers. And so we took a bus to Guadalajara, planning to continue on to Puerto Vallarta, then an unspoiled paradise on the Pacific.

In Guadalajara we looked up Charles Roberts, one of Scott's PC clients. I'd worked with Roberts during my brief swing on the PC desk, and had buoyantly assured him we were taking his manuscript right out to market, as others had told him we'd done with the other masterpieces he'd produced that way. (Roberts, I should say, was not utterly inept, and had sold to *Bluebook* or *Argosy* previously. Why he fell for the PC dodge is beyond me.) I don't know why I thought it would be a good idea to go see him, but I called and introduced myself and he invited us over.

It turned out that he was wheelchair bound, crippled by MS or something like it. He'd retired to Mexico because it was a place where he could live decently on his savings. Not only was the exchange rate favorable, but you could lend out capital in Mexico at positively usurious rates of interest. And you could write your lousy stories, and wheel yourself out to the mailbox each morning, hoping for word that Scott had sold something for you.

What a depressing visit. I assured him that Scott thought highly of his work, and that it was just a matter of time until his stuff started to sell. Then Steve and I got away as quickly as we could. It was much easier to strike a cavalier attitude toward Scott's various victims, I found out, if you didn't have to meet the poor bastards.

THE NIGHT BEFORE we were supposed to leave Guadalajara, we were on our way back to the hotel after dinner when we walked into the middle of a riot in the public square. There was a national election scheduled, and as usual the result was a foregone conclusion. PAN, one of the opposition parties, had evidently decided not to wait until Election Day to register their protest. All around us, people were flinging Molotov cocktails and the cops were blasting them with tear gas.

If we'd been bright enough to get the hell out of there the minute we saw what was going on, we'd have been all right. But it was far too fascinating and we couldn't tear ourselves away. The next thing we knew we were under arrest.

I suppose they might have thought at first that we were agitators, but the minute they scooped us up they knew better. They also realized we were a nice potential source of income, and they made the most of us, letting us sit incommunicado overnight in jail, then taking us back to our hotel and playing good cop-bad cop with us. (The bad cop looked at the Religion entry on our passports and was outraged. I had put "Jewish," while Steve had put "None." "To be a Jew is bad enough," he thundered, "but to have no religion at all is much worse!" He read an account of a visit to 9 Medellín in a diary I'd been keeping, accused us of moral turpitude, and confiscated it. He also took Steve's copy of *The Brothers Karamazov*, which he was sure had to be a communist tract. Then he acted his way into a frenzy and stuck his gun in our faces; we knew it was an act, but felt there was a good possibility he would get carried away with himself and blow our brains out.

Looking back, I'm sure we were in no real danger. I have a feeling the son of a bitch did this all the time.

The good cop said next to nothing, contenting himself with confiscating my new camera. Then the bad cop went out in the hall, and the good cop suggested that we might want to bribe our way out. He'd found our traveler's checks and had us sign them over to him, then kept us company while his buddy took them out and cashed them. They left us enough money for two bus tickets to Laredo and told us not to come back.

We called home from Laredo. Steve's dad wired us a couple hundred dollars and we flew home.

LATER, I FOUND myself wondering why we'd hurried home. It was understandable that we wouldn't want to step onto Mexican soil again, but we could have spent the next two months knocking around the Southwest. We didn't have any money, but we were able-bodied and could have found work. Why end the summer prematurely? Where was our sense of adventure?

All I can say is that it never once occurred to either of us. And, if one of us had suggested it, the other would have told him he was out of his mind.

It was just as well. I didn't know it yet, but I had things to do in Buffalo.

THE FIRST THING I did was write a story. It had nothing to do with Mexico or police brutality. It was just an ordinary crime story of the sort I'd been writing. I sent it off to Henry and he sent it back, saying he didn't think it worked.

I read it and decided *I* thought it worked, so I sent it to W. W. Scott and he bought it. I made sure to mention as much in my next letter to Henry, and he responded gracefully enough. "Congratulations," he wrote. "I always said W. W. Scott was a hell of an editor." I wasn't entirely certain what he meant by that, but I'd cashed W. W. Scott's check for $35 instead of one from SMLA for $31.50, so I was happy.

Then I got another letter from Henry.

"Dear Larry," he wrote, "I certainly hope you know what a sex novel is, and how to write one, because we've got an assignment for you." He went on to explain that a new paperback publisher was starting up, and would be bringing out 60,000-word novels not unlike those being published by Beacon Books. If I would send in thirty pages and an outline of the remainder, he thought he could get me a contract.

I knew the kind of books he meant, and I found a drugstore that carried them and bought a couple by Beacon's leading light, one Orrie Hitt. I skimmed them and figured I knew what was required. I sat down at my desk and produced thirty or forty pages and an outline. For a title I chose *Carla*, the name of the lead character. I used Sheldon Lord as my pen name.

I sent off the portion and outline, and within days I got a green light to go ahead and finish the book. There was no contract in the formal sense, unless Scott signed some letter of agreement on my behalf and kept it in his files. I never signed actual contracts on any of the books I did for Harry Shorten, who published *Carla*, or for any of the many books of mine Bill Hamling would publish.

A note from Henry spelled out the terms. I would get $600 for the book, $200 immediately and the balance when I turned in the completed manuscript. That sounded good to me, and I got to work right away. I wanted to finish the book before I went back to Yellow Springs.

That turned out to be easy enough. I suppose I must have written something like fifteen pages a day. I kept at it, and didn't find it particularly onerous. I got it done and mailed it off.

Did I read it when it came out? Probably not, and I certainly haven't looked at it since. I know it must have been awful. Carla, my heroine, was a hot young thing married to a rich older man. She has an affair and falls in love with the guy, or he falls in love with her. Or both. I think she winds up leaving her husband for the young guy, but I wouldn't swear to it, and I can live without knowing.

There were a couple of interesting things about the book. One was that I somehow knew how sexy to make it. I hadn't read much in the way of soft porn, except for a couple of hardcover examples by Joe Weiss and Jack Woodford that had turned up in the freshman dorm at Antioch. But I got the hang of it right away, making sex the dominant motif of the book, including a sex scene in virtually every chapter, and writing as erotically as possible without describing genitalia, using any expletive stronger than *hell*, or otherwise exceeding the bounds of the permissible.

And I wrote one scene that was a sort of interesting technical exercise. In one chapter Carla goes out on the prowl and picks up a black lover named Lou. They go off somewhere and there's an extended sex scene. At the end of it, Lou says, "You know, that was my first time with a white girl." And Carla says, "Well, it was my first time with a woman." Whereupon you realize that, although you'd assumed Lou was a man, the writer had never said so, or used any telltale pronouns. I was pretty proud of myself for thinking that one up, and carrying it off.

In another scene, Carla's initial encounter with her young lover, she gets her car serviced at a gas station where he's working. At her suggestion, they screw in the grease pit.

A year or so later I met Harry Shorten, the publisher of Midwood Books. He couldn't stop talking about that grease pit scene. How had I ever come up with something like that? Jesus, where'd I get the idea?

The thing is, I didn't really know what a grease pit was. I mean, I knew it was a pit, and that there was grease in it, but I didn't appreciate what a disgusting experience it would be to roll around in a grease pit, with or without a partner. For God's sake, I had Carla go home, take a quick shower, and come up smelling like a rose. If I'd ever had a job pumping gas I'd have known better, but then I'd have missed out on a scene that made me Harry Shorten's favorite writer.

I FINISHED THE book and sent it in, and then something happened that provided Don Westlake with a story he delighted in telling. I got a note from Henry saying Shorten liked the book, and then another note a few days later adding that Shorten had sent it in for typesetting and that it looked to be a little too short. Could I please provide an additional chapter to be inserted anywhere in the book?

I could and did. Because I couldn't find room anywhere in the story for an additional incident, I wrote a flashback chapter in which Carla recalled something that had happened to her long ago—some occasion when she got laid, obviously. Then I checked the manuscript to see where it belonged, and I realized it didn't matter. So I wrote Henry a note saying here's the chapter you requested, to be inserted anywhere in the book.

I thought, and still think, that I was taking the easy way out. A harder task by far would have entailed wedging a current-time chapter into the novel. But Don prefers to see what I did as an example of true professionalism, a stunning tour-de-force on a par with the time I wrote Page 39.

But I'll save that one for later.

9

IT WAS GOOD to get back to Yellow Springs. I returned feeling pleased with myself. I had written two novels and sold one of them. Now I would be taking courses again, and helping Bob Zevin with the school paper so that I'd know what I was doing when my turn as editor came up in January. I had left Antioch as an unimposing sophomore and returned as a prominent campus figure.

That particular year they were encouraging upperclassmen to find off–campus housing, and that was fine with me; after a year on my own, I wasn't eager to return to dormitory living. I found a furnished room in a house owned by three sisters who'd been out of work since *Macbeth* closed. One was a widow, the other two had never married, and they lived together in a large old house a few blocks from the campus. They had two or three rooms they rented out, and I took one of them. I bought a '50 Chevy coupe from another student for $135, and learned how to open the hood and pop it back in gear when it balked. I scouted the entering freshmen, and began keeping company with a nice girl from Bayonne named Carole.

I signed up for classes, and managed my schedule brilliantly. I took a course on Milton with Albert Liddell, another on the early English novel with Milton Goldberg, and a psych course called Workshop in Small Group Functioning which looked as though it might be interesting. (Not!) There were only two of us reading Milton, Adam Fischer and I. (Adam was the son of Bruno Fischer, a onetime editor of *The Socialist*

Call whose crime stories I'd read in *Manhunt*.) That class was essentially a tutorial, and only met formally two or three times. My other classes both met in the afternoon. I had so arranged things that I never had to get out of bed before noon.

In no time at all, I realized I'd made a tragic error. I should never have tried to come back.

IT MIGHT HAVE been different if we'd been quicker to get away from that riot in Guadalajara. If our Mexican trip had gone as planned, I might have been safely out of the country when Henry was looking around for people to write books for Harry Shorten.

I'm not suggesting that I owe my career as a pornographer to a couple of thieving cops. Sooner or later I'd have been offered the opportunity to write sex novels. But if I hadn't already started before I returned to college, maybe I wouldn't have felt so thoroughly out of place.

As it was, I looked around and couldn't figure out what I was doing there. What did I care about Milton? What did I care about *Humphrey Clinker*, or *Pamela*, or *Joseph Andrews*?

I didn't, and I cared even less about them when Henry wrote to say that Harry Shorten would love to have another book from me. He knew I was busy at college, but did I think I could find the time to write something?

Of course I could. There were typewriters in the *Record* office just like the one I'd had on my desk at SMLA, and at night I could have the place all to myself. I picked out a typewriter and started in on a book about an old writer. (He must have been well up in his thirties. This dude was really ancient.) He was a drunk, and he hadn't written anything in years, and then he met this woman and fell for her and cleaned up his act and knocked himself out writing the best book he'd ever written in his life. And then something tragic happened. I forget what exactly, but I think she must have died. And he joined some bums in an alley and took a deep drink from the bottle when it came to him, knowing he was back where he belonged.

That's as much as I remember of the plot, and I'd say it's enough. I wrote the book in the first person, which made a nice change, and it seemed to me that it was a whole lot better than *Carla*, for whatever that was worth. Henry thought it was okay, and Shorten was happy, and I had earned another $600.

I called the book *The Long Road*, a title nobody liked much. Midwood published it as *A Strange Kind of Love*.

WHEN I WASN'T staying up working on the book for Shorten, I was in the *Record* office helping with the newspaper. Because editing it was a full-time co-op job, and because no one else connected with the paper got paid except for the guy who sold the ads, the editor wound up doing virtually all the work. It probably didn't have to be this way, but that's how it always seemed to work out. I helped out a good bit during the fall quarter, though, because I wanted to learn what it was you had to do.

The *Record* was a weekly, and it was supposed to come out in time for dinner Friday night. (You hauled a stack of papers over to the cafeteria and set them on a table by the door. That was our distribution.) The paper ran to four pages, and was run off on an old flat-bed letterpress printer at the Yellow Springs *News*. If you were the editor you generally stayed up all of Thursday night, cutting up galley proofs, pasting up the pages, writing heads, and knocking out last-minute news stories to fit. At two or three o'clock in the morning you would drive on a back road to Fairborn, where any artwork was dropped off so that cuts could be made. Friday during the day you generally had things to do at the *News*, and after you dropped the papers at the caf you could go somewhere and collapse. The job probably didn't run to more than forty hours a week, but they all came at once.

I helped Bob some, writing news stories and features, rewriting other staffers' stories, riding shotgun when he drove to Fairborn. I figured I would be able to handle it when it was my turn to do the job, but I wasn't looking forward to it.

I didn't want to be there.

By late November I couldn't stand it. I wasn't going to any of my classes. It didn't even help that none of them met before noon, because I'd perversely shifted my own sleep pattern around, and rarely got to bed before eight in the morning. I would roll out of bed around four and realize I'd somehow managed to sleep through all my classes.

Even if I was awake I rarely went, and when I did I couldn't figure out what I was doing there. I didn't want to do the reading for my English classes, and when I tried I fell asleep over it. I couldn't bear to go to the psych class because I couldn't even figure out what they were doing there. Splitting up into small groups, I guess, and functioning. They were mostly exchange students from Germany, older fellows here as part of some sort of management training program, and I couldn't understand what they were saying half the time, anyway.

I was stupidly arrogant. There were things I might have learned in all those classes, but I decided none of it was important, and anyway I didn't give a rat's ass about it, any of it. What did I need it for? If I could just get away from the goddamn place I could earn $600 a month (well, $540 after commission) writing a book a month for Shorten. Add in a short story now and then and I'd be doing better than most college graduates.

I decided to leave. I wasn't going to tell anybody. I would just withdraw from the college, ship most of my belongings home to Buffalo and give the rest away, get in the car and point it toward New Orleans, and hope it stayed in one piece long enough to get me there. I'd never been to New Orleans, but I liked the sound of it. I figured I would get a room in the French Quarter, one with a table I could prop my typewriter on, and I'd do what I seemed to be best at.

It struck me as romantic as all hell. It also struck me as eminently practical. Why should my father have to scrape up money to keep me in a place where I no longer belonged? Why should I have to write in my spare time, when writing was the most important thing I could do to advance my career?

I packed a trunk and shipped it home. I told the registrar of my intention to withdraw. I had recently stopped seeing Carole, but I saw her long enough to give her my records and record player. And then, because he was the closest thing I had to a mentor on the faculty, I told Nolan Miller what I planned to do.

He didn't like the idea. He thought I should stick around, and offered what I suppose he thought was a powerful incentive. He was not without influence, he assured me, and if I just hung in there long enough to graduate, he could almost guarantee that I'd be able to get into the Master's program at the University of Iowa.

What a fine, decent man Nolan Miller was, and what a considerate and generous offer he made me. But how could he possibly have thought it would appeal to me? All I wanted to do in the world was get the hell away from academic life, and he was telling me to stick it out and I could go to graduate school as a reward. "Eat your spinach, kid. Then you can have some dessert. What's for dessert? It's your favorite—broccoli."

WHEN NOLAN'S OFFER fell flat, he did something I wished he hadn't done. He called my parents in Buffalo.

He'd never met them, but of course they recognized his name. He told them he thought I was about to make a big mistake and suggested they use their influence. They called, and we had the phone conversation I had hoped to postpone until I was holed up in New Orleans. It ended with their insisting I stay put in Yellow Springs until they had driven out to discuss it with me.

I couldn't refuse. We spoke right before Thanksgiving, and they spent the holiday weekend driving to Yellow Springs and back to Buffalo. I knew I didn't want to stay in school, I was very clear on that point, and I didn't change my mind, either. But they wore me down—with tears, with arguments. They won, and I told the registrar to withdraw my withdrawal, and they drove back to Buffalo.

And I stayed at Antioch, and I decided two things. I'd pass those fucking courses, and I wouldn't speak to my parents.

I SPENT THE month of December catching up in courses that I'd essentially given up on in early October. I had a ton of reading to do and a lot of papers to write. So I put myself on a very strange regimen.

Each morning I got up around eight and breakfasted in my room on a glass of Tang. Then I read a chapter from George Macaulay Trevelyan's *History of England* so that I wouldn't forget how English ought to be written. Then I went to the library and worked.

I worked all day, reading books and writing papers. Then I went to the Tin House, which was a little pre-fab house off campus rented to three or four second-year women. I didn't have designs on any of them, nor they on me. It was a place to hang out, and I increased the odds that I'd be welcome by bringing along a half-gallon of Almaden Mountain Red. I would sit there and numb myself out with wine until I figured I could sleep, and then I would drive back to the old ladies' house on Phillips Street and do just that.

Then I'd wake up in the morning, drink my glass of Tang, read my chapter of Trevelyan, and do the same thing all over again.

Throughout December, I never communicated with my parents. I got letters from them, mostly from my father, who typically wrote me a couple of times a week, generally brief letters in his unmistakable and wonderfully precise hand. He wrote more often than not in little memo books with his name and address on them, giveaway items from his days as an agent for Connecticut Mutual Life Insurance. (He had hundreds of automatic pencils around the house, too, with an 8-ball on the tip and the legend, "I'll never be behind the 8-ball with friends like you." I think he'd given those out when he was with Penn Mutual. I took a couple dozen with me after his death, and expected to have them around forever. But of course they're long gone now. What you're sure will last never does.)

I read his letters, but I didn't answer them. I was punishing them, but I don't know that they were aware of it. I often let a lot of time go by without writing a letter, and this was only a month we're talking about, although it was one of the longer months I can recall living through. They didn't call—there wasn't really any way to reach me by phone—and it would have been unusual for me to call them.

This was, after all, 1958, and people didn't make long distance calls the way they do now. I understand that it's now commonplace for college students to have private phones in their dorm rooms. When I was at Antioch the dorms had one phone per floor, and there was never a wait to use it. Back then, when you went on a long trip, you called home on arrival to let them know you'd made it safely. And you made the call person-to-person and asked for yourself, and the person at the other end heard your voice and knew you were okay, and told the operator that So-and-so wasn't in at the moment, so you got to hear *their* voice, and knew they were okay. And the call didn't cost anything.

So I didn't write and I didn't call, and maybe they knew they were being punished, and maybe not.

*   *   *

MY REGIMEN WORKED. I stuck with it until the end of the month, and got all my work done. Milt Goldberg gave me a B in his 18th Century Novel class, and I must say I earned it. Albert Liddell gave me a B in Milton, and it seems to me that was out of the goodness of his heart. I don't remember what happened in the Small-Group class, which was only a three-credit course and not one I needed for graduation. But I must have received some sort of grade, and I have no memory of it whatsoever. What could it have been? An F? An incomplete?

Maybe it was an Umlaut.

10

WHEN THE TERM ended the campus emptied out. Even the handful of students who would be staying in Yellow Springs for the coming semester went home to see their parents over Christmas vacation. But I was still punishing my folks, whether they knew it or not, so I stayed where I was.

Until Christmas Eve, when I had a few drinks and decided to go to New York. I drove to Dayton, and a fellow in the waiting room had a bottle of what he called Christmas cheer, but which the world recognizes as rye whiskey. He was inclined to share it, and the next thing I knew I was awake and the train was pulling into Pittsburgh.

I had a handful of coins in my pocket. I bought a packet of peanut butter crackers in the rail station and got back on the train to New York. On arrival I found a friend who gave me a place to stay, and the next day Steve came into the city and lent me ten dollars.

A day or so later I went to the Scott Meredith office. Henry had a small check for me, payment for some short story they'd sold. Don Westlake was working there by then, writing fee reports, but we didn't meet. He got a glimpse of me, though, talking to Henry through the little window. This is the conversation he remembers:

Me: "Is it too late to change the dedication of *A Strange Kind of Love*?"

Henry: "I'm afraid so. Why?"

Me: "I'm not going with that girl anymore."

"*This is for Carole*," I'd written, "*and it is not nearly enough.*" Which was true, but don't forget she'd got my records and record player, too. When

I'd caved in and stayed in school, she asked me if I wanted them back. I told her to keep them.

I STAYED IN New York for most of Christmas break, and while I was there I managed to start a relationship with a girl named Gail. She was an old-time friend of Steve's who had transferred to Antioch that fall; having completed an academic semester there, she was now ready to spend three months at a job in New York. My timing was thus less than ideal, but we had a couple of days together and agreed that we'd see each other in the spring.

I took a train to Buffalo and spent a day or two with my parents, having decided I was speaking to them again. We never discussed the month I'd spent not speaking to them, and acted as if there was nothing to discuss. And maybe there wasn't.

Back in Yellow Springs, I threw myself into the business of editing the newspaper, which was as I've already described it. I had one enormous advantage over Bob Zevin, my predecessor; he'd had me as a helper, while I had Peter Hochstein.

Peter was scheduled to succeed me at the *Record*. He'd spent the fall term as a reporter for Matzner Publications, in northern New Jersey, and this practical experience put him way ahead of me or Zevin—and, indeed, most of the other editors in the paper's long and undistinguished history. He brought back some wonderful stories, the best of which may have been the one about the time he'd been assigned to write a series of articles on garbage collection in the area. His first article appeared, and he got a phone call from a fellow who proposed a meeting at a diner in the area. He wound up sitting in a booth with a man who looked about as compromising as an anvil. The fellow stared at him for a long moment and then said, "Some people think you should stop writing about garbage." "Okay," Peter said. "I'll never write another word about garbage again. It was a stupid idea in the first place. Garbage—who needs it? The hell with garbage." The guy nodded, pleased. "Here," he said, and handed Peter a small package. Peter unwrapped it in his car, and it was a bullet.

Nobody gave Peter any bullets in Yellow Springs, and he revealed a talent for investigative journalism that scared the shit out of the school administration. We had a lot of action that quarter—a fire that destroyed the Science Building, a great foofaraw about a loyalty oath provision that had snuck into the Student Loan bill in Washington, and other stories that seemed incredibly important at the time, and that have slipped quietly out of my memory. I know, though, that I never had trouble filling the paper.

One of the things Peter had learned was that you didn't wait for news to walk in the door, you went out and created it. One story he created concerned unsafe conditions in the housing provided for married students; we called the little huts firetraps, and ran a photo of hazardous electrical wiring. This infuriated a lot of people, who were quick to accuse the *Record* of tabloid sensationalism and irresponsible yellow journalism. Within a week a child died in a fire that broke out in one of the homettes we'd written about; the cause was found to be defective wiring. I'd have preferred not to have been vindicated in that fashion, but there was no question that our story made things happen. The unsafe conditions were corrected in short order.

THAT WAS ONE of my two accomplishments as *Record* editor. The other resulted from an editorial I wrote lamenting the fact that the 68 Grill, a greasy spoon in downtown Yellow Springs, had abandoned its longstanding policy of staying open all night. Someone showed the editorial to the restaurant's owner, and damned if he didn't change back to around-the-clock operation.

*   *   *

I WROTE ONE book during my three months as editor, hammering away at it in the *Record* office on those nights early in the week when no news was good news. I called it *Born to be Bad*, and Shorten used my title, although in a later edition he changed it to *Puta*. The book featured Rita Morales, who was either Mexican or Puerto Rican, and who led an active life. That's as much as I can remember about the book, and, I shouldn't wonder, all ye need to know.

My mother suggested the heroine might better have been named Rita Immorales.

EVERY FRIDAY NIGHT, after I'd safely delivered the papers to the distribution table in the cafeteria, I'd go to the freshman dorm where Steve Schwerner and Andy Gardner were serving as hall advisers. We'd close the door of the room that they shared, shove the bunk bed so that it blocked the door, and get stoned.

Steve had managed to find a local marijuana source, and the three of us got high once a week. We could hardly have been more secretive if we'd been plotting to assassinate the Dean of Students. For three months we smoked only on Friday nights, and always behind closed doors. We told no one. As far as we knew, we were the only ones at Antioch who smoked. It seems to me now that there must have been others, but if so they were as covert about it as we were.

In the spring semester, the circle expanded, and we stopped limiting ourselves to one night a week. An additional six or eight fellows were carefully introduced to the pleasures we had discovered, and some of them contributed expertise of their own. A fellow named David Sepsonwall came back from spring break and turned us on to a cherry-flavored cough syrup called Teek. He said his father used it.

Half a dozen of us trooped off to the drugstore downtown, and each of us bought a bottle of Teek. The pharmacist seemed surprised by such a run on what must have been a slow-moving item—the bottles were coated with dust—but he wasn't alarmed, and I don't think we had to sign the narcotics register. We went back to the campus, and one of us read the label. "Uh-oh," he said. "Dave, it says right here, 'Warning: May be habit-forming.' And it contains codeine. Can we get addicted to this stuff?"

Sepsonwall gave him a look. "Don't be ridiculous," he said. "My *father* drinks this stuff. He's been drinking a bottle every day for thirty years. If this stuff was really habit-forming, don't you think he'd be addicted to it by now?"

His logic was irrefutable. Reassured, we drank our Teek.

MOSTLY, THOUGH, I just drank.

As far as I've ever been able to determine, there was never any alcoholism in my family. My parents were both light social drinkers. They'd have one or two drinks with friends, but that was the extent of it. My father over the years developed a palate for good Scotch, and had a special liking for Ne Plus Ultra, a limited-run premium label of Dewar's. At the time I believe it was only available in Canada. He was very fond of it, but one small glass of it before dinner was all he ever wanted.

I only once saw him drunk. It was after an office Christmas party, and he came home giddy and lighthearted. On social occasions he would have two drinks, and almost never had a third; when he did, he would fall asleep in his chair.

After she was widowed, my mother got a job as a librarian. When she came home at the end of the day she got in the habit of having a drink before dinner. Then one day she realized that she had increased to two drinks, so she cut it out altogether, limiting her drinking to social occasions.

If, as seems likely, there's such a thing as a genetic predisposition to alcoholism, I didn't have it. Nor did I drink anything to speak of in high school, except for getting ritualistically stupefied the night of my graduation.

But I drank when I got to Antioch, and I drank while I lived in New York and worked for Scott Meredith, and I drank more often and more heavily now that I had returned to Yellow Springs. One time I went to a party and woke up in my bed on Phillips Street with no memory of having come home. My car was parked at the curb, and I was horrified at the thought of having driven in the condition I must have been in. But a friend who'd been at the same party told me I'd seemed perfectly fine when I left, not even observably high, so I concluded that I must have been all right.

Another time I drank heavily on a Saturday night and woke up expecting the hangover I knew I deserved. But I didn't have a hangover because I was still drunk. I reached at once for the Scotch bottle, grateful for this miracle and determined to keep the ball in play.

MY ROMANCE WITH Gail continued in her absence. I spent some time with other women, but wrote to her with some regularity. Around the middle of the semester she flew out to Yellow Springs for a weekend and we spent it together.

Then one morning, with less than two weeks left in the term, I got a letter from her. She explained that would not be coming back to Antioch, that she was going to marry a former Antiochian now living in New York. "Give my best to the gang," she concluded.

I was absolutely devastated. I don't know why—I'd spent very little time with her, and we didn't really know each other at all. But I reacted immediately and decisively. I went over to Steve and Andy's room to tell them what had happened. They weren't there, but their booze was. There was a fifth of Scotch on Andy's desk and a bottle of rum on Steve's.

First I drank the Scotch. Then I started in on the rum.

Then I woke up in the hospital.

IT WAS A new experience. I had a cord around each ankle and was tied to the foot of the bed. I had an enormous bandage on my right hand that covered the wrist, the palm, and the middle finger. I had a narrow plastic bracelet on my left wrist, and it said two things, "Lawrence Block" and "Springfield City Hospital."

Later, people told me what had happened. After drinking all of Steve and Andy's liquor, I'd reeled around the campus, making a spectacle of myself. Then I'd disappeared, and sometime in the middle of the night the police had been called when I'd attempted to break into a house in Yellow Springs. I'd broken a small window in the front door and had cut my finger on the broken glass, nicking but not severing a tendon in the process. The cops had taken me to the hospital, where they'd pumped my stomach, sedated me, and tied me down.

The house I'd attempted to enter was occupied by Harry Steinhauer, an Antioch professor of German language and literature. Much was made of this, but, since I'd never had a class with Dr. Steinhauer or had a conversation with him, and would not anyway have had the faintest idea where he lived, I don't see any significance there. My guess is I got disoriented, thought I was back at 504 Phillips Street, and broke the window in frustration when my key wouldn't work in the lock.

A doctor from the clinic in Yellow Springs came to see me. He seemed concerned about my behavior, and I couldn't understand why. It seemed pretty clear-cut to me. I'd had unsettling news and I'd responded by getting drunk. Isn't that what people did? Wasn't that why they bottled the stuff? He was concerned, too, that I'd had a blackout, and asked if that had happened on other occasions. Only when I drank, I told him.

Nowadays I suppose he'd recommend treatment, some 28-day program somewhere. All he did was ask me if there was anything he could get me, and at least I had the sense not to tell him I could use a drink. They kept me in the hospital one more night, then let me go. The term ended and I went back home for spring vacation.

I was a little embarrassed by the way I'd behaved, but I probably got off on the drama of it. And I thought it was pretty amusing the way the doctor had overreacted. "I guess he never ran into an alcoholic before," I would say, and my friends thought that was pretty amusing.

11

FOR THE SPRING semester, I moved out of my furnished room on Phillips Street. Pete Hochstein and I took an apartment together, the entire second floor of a two-family house on the edge of town. Our landlord had picked the place up—literally, when it was scheduled to be torn down and a commercial building thrown up on the site. He trucked it to a foundation on a piece of land he owned, rented out the lower half to a young married couple, and was fool enough to let us have the top half. We furnished it for next to nothing with used furniture from Springfield, one item of which was a $10 refrigerator that proved unreliable. It died in late May, and by the time we realized what had happened we'd missed our chance to clean it. Everything was too far gone to go near. Until the end of June we stayed away from it. Every once in a while some unwitting visitor would open the door by mistake, and then we'd quick close it and open every window in the house and go away for a few hours.

We moved out just hours before the landlord's agent was scheduled to show the place to a prospective tenant. I can imagine them walking through the rooms, bravely ignoring the detritus we'd left behind, until someone, agent or tenant, opened the fridge.

I HAD A full schedule of courses to take that spring, and they were the least of it. The important thing I had to do was revise *Shadows*.

Because, incredibly enough, my lesbian novel had sold to Crest for an advance of $2000.

Thinking back, it's hard for me to understand why it took so long. That may sound arrogant, but I can assure you that arrogance had nothing to do with it. As a matter of fact, I'd almost forgotten about the book, and didn't expect it to sell. I'd written it the previous June, and, while it wouldn't have been unreasonable for the book to take nine months or more to find a publisher willing to take it on, it seems to me that Crest would have been the first place Henry'd have sent it. Could it have been sent to several other markets first? Or did it go straight to Crest and languish in a corner of somebody's office, with never an inquiry from my agent as to when they were going to shit or get off the pot?

I know it couldn't have sold until sometime around the end of the second semester, because I specifically recall doing the revisions at a table in the living room of the new apartment. I remember, too, that I had to learn how to type all over again.

I was a self-taught typist, having learned during high school by typing all my papers. I was used to looking at the keyboard, which made copying other text a pain in the neck, and I only used the first two fingers of each hand on the keys, and a thumb on the spacebar. Though my approach was unorthodox, I was as fast as a good stenographer.

But now I had to accommodate the finger I'd injured. It was too sore to hit keys with, and indeed remained slightly numb for years. So I rewrote my lesbian novel with the index and ring fingers of my right hand (and, of course, the first two fingers of my left hand). And I have never been able to switch back. In every other respect I quickly recovered full use of the afflicted finger, but to this day it just hovers there while its fellows on either side do all the work.

How much revision did the book require?

Less, I suspect, than it got. My editor at Crest was in her early twenties, a recent graduate of a good eastern school, and I suspect she had less experience in the publishing world than I did. They gave her my book to practice on, and she gave me a batch of suggestions, and it never occurred to me that I had any say in the matter. I did what I was told.

The book made a second trip through the typewriter, but it doesn't seem to me that there were many changes. There was one thing she wanted that bothered me, however. Peggy, Laura's love interest before Jan turned up, had a chapter of her own, like all the other key supporting players. "Her name was Peggy Corcoran and she was drunk," was how that chapter began, and by the chapter's end Peggy had been waylaid and raped by a group of young neighborhood punks. My editor said it didn't advance the story, but she was full of crap. It was a good scene, it belonged in the book, and I knew it. I should have fought for it.

Part of the problem, I suppose, was that I was used to magazines, and low-level magazines at that. They did what they wanted with the stories they bought, trimmed them to fit the available space, changed the title, even changed character names if there were two many stories in that issue with the same name. Pontiac, as I've said, even made up pen names for you without consulting you. If you were Faulkner, I knew, you didn't have to let them get away with this shit. But I also knew I wasn't Faulkner.

My title was *Shadows*, my pen name Rhoda Moore. My editor reported that they were changing the title to *Strange Are the Ways of Love*. Okay, I said. I didn't like it much, but nobody asked me. A little later she informed me that they were also changing my pen name. They were changing it to Leslie Evans, so that the author's gender would be indeterminate. Okay, I said. Then, by the time they finally published the damned thing, they'd second-guessed themselves and made it Lesley Evans.

Thirty-odd years later, when Lynn Munroe published his catalog of my pseudonymous work, he had a few observations on this book. The title, he said, showed my fascination with the word "strange"—viz. the second Sheldon Lord novel for Midwood, *A Strange Kind of Love*. Both titles, of course, were supplied by the publishers. And Lesley Evans, he proposed, might be an homage to Evan Hunter. News to me.

MY REVISIONS WERE accepted, and I remember I got a check for $1350—$1500 less Scott's 10% commission. (They must have paid $500 on signing. Either that or I got $1000 on signing and a total price of $2500.) Whatever the total and however I got it, $1350 was the largest check I'd ever seen with my name on it.

It was becoming increasingly evident that I could make a living this way. Harry Shorten kept asking when he was going to see another book by Sheldon Lord, and it was reasonable to assume that Crest would be happy to see something new from Lesley Evans. I couldn't run out and buy a Cadillac, but it looked as though I could realistically expect to support myself.

Meanwhile, I had to get through college.

I still didn't know what I was doing there, but I figured I'd made my bed and I could lie in it until somebody handed me a diploma. I had three months of study to get through, and then I'd be on my own for six months—the new calendar, bless its heart, called for a co-op job period from July through September. I applied to spend that period as a freelance writer in New York, arguing persuasively that no job on the school's list could do as much for me at this stage of my career. The co-op department agreed, my project was approved, and all I had to do was sit tight and pass my courses.

Ah, Jesus, it was hopeless. I swear I set out with the best will in the world, and I didn't have a snowball's chance in hell. I don't even remember what courses I took, except for one which I shall never forget. It was called "The Development of Physical Ideas" and the description in the catalog made it sound like a science course for a non-scientist. I was emphatically the latter, and I needed one physical science course in order to satisfy the General Education requirement, and this was the only one available to me. It met three times a week at 8 am, but I signed up for it anyway and made sure I was there on time every morning, with a seat in the front row so I wouldn't miss anything.

On the first day the professor said, "Now we'll be starting off with a quick review of Newtonian mechanics for those of you who've gotten a little rusty, and then we'll move on to quantum theory and relativity."

I didn't even understand the words he was using.

But I figured I was bright, and I ought to be able to handle this. I took the textbook home and tried to read it. I couldn't do it. I'd force my way through two or three incomprehensible pages and then my eyes would glaze over and I'd be gone. It was hopeless.

There was a way out. If you wanted to change your mind about a class, you could transfer out of it and into something else anytime during the first two weeks of the term. But the two weeks had passed before I knew for sure that I was never going to be able to cope. For two more weeks I had the option of dropping the course without a penalty, but I couldn't replace it with something else, so what was the point? Anyway, I still believed in miracles.

By the end of the fourth week I knew that a miracle was out of the question. But what could I do? Nothing. I'd stopped going to the class, and I'd get an F, and so what? I'd already handed in a blank test paper because I couldn't even guess at the answer to a single question. And, when called upon to submit a proposed topic for a paper I knew I'd never be able to write, I came up with an unusual one: "The Relationship of Twentieth-Century Physical Ideas and Hypermodern Chess Openings." I actually had some sort of intuitive sense that there might be such a re- lationship, that those openings which gave up control of the center might bear a philosophical kinship to whatever the hell it was we were learning about, but I wasn't prepared to take it any further than the title.

I did what I had to in my other courses. I drank a lot, I smoked a fair amount of dope, and I developed an abiding fondness for Teek. When the drugstore ran out, we learned to make do with terpin hydrate and codeine, and I got so I even liked the taste. But I was no match for Dave Sepsonwall's father. I only drank the stuff for another seventeen years.

BY THE BEGINNING of July I was back in New York. I knew I wanted to live in a hotel, and I knew exactly where I wanted to be—on West 47th, right down the street from Scott's offices. I checked out the hotels on the block between Sixth and Seventh. There were a lot of them then, and at least fifteen restaurants; most of the block got leveled a few years later when the Rockefeller interests threw up high-rise office buildings just west of Rockefeller Center.

The hotel I chose, the Rio, is still there to this day. It was family-owned and operated at the time, and was reputable for the neighborhood it was in. No hookers lived there, and you couldn't get a streetwalker past the front desk. There were Greek sailors who stayed there regularly when they hit town, and residents who'd lived there for years, along with a mixed bag of transients and travelers on a budget.

I had a nice enough room for $12 a week. The window opened on a narrow airshaft, so the room was not much brighter at noon than at midnight, but this didn't seem to bother me. There was a church next door, and that did bother me a little on Sundays, when they rang bells all day long. But it wasn't that bad.

I moved in and went to work. I was a block and a half from Scott's offices, a five-minute subway ride from the Village. I could have dinner at a different restaurant every day for the next six months without walking more than two blocks. I could go around the corner and stand in front of the Metropole and listen to Gene Krupa, and when I tired of that I could walk across the street and pick up a hooker, even if I couldn't get her past the front desk at the Rio.

I had a lot of friends in town, too. Friends from the Village, Antiochians on co-op jobs, writers I'd met while working at SMLA. Early on, I dropped by the agency to deliver a manuscript or pick up a check and met Don Westlake, who'd come by on a similar errand. He'd quit working there some months earlier and was now writing full-time, doing books for Harry Shorten and working on a mystery. We got to talking and he invited me to drop over for a beer.

Don was living with his wife and infant son in a run-down tenement on 46th between Ninth and Tenth. (There's a redundancy there. On that block, either you lived in a run-down tenement or you were sleeping on the street.) He and I had instant rapport, and no end of things to say to each other. That first night we sat up talking until two or three in the morning, and that's what usually happened when we got together. (And still does, thirty-five years later.)

I couldn't have asked for a better situation. I knew I was set for the next six months, and figured I'd have a tough time tearing myself away come the end of December.

By the middle of August I was back in Buffalo.

BEFORE THAT, THOUGH, I wrote a couple of books. First was *69 Barrow Street*, set in the Village on the very block where I'd lived while working at Pines Publications. (I'd lived at 54 Barrow; there was no 69 Barrow.) The book concerned the various couplings of the various residents of a Village brownstone, and I don't imagine there was anything very original about it, except for the title, which was a nice uncensorable way to get a hint of lewdness right out there on the cover.

And that, I subsequently found out, wasn't entirely original either. Years earlier Harold Robbins had had the same bright notion, until some killjoy publisher made him change his title to *79 Park Avenue*. There was a party scene in my book that was a minor tour de force; I suspect it owed something to the New Year's Eve party sequence in James T. Farrell's *The Young Manhood of Studs Lonigan*.

When I'd finished that book, I wrote one called *Campus Tramp*.

I can't say I remember a great deal about the story line of *Campus Tramp*. It was set in a small midwestern college something like Antioch, but without the work-study program. (I could never figure out how to put the work-study program in a book. It took too long to explain it.) The title character, if you will, was an innocent freshman girl named Linda Shepard who led a checkered career at Clifton College. One of the other characters, Don Gibbs, was the editor of the college paper.

More significant than the plot or characters was the fact that the last name of every character in the book was that of an Antioch dormitory, while all of the buildings in the book bore the names of friends of mine from school. This seemed harmless, and made it easy to come up with names.

I thought my friends would get a kick out of it, if any of them ever happened to come across the book. What I never anticipated was that it would become scandalously successful at Antioch, with a whole myth springing up around it, or that it would retain its notoriety for years on end. I've been given to understand that tattered copies of the book change hands at Senior Sales for $25 or more.

I've been told, too, that it was common knowledge I'd written the book to revenge myself on the school, and that various characters had real-life counterparts. I heard that one fellow, Arno Karlen, was bemused or flattered or outraged—it depended who was telling the story—because Don Gibbs had clearly been based upon him.

Someone asked Arno why he thought that. Why, it was obvious, he said. Gibbs edited the school newspaper, and was described as having a beard and a crewcut. And wasn't he himself the editor of the *Record*? And didn't he have a beard and a crewcut?

It was pointed out to him that, when the book was written, he had not yet begun editing the paper. Furthermore, the book's author had spent a term editing the paper, and also had a beard and a crewcut. So if Larry had based Don Gibbs on anyone, wasn't it reasonable to assume he'd based him on himself?

Oh, he said.

There were professors who felt they'd been ill-used in the book, I was told, and in one or two cases they may have been right. I couldn't believe any of them ever read the silly thing. I had trouble believing *anybody* ever read it, truth to tell. And I certainly hadn't meant the college itself any harm. At the time I began the book, I fully expected to return in January and graduate in June. I can't say I was looking forward to it, but I thought that's what I was going to do. By the time I finished the book I knew I wasn't going back, but I wasn't angry about it. If anything, I was grateful. I can assure you I didn't bear the school any ill will, and if I'd wanted revenge I wouldn't have sought it by writing a sex book set there, for Christ's sake. I'd have learned how to make a bomb so I could blow the place up.

CAMPUS TRAMP WAS never submitted to Harry Shorten. Instead, it was one of the first books sold to Bill Hamling. Hamling, originally a science fiction fan, lived in Evanston, Illinois, and published a *Playboy* imitator called *Rogue*, and a few other magazines as well. Now he was starting up a line of sex novels, and his imprint was Nightstand Books. (His books carried various other imprints over the years, including Midnight Reader.) The books were to be a little more graphic than Shorten's Midwood line, and more cheaply produced. The perfect binding (a printing-trades misnomer if ever there was one) was sufficiently cheesy that the pages came loose on the book's second or third reading. Everyone I knew figured this was intentional, a form of planned obsolescence not unheard of in American industry.

Hamling thought *Campus Tramp* was just fine, and wanted more of the same. And he was paying more than Shorten, too. He was willing to pay $750. Henry said I would need a new pen name for the books I did for Hamling. I thought about it and settled on Andrew Shaw.

WHILE I WAS finishing up *Campus Tramp*, I got a letter from J. D. Dawson, the Dean of Students back in Yellow Springs. He wrote to advise me that, at a recent meeting of the Student Personnel Committee, the consensus had been that I would be happier elsewhere, and thus I need not think in terms of coming back to Antioch in January.

Reading the letter, all I could think of was how perspicacious it was of them to see that I would be happier elsewhere. Indeed I would, and I'd come to the same conclusion myself the previous November. I didn't leap into the air and exult at my expulsion—it is, after all, never entirely a treat to be told to go shit in your hat—but I was not by any means dismayed.

J. D.'s letter was gentler than my summary of its contents may suggest. Reading between the lines, I suspected it wouldn't have been terribly difficult for me to talk my way back into the school's good graces. Antioch was a pretty lenient institution, and Nolan Miller would have been happy to go to bat for me if I asked him to. I never even considered it. They were right, by God. I'd be a whole lot happier elsewhere, and I was out now, free and clear, and I wasn't going back.

I called my parents and told them the school's decision, and they didn't seem dismayed, either. I'd given it a shot and it hadn't worked, and they weren't inclined to ask more of me than that. Then too, I had a lot more credibility as a self-supporting freelance writer in August of '59 than I'd had the previous November.

One thing, though. They didn't see any need, really, for me to say that I'd been expelled, or asked to withdraw, or whatever you wanted to call it. They thought it would be just as well to tell their friends and the rest of the family that the decision had been mine, not the school's.

Well, what the hell, what difference did it make? I told the truth to everybody else, but in Buffalo I let them have it their way. Not that I figured to be spending much time in Buffalo.

A COUPLE OF weeks later I was back in Buffalo, living once again in my parents' house.

I don't know that I can explain it, but I can certainly tell you precisely what happened. One Saturday morning I got up as usual and started writing the day's chapter of *Campus Tramp*. I was close to the end of the book, and around the middle of the day's stint I poured myself a glass of bourbon and tap water and sipped it as I worked.

This was not standard procedure. I generally took a drink when I was done with the day's work, but I never drank while I was working. This particular day, though, it seemed appealing enough. I kept writing, and when the glass was empty I filled it up again. When the chapter was done I had another drink to celebrate.

I was invited to a party that night, and I must have been pretty well lit by the time I got there. The hosts were people I didn't know, and I couldn't have made a very good impression. I hit on a young woman who was not unattached, and did not let her attachment dim my enthusiasm. I blacked out somewhere along the way, and came to as I was being forced out the door. Then I went back into a blackout and came to somewhere in Harlem, with a couple of cops suggesting that I'd picked a bad neighborhood for a midnight stroll. I suppose they put me in a cab or steered me to the subway. One way or another I found my way home, and I woke up the next day praying that what I was experiencing was a hangover. Because if it wasn't I was dying.

No mad burst of creativity this time around, no Great American Lesbian Novel outlined in a couple of furious hours. I couldn't move, and everything hurt, and I felt horrible.

There's no need to work up a description, or hunt out the right metaphor. I had an awful hangover, and it had a surprising effect. It got my attention.

Something, I realized, was wrong with this picture. I had started drinking early in the day for no reason whatsoever. I had behaved in an uncharacteristically loutish fashion at the party. I had risked my life staggering around in a notoriously unsafe part of town.

I made a decision. I was going to stop drinking. And I was going to get out of New York.

"New York's not working for me," I told my friends. "I love this city too much to stay here and hate it."

FIRST I FINISHED the book I was working on. Then I went home.

My parents seemed pleased by my return. Many years later my mother confided that she'd never understood why I hadn't stayed in New York, but she certainly never said anything to that effect at the time. I moved back into my bedroom, put my typewriter once again on my little maple desk, and got on with the business of writing.

I don't remember all the books I wrote there. For Harry Shorten I wrote *A Woman Must Love* and *Of Shame and Joy*. (I'd called the latter *Of Crimson Joy*, wanting to use as an epigraph quote the lyric of Blake's that starts "O rose, thou art sick." It wasn't a very good title for a sex novel, and Shorten was probably right to change it. Years later, Robert B. Parker wrote a detective novel called *Crimson Joy*. Lucky for him he didn't have to get it past Harry Shorten.) For Bill Hamling I wrote *The Adulterers* and *High School Sex Club* and *The Wife Swappers*.

I gather both lines were hugely successful right from the jump. On 42nd Street, both Midwood and Nightstand titles sold at a premium. The early Midwoods had 35¢ as a cover price, but the porn shops marked them up to 75¢. The Nightstands, priced at half a dollar, were cello-wrapped and tagged at double that. They were hot stuff by the standards of the day, and the public snapped them up.

So the publishers needed a steady supply of product from writers they could count on. Somewhere along the way, Hamling increased his rates to $1000 for writers who would deliver a book a month. His was a closed shop, buying only from Scott, and, I learned years later, paying Scott a substantial under-the-table packaging fee in addition to the 10% commission he was taking off the top. (This was by no means ethical, and may not even have been legal, but when was that ever a consideration?)

So I was writing a book a month for Hamling, and whatever I could fit in for Harry Shorten, who had raised his rates to $800. This probably sounds like a lot of writing, and it was, but I never had trouble getting the work done on time.

At first I kept to a fairly standard schedule, writing by day, sleeping by night. Then I began sleeping later and staying up later, and reached a point where I was getting up in the early afternoon, amusing myself during the day and evening, having a cup of coffee with my mother before she went to bed around midnight, writing all night, and having breakfast with my father around six in the morning. Ours was a curious household, but it worked surprisingly well that way.

Away from the typewriter, I found things to do in Buffalo. I had a few dates with a girl named Ruth Opler, but that ended when she went off to Cornell. Then I began dating Loretta Kallett, and around that time had an opportunity to purchase a half-interest in a jazz coffee house called the

Jazz Center. A fellow named Frank St. George had started it a couple of years previously, and he couldn't make a go of it, so he was looking to take in a partner. I was going there all the time anyway and thought it would be more fun if I owned the place.

Frank wanted $2500 for a half share, and I had $2500 I didn't know what to do with, so we were made for each other. My father told me he figured we would probably go broke, but that was something everybody did sooner or later, and I was at the right age for it. If I could get it out of the way this early in life, I'd be ahead of the game. So I bought in, and while we didn't go broke, neither could we make any money there. We couldn't get a liquor license—the premises were within 200 feet of a church, or however the law read, and the Monsignor had to sign off in order for us to get a license, and he wouldn't. He didn't like the fact that we had a racially mixed clientele. I have a feeling a little grease in the right place would have worked wonders, but you have to know how to manage that sort of thing, and we didn't.

Frank was a sweet guy. He'd been involved in left-wing politics years previously—I think he was at Bell Aircraft—and he now had his own business installing floor tile. He opened a jazz club because he loved the music. I don't think he knew the first thing about business. One thing I remember is that we served cider, among other non-alcoholic beverages, and every Friday afternoon Frank would drive way the hell out to Niagara County because there was a place there where you could get really good cider. I didn't know the first thing about business myself, but even I realized that was crazy.

WHAT I MISSED in Buffalo—what I would always miss in Buffalo—was people to talk to. I was doing solitary work of a sort no one around me could really understand, and I didn't have anybody to discuss it with. I filled the gap by correspondence, exchanging letters with several friends, especially Don Westlake and Larry Harris. To each of them I wrote, and from both of them I received, long thoughtful artful letters, most of them answered on either side within a day or two of receipt. Don and I wrote letters as long as fee reports—and, in a running gag, closing with some variation on "all best wishes."

I wish I'd held on to those letters. I kept them for quite a while, but I was to move many times in the coming years, and somewhere along the way I let go of them, as I trust they did of mine.

The letters are gone. The book Don and I wrote by mail lives on.

I DON'T REMEMBER whose idea it was.

I was at his place on 46th Street, either just before my move back to Buffalo or on a brief visit in early autumn. We decided to try writing a book in collaboration, but not as most collaborators are wont to do, batting ideas back and forth, working out the details of the plot together. We'd collaborate on a book for Harry Shorten, and it wouldn't require any more forethought than anything else we did for the man.

I went back to Buffalo and wrote a first chapter about a girl named Honor Mercy Bane. I wrote with the delicious freedom that comes of knowing you're not going to have to figure out what happens next. I kept my carbon copy, mailed the original to Westlake, and got back to my real work, sure I wouldn't hear from him for a while.

I got a chapter from him by return mail. He introduced another character, a whiny, sniveling punk named Richie. I didn't much like Richie, but I liked the chapter, and got right to work on chapter three.

And so on. As the book gathered momentum, we had more and more fun with it, each leaving the other with increasingly impossible cliffhangers. Eventually I got so I couldn't stand Richie, and I killed him off. In the following chapter Don got even; I'd introduced a counterbalance to

Richie early on, a middle-aged lawyer named Joshua Crawford who was the other man in Honey's life. (That's what Honor Mercy called herself when she turned bad.) Don promptly killed Crawford, leaving us with a fourth of the book still to be written and nobody for our heroine to go to bed with.

We worked it out. The book got finished in not much time at all, and the best part was that it didn't really feel like work. We wanted to call it *Piece With Honor*, but that was out of the question. I don't remember what title we hung on it. Shorten published it as *A Girl Called Honey*. It bore a joint byline, Sheldon Lord & Alan Marshall. The dedication read: "To Don Westlake and Larry Block, who introduced us."

On my fall promotional tour in 1992, a fellow turned up at Book Carnival in Orange, California, and presented a copy of *A Girl Called Honey* for my signature. "I know you don't sign books by Sheldon Lord," he said, "or even admit to being Sheldon Lord, and that's your business. But I happened to notice that Lord and Marshall dedicated this book to you and Westlake, so I thought you might be willing to sign the dedication page, as one of the dedicatees."

Foxy bastard. I signed the book.

I'M NOT SURE how long I went without drinking.

From that hungover morning on, I certainly didn't find it hard to say no. I may have known intuitively that abstinence would be easier than moderation, or perhaps I'm just given to extremes. Or both. In any event, I stopped drinking entirely. No wine, no beer, nothing.

I think I got off on it. If drinking was worldly, consider the cachet attached to having given it up. I'm sure I enjoyed the surprised looks that greeted the news that I was on the wagon.

After I'd been back in Buffalo a couple of months I was out somewhere with Loretta and thought I'd order a drink and see what happened. I did, and nothing happened. I figured I'd cured whatever had been wrong with me, and that was the end of being on the wagon.

MY ROMANCE WITH Loretta continued apace. We went to New York for a weekend, and I introduced her to the Westlakes and to Steve Schwerner and Nancy Hayes. We were both living with our parents, so I rented a furnished room downtown where we could have some privacy. (I decided I ought to do this under a false name, and used Nat Crowley. I had my protagonist assume that name in a crime novel I was trying to write, and I can't honestly remember which came first, the book or the rented room.) Around Christmas time I proposed, and we had a wedding date set in June.

Loretta's folks didn't have a pot to pee in or a window to throw it out of, and were preparing to go deeply in debt for a wedding we wanted less and less the closer we got to it. Accordingly, when we made another weekend trip to New York in March, we looked at an apartment on West 69th Street, signed a lease, then added on a side trip to Baltimore, where I knew there was no waiting period, and we got married.

Like Bogart in *Casablanca*, I was misinformed. Baltimore had a 48-hour waiting period for marriages. We waited out the waiting period, exchanged our vows, and returned to Buffalo to pack for the move to New York.

IN THE HALF year I spent in Buffalo, then, I wrote a lot of books, wrote and received a lot of letters, took a flier in the nightclub business, stopped drinking and started in again, and fell in love and got married. What I didn't do, as you may have noticed, is write another lesbian novel for Crest.

I barely noticed. I thought about doing a college novel for them, but that turned into *Campus Tramp* instead, and got me started with Hamling. After that, I never even considered it.

It's not as though I lost interest in lesbians, or decided it was not meet for me to write about them. As a matter of fact, I don't believe I ever wrote a book for Shorten or Hamling that didn't have at least one lesbian sequence in it. Later, when I employed ghostwriters to produce sex novels as Andrew Shaw or Sheldon Lord, I instructed them to include a lesbian scene in every book.

What was it, then? Crest paid twice as much, put out a far more respectable product, and even paid royalties. (I never earned any with *Strange are the Ways of Love*, but would have if the book had gone into a second printing.) There was more satisfaction, more prestige, and more money writing for Crest, and I'd sold them first time out. Why didn't I try them again?

I'd have more trouble figuring it out if the pattern were not one I can see repeating endlessly over the years. I didn't try to write another book for Crest because I was afraid I couldn't do it.

This may seem curious, in light of the fact that so much of my behavior was fearless to the point of stupidity. But mine was a very particular sort of fear. I was scared to risk failing at something at which I had previously succeeded.

Thus I could write the first lesbian novel because I had nothing to lose; no one expected me to be able to do it, least of all myself. In the months it took *Shadows* to sell, I didn't sit around agonizing over it. Indeed, by the time it sold I had almost forgotten it was out there.

But if I tried to do it again, and I couldn't, well, that would be pretty disappointing. And if I didn't try, I could guarantee I wouldn't be disappointed.

Hamling and Shorten were sure things. It was heartening to know, when I rolled the first blank page into the typewriter, that I would be able to see the book through to the end, and that it would be bought and published and paid for. The money was important, it was how you kept score, but it was really the least of it. Far more important was the certainty of success.

12

LORETTA AND I were married on March 10, 1960. We set up house-keeping in a furnished one-bedroom apartment at 110 West 69th Street. On West 23rd Street for $40 I bought a five-foot mahogany desk, not unlike the one I'd held down at Scott Meredith, and set it up in the bedroom. Loretta got a part-time job, working afternoons in a small midtown office, and I wrote. I was turning out a book a month for Hamling, an occasional book for Shorten, and now and then a short story.

Within a couple of months I'd unloaded my interest in the Jazz Center. My uncle Jerry Nathan, a jazz fan and a good amateur pianist, considered buying me out but concluded that the club's prospects weren't good. (Still, he'd caught the virus; shortly thereafter he began putting on jazz concerts, eventually establishing himself as Western New York's leading concert promoter.) When he took a pass, I sold my share back to my partner, Frank St. George. He gave me $1500, so I only lost a grand on the venture, which now strikes me as miraculous. The place never did make money—at one point Frank took in the musicians in the house band as partners because he couldn't afford to pay them. He went on to do very well as a manager of David's Table, one of the city's better restaurants; in time he bought it, moved it to a better location, called it St. George's Table, and did very well with it.

I HAD WRITTEN a crime novel while I was in Buffalo. I called it *Sinner Man*, and it concerned an ordinary middle-class guy in Danbury, Connecticut, who has an argument with his wife, takes a swing at her, and she hits her head on something and dies. Instead of calling the cops he panics and runs for it.

He changes his appearance, his hair style, and his name, calling himself Nat Crowley, the very name I'd used to rent a room on Franklin Street. He comes to Buffalo, where he hangs out in mob joints and acts like he belongs, and winds up being taken on by a local organized-crime operation. He thus becomes the criminal he's pretended to be. I don't know how I ended the book, but it seems to me he must have come to a bad end. Doesn't everybody?

The plot strikes me as preposterous now, but it didn't seem that way when I wrote it, at least not to me. Henry thought it was promising enough to send around, and it kept getting the same reaction from just about everybody who saw it. They all really liked the way I wrote, and would be very interested in seeing my next book. But they would have to pass on this one.

I found this infuriating, of course, but now it makes perfect sense to me. They liked the way I wrote because I wrote well, with good sentences and good dialogue and interesting characters doing interesting things. They figured I'd eventually write a book that worked, but this wasn't it.

In New York, I did write a publishable crime novel. It happened while I was trying to do something else.

What I was trying to do was write a sex novel for Harry Shorten. I'd done my book-of-the-month for Bill Hamling, so this would be an extra book. I wrote a couple of chapters about a con artist down on his luck. He skips a hotel bill, then steals a suitcase at a railroad station so he'll be able to check in at another hotel. (This was before credit cards, and if you looked presentable and had decent luggage, hotels didn't ask for money up front.) The suitcase turns out to be full of heroin, and belongs to a presumably respectable businessman who's actually a drug trafficker, and who has a beautiful wife.

And away we go.

Two or three chapters in, it seemed to me that I was writing something with possibilities. Don Westlake came over and I asked him to read it. (He'd moved to Canarsie, at the very end of the 14th Street line, but we still saw each other a couple of times a week.) Don encouraged me to forget about Shorten and write the book as a Gold Medal-type suspense novel. The book I wrote probably owed a lot to James M. Cain, and to such literary heirs of his as Charles Williams and Gil Brewer. The narrator finally winds up with the woman, and to make sure he can keep her he addicts her to heroin. At the end he's toying with the idea of trying it himself.

(After the book came out, I ran into Bob Aronson, who pointed out that I'd worked a variation on "Ride a White Horse," a *Manhunt* story I'd written while we were roommates at the Alexandria. He was right, of course, but I hadn't even realized it. I'd forgotten all about that story.)

Henry sent the book to Knox Burger at Gold Medal, far and away the best market for this type of book. Knox bought it, and liked pretty much everything about it but the title. I'd called it *The Girl on the Beach*, and he wanted to change it to *Grifter's Game*, which was fine with me.

When it came out, the title had become *Mona*. It seemed that Ralph Daigh, who ran the company for the Fawcett brothers, had bought a piece of art he wanted to use for the cover, a drawing of a woman's face. The woman in the book was named Mona, so that's what he decided to call it.

Jove reissued the book in the early eighties and called it *Sweet Slow Death*. Sounds like a bodice-ripper with a dark ending. I know where they got the phrase; it was part of the back-cover blurb on the original Gold

Medal edition. As I write this, Paul Mikol at Dark Harvest is preparing to publish the book in hardcover for the first time, in both a limited and a trade edition. "Ride a White Horse," which I've never collected in any of my short-story collections, will be included in the volume. It seems remarkable to me that the book should have had so many lives, and I'm by no means sure it deserves them. This time around I could call it *Grifter's Game*, I suppose, or even *The Girl on the Beach*, but some people might think it was a new book, and they'd read the first chapter and figure I'd lost it. I'll stick with *Mona*.

IT WAS AROUND this time that I became the notorious publisher of *Confidential*.

Well, the former publisher. His name was Bob Harrison, and he'd made a pile of dough with the scandal magazine during the fifties. It was the climax of a truly tawdry publishing career, which included a couple of girlie books called *Wink* and *Titter*. This was a class act.

Harrison had some sort of deal to do a book, which would be essentially a distillation of the best of *Confidential*. They could have called the book that, but it would have been too oxymoronic for words. Besides, no one wanted to tip the fact that the book had nothing new in it, that it was just old magazine garbage tucked between hard covers.

The book was going to be limited to material with some sort of connection to New York, and Harrison would have loved to call it *New York Confidential*, but unfortunately that title had been used by Jack Lait and Lee Mortimer, two journalists who were more respectable than Harrison, though less respectable than almost anyone else you could name. This really pissed Harrison off, as he figured he ought to have a proprietary interest in the C word, but he let it go.

He might have called it *Inside New York*, but then he'd have John Gunther mad at him. So he settled on *Naked New York*.

Now all he needed was somebody to write it for him.

That was where I came in. Harrison had called Scott, and Henry called me, and I went over to Harrison's suite at the Hotel Madison, on Madison Avenue in the 30s. Harrison was a tall, well-built man in his sixties, always attired in a conservatively cut suit. He was accompanied by a woman of a certain age who was his assistant and, if I remember correctly, his sister. The two of them had a folder full of clippings of old stories from the magazine, and it would be my job to seek out the best of them and write them anew so that they would be fresh and timely.

Harrison couldn't possibly do this himself. I'm not sure the son of a bitch could read.

I've thought about this, and my guess is he was dyslexic, or something like it. Whenever you wanted him to look at something, he would insist that you read it aloud. He had to hear it. It was easier for him to evaluate material that way.

"This is great," he'd say, shuffling through the folder and pulling out some article about B-girls serving watered drinks in 1952. Then he'd hand it to me or his sister. "Here—read it to me." And we'd read it and agree how great it was.

Many of the articles had nothing to do with New York—"But you could make it New York, couldn't you?"—and managed to be tacky without being sensational. Anyone with an IQ higher than his birth weight could have told him he didn't have the makings of a book. But he had something more important than that, he had a deal, and if you've got a deal you can always come up with a book, and it was my job to write it.

Somehow or other I did. I took the stories we selected back to my apartment and got the job done. I know it was one of those deals where they needed it yesterday, and I was certainly anxious to be done with it myself, so it didn't take long.

Then the fucker welshed. He told Scott that the script I'd delivered wasn't long enough, and that I hadn't done it right, and he wasn't going to pay the balance. He'd paid half, with the rest due on delivery. He was screwing me out of $750 or thereabouts. Scott said you had to stand in a long line to sue Harrison, so we let it go.

Naked New York. I don't think I ever saw a copy. Was it ever published? Did Harrison ever get somebody to read it to him?

AROUND THIS TIME, I began writing for Charles Heckelmann.

Heckelmann was an editor at Popular Library while I was working as a mailboy at Pines Publications, but I never met him then. I never met him afterward, either, although I wound up writing upwards of a dozen books for the man.

As a matter of fact, I never met most of the people I wrote for, and it was a long time before I realized that this was unusual. There were two reasons for it. First and foremost, it was a policy of Scott Meredith's to discourage any direct contact between the writers he represented and the editors and publishers with whom he placed their work. One might rub the other the wrong way and ruin what had been a perfectly satisfactory relationship. More to the point, the greater the distance between author and publisher, the more indispensable that made the agent.

In my particular case, Henry was especially disinclined to put me face to face with editors. He didn't want them to realize how young I was.

There were times when Henry had to bite the bullet and let me meet somebody. He'd kept me away from Knox Burger with *Mona*, but would have to send me over to Fawcett's 44th Street offices when Knox wanted to discuss changes in the second book I sold him. And, when Harry Shorten had insisted on meeting me, Henry grudgingly set up a date. I went to Shorten's office, and he had two questions to ask, and I don't think I answered either of them satisfactorily. First, he wanted to know how I intuitively knew just how hot to make a sex scene. Henry had told him that I was a professor of English ("Tell him you're a professor of British," Larry Harris counseled me. "It'll impress him more.") and I gave some artsy-fartsy answer, the equivalent of a starlet's explanation that she'll fellate an orangutan on camera but only if the integrity of the script demands it.

His other question? "That grease pit scene in *Carla*. Jesus, how'd you ever come up with that one?" I mumbled something vague. It was a pity the New Age hadn't dawned yet. I could have said I channeled it.

IN 1960, HECKELMANN WAS editor-in-chief at a low-level paperback house called Monarch Books. Monarch wasn't in a class with Nightstand and Midwood, but it was still pretty sleazy in its own right. Heckelmann had a penchant for quickie books produced to hitch a ride on the coattails of a popular success. He kept an eye on the headlines, too; when Elizabeth Taylor fell seriously ill, he commissioned Don Westlake to knock out a quick cut-and-paste biography of the actress. (When she pulled through he published it anyway, but I'm sure he wasn't happy about it.)

The first thing I did for Heckelmann was a literal piece of ghostwriting. William Ard, a Scott Meredith client, had recently died young of cancer, and he'd stuck Heckelmann with a portion and outline of a mystery novel before bowing out. If I could complete the book from Ard's outline, Heckelmann would have a book to publish, Ard's widow would pick up a couple of bucks, and I'd make some money and have one more cover for the wall.

I'll tell you about the wall in a minute.

William Ard was a pretty good writer, and got consistently good reviews from Anthony Boucher in the New York Times Book Review. Boucher was particularly pleased by Ard's ability to get a story told economically. Brevity, I sometimes think, is especially endearing to reviewers, who have so damned much to wade through day in and day out that they're grateful to anybody who gets them home early. Ard's mysteries were on the short side, all right, most of them a scant 50,000 words if that.

I trust my contribution to Ard's body of work was a slender volume. I certainly wanted to be done with it as soon as possible. All I recall of it was that there were twin sisters named LiLi and LoLa; putting those extra caps in their names was a real pain in the ass, and keeping them straight was out of the question. The opening chapters were not a terribly hard act to follow, but the outline, which I somehow thought I had to stick to slavishly, was awful. I'm sure if Ard had lived to finish the book himself he would have felt free to stray from the outline, and would have made the whole thing work. About all I managed was to get the thing written.

Besides, they needed it in a hurry.

I'll tell you, I was a real sucker for that approach. All Henry had to do was tell me somebody was racing a deadline and needed something as fast as possible, and I'd have the sucker half written before he could hang up the phone. To meet Heckelmann's ostensible deadline on the Ard project, I rented a room at the Spencer Arms, a hotel half a block away at the corner of 69th and Broadway. I pounded away at the typewriter and finished the book in three or four days, stupidly convinced that such a pace was essential. I'm sure it was a week before Heckelmann even looked at it, and another month before it went to typesetting.

I never looked at the manuscript after I wrote the last page, and never read it after it came out, but I'm sure it was terrible. Heckelmann must have thought so, because I wasn't asked to be part of the team when they decided to keep poor Bill Ard dead and writing. Another of Scott's faithful retainers got the job, and produced three or four more masterpieces under Ard's name before the project was aborted.

What's extraordinary about the whole affair is that anyone could have thought this deception was worth the trouble. Ard was a pretty decent writer, certainly, but it's not as though he had a host of readers out there clamoring for more of his work. If he'd had any kind of a following, he wouldn't have been writing for Monarch. One reason for continuing the series, of course, was so that the widow Ard wouldn't have to take in washing. (I presume she got a quarter of the earnings on the posthumous books. That was the usual arrangement Scott worked out when he breathed fresh life into a writer's corpse.) Somehow I can't believe anybody at 580 Fifth wasted a lot of sleep over the state of Mrs. Ard's finances. It was an easy sale, that's all, and Scott never let one of those get away if he could help it.

But it wasn't a *good* sale. It was John Jakes who ghosted those books for Ard, and in years to come he established himself as a writer of popular historical fiction and had a string of books on the bestseller list. His talent might have had a chance to develop far sooner than it did if his agent hadn't handed him every piece of low-level hack work that came along.

I don't know of a case where Scott helped a writer to improve, or even encouraged it. He never took the long view, never thought in terms of building a career. The point, as he saw it, was not to get his clients writing better books for better markets. The point was to keep everybody writing, so that they were all generating commissions.

I DON'T KNOW if I was called upon to make any changes in the Ard book. It seems to me there must have been a letter from Heckelmann, imploring me to flesh out a couple of scenes.

Everyone who wrote anything for Monarch was familiar with that phrase. It was a favorite of Heckelmann's, and he rarely got through a letter without it. I used to have this mental picture of the Heckelmanns sitting down to dinner, all of them fleshed out like regular little porkers. "Have another helping!" he'd urge them. "I want you fleshed out!"

I don't know how many books I wrote for him after that. Ten? Twelve? More?

I couldn't say, but I can tell you this. He never knew it was me.

I PROMISED TO tell you about the wall.

It was Don Westlake who first took to mounting the covers of his published works on his office wall. He'd acquire a second copy of every book or magazine as it came out, cut off the cover, and affix it to the top of the wall where it met the ceiling. The parade of covers worked its way around the room, each specimen a proud proclamation of a burgeoning career. (Several of the covers were upside down, Don's way of indicating that, while a publication had indeed used his story, they'd neglected to pay him; I remember three or four such covers from *Mystery Digest,* but there may have been others as well.)

My own first venture into the wallpaper business came in the first apartment Loretta and I shared, at 110 West 69th Street. Instead of circling the room with the covers, I started at eye level directly above my desk, and let the covers fan out in a sort of montage. Double-sided tape would have been ideal for my purpose, but I'm not sure it existed in 1960, and if it did I didn't know about it. I made little circles of masking tape, and they worked well enough.

When we moved to 444 Central Park West, the wall montage made the trip with us, and was promptly installed over my desk in the dining room. It would move again, to Tonawanda and Racine and Lambertville, until one relocation proved to be A Move Too Far. The covers, dozens of them by then, came down from one wall but went not onto another but into a file folder.

Until then, the wall served a purpose. It furnished graphic evidence that I was turning out work and getting it published. While my books and stories put food on the table and kept a roof over our heads, they had little presence in the outside world; most of what I wrote was pseudonymous, and the rest might as well have been, for all the attention anyone paid to it.

The wall was evidence of accomplishment. Every time I wrote something, I covered some more square inches of wall space. And it was, to be sure, more satisfying to look upon than those rejection slips I'd mounted in my Antioch dormitory.

And, when Ted Hecht reprinted an article in another of his magazines, well, he might not pay me anything for running it a second or third time, and indeed I might have to buy my own copy at a newsstand, but that's not to say I didn't get anything out of it. It was, by God, one more cover for the wall.

ONE OF THE first books I did for Heckelmann—it may have preceded the Ard mystery—was the purported autobiography of a prostitute, *I Sell Love*, by Liz Crowley. That's all I remember about it, that and the fact that I got $1250 for writing it. It was like writing a novel, except that it purported to be true. If anything, that made it a little easier to plot.

Then one day I got a call from Henry. Heckelmann had read a book called *The Power of Sexual Surrender* and wanted to knock it off. For this one, though, I would have to be a doctor, and the working title was *Sexual Surrender in Women*.

"That's nice," I said. "What does it mean?"

"It's a way of overcoming frigidity by giving up control," he said.

"Control of what?"

"I'm not sure," Henry said. "You can read the book and then write your version. You just make up case histories to illustrate the points you're trying to make."

I looked through the book by Marie Robinson, then sat down and wrote *Sexual Surrender in Women*, by Benjamin Morse, M.D. Heckelmann knew this was a pen name, but he was given to understand that the real author was Morton A. Benjamin, a Chicago-area psychiatrist. If he'd found himself in Chicago in the middle of a psychotic break, he'd have had to seek out a couch to lie on other than Dr. Benjamin's, who was as much a figment of my imagination as was Dr. Morse.

It seems to me that first Benjamin Morse book must have been on the lame side, because I wrote it without a very clear understanding of what Marie Robinson was getting at. It was full of case histories, though, in each of which some patient of the good Dr. Morse managed to get her rocks off as a result of his therapy. Heckelmann liked it enough to ask for more.

Morse's next book was *The Lesbian*, followed by *A Modern Marriage Manual* (dedicated by that cunning Mort Benjamin "to my wife Sylvia, who could write a book of her own"), *The Homosexual*, and a few others.

At one point, Heckelmann decided a clinical knock-off of Helen Gurley Brown's *Sex and the Single Girl* was in order. I'd just finished a book for him, and for Dr. Morse to knock out another right away might strain the bonds of credulity some. After all, Mort Benjamin presumably had a big clinical practice. How did he find the time to write so much?

This time, Henry explained, I would be Dr. Walter C. Brown. I went out and marked the occasion by buying a second typewriter, which wasn't a bad idea anyway. My standard model had pica type, so I got a portable with elite type and used it to write *The Single Girl*.

Heckelmann took it and paid the $1500, but it didn't knock his socks off. "Brown's all right," he told Henry, "but he's nowhere near the writer Mort Benjamin is, is he?"

I decided Heckelmann preferred a larger typeface. And that was the end of kindly old Dr. Brown. He never wrote another word.

*   *   *

DON MARQUIS ON one occasion likened publishing a volume of verse to "dropping a rose petal into the Grand Canyon and waiting for the echo." The books I was writing may have been less than fragrant, but they were definite rose petals in the echo department. I wrote them, I handed them in, I got paid for them, they came out—and that was that. They didn't get reviewed, and were rarely read by anyone of my acquaintance.

I did get a handful of letters from readers. When *Strange are the Ways of Love* came out, Crest forwarded a letter to Lesley Evans from a lesbian reader in Corvallis, Oregon. And Benjamin Morse received perhaps half a dozen letters from readers who wanted his professional advice.

I never answered any of these. Dr. Morse also got an invitation to speak at a symposium at Dickinson College, for which service an honorarium would be provided. That was tempting, I must admit, but I wasn't quite crazy enough to attempt it. I never responded.

My favorite letter, and one I showed to all my friends, was from a gay man in the Village writing in response to Morse's *The Lesbian*. He didn't have a problem, just wanted to boast about his sex life, and to advise me that a surprising number of lesbians welcomed a man's attentions now and then. He himself, he reported, was known as "King of the Fish Queens" because of his occasional dalliances with such women.

I was tempted to reply, but it was easier to let the letter go unanswered. Years later, when I was corresponding actively with readers as John Warren Wells, and even meeting some of them face to face, as it were, I thought from time to time of the King of the Fish Queens and wished I'd managed to hear more from him.

13

March 10, 2020
Newberry, South Carolina

MY GOODNESS, WHAT a place to stop. What could have led me to give the last word to the King of the Fish Queens? It was certainly not a deliberate choice, but one brought about by lack of time. My stay at Ragdale had run its course. I had to leave so that some other writer could occupy my room and take my place evenings at the communal dining table. I had to get back to New York, where I could delight in the company of my wife and give in to the exhaustion which was already creeping in like cat-footed fog.

That was 1994. This is 2020.

For God's sake, where do I go from here?

I COULD JUST stop. I have, after all, fifty-five thousand words to place between actual or virtual covers. That's enough for a book.

Indeed, it's already as long as most of the books I've been telling you about, and longer than some.

Is it worth a brief digression to make a point about word count then and now? Let's find out.

I always thought of my early books as running around sixty thousand words. That was what I understood to be a sort of average minimum for a novel. Some, surely, were shorter, and *War and Peace* was a good deal longer, but if you gave them 60K you weren't short-changing anybody. (Not in terms of length, anyway. Whether your words were well- or ill-chosen was another matter, and—for some editors—barely a consideration.)

With short stories, where the writer was paid by the word, I'd sit down and count the words, tapping each one with a pencil tip and making a little mark on my carbon copy every hundred words. Then I'd return the first page to the typewriter and, beneath

Lawrence Block

Scott Meredith Literary Agency

580 Fifth Avenue

New York 36, New York

I would type the word count:

3823 words

Except, of course, I would know better than to be that OCD-ishly specific. I'd round the figure off. Perhaps to 3800, if I wanted to feel righteous, or to 3900, because my own wallet might as well have the benefit of the doubt. Or I could decide that we're all grownups here, and word counts are only approximations, even if I happened to be ninny enough to tap away with my pencil, so why not deal in round numbers and make it an even 4000 words?

That was fine with short stories, and I know I'm by no means the only writer who went through this ritual. Word count was important. That number you typed beneath your name and address determined the number on the check they sent you. You certainly didn't want to cheat yourself, but neither did you want to get caught trying to cheat the magazine. So you counted the words and acted accordingly.

But book publishers weren't buying words. They were buying books.

Length still mattered. It mattered to low-level paperback houses like Midwood and Nightstand, because they wanted to fill a certain number of pages. Too short and the reader would feel cheated, too many and their production and shipping costs would climb.

It mattered to far more respectable operations as well, like Doubleday's Crime Club line; they published hardcover mystery novels, averaging three a month for over sixty years, and a substantial portion of their output went straight to public and lending libraries. While it would be going too far to say the books were bland, they were certainly not particularly spicy or hard-boiled. Were they formulaic? Some of them probably were, but that was not a requirement. What they couldn't be, though, was too long or too short. I never inquired too closely, but always understood that their books were never very much longer or shorter than sixty thousand words.

But I don't think anybody counted each word in a Crime Club novel, any more than I counted the words in *Carla* or *Campus Tramp*. There was a more efficient way to know where you stood, and it was called *printer's measure*. It was based on the notion that nobody publishing a book gave a damn how many individual words it contained, that what mattered was how much space they took up on the printed page. The accepted formula for printer's measure was that a word was six characters long, five letters plus a space, and you computed that on the basis of the number of lines on the typewritten page and the average number of characters per line.

This of course would vary with the typewriter you used—Dr. Walter C. Brown's typewriter, with its *Elite* typeface, put more words on a sheet of paper than did the *Pica* type that served Benjamin Morse, M.D. It would also vary with the width of the margins you set, and if you started at the top or middle of the first page, and how much space you left at the top or bottom.

(When I worked at Scott Meredith, one of the pro clients was a fellow named Hal Ellson, who spent his days as a social worker and therapist at Bellevue Hospital, where he dealt with the troubled adolescents whose life experience wound up in his novels and short stories. *Duke* and *Tomboy* are the titles I remember, and his biggest successes. I never met Ellson, but I think of him now because his manuscripts bore the largest margins I've ever seen, with his typing confined to a column in the center of the page that couldn't have been more than three inches wide.)

So you worked out what your pages added up to in printer's measure, and if that was 300 words to the page, then two hundred pages of manuscript would bring you in at sixty thousand words. And so on.

That was my own rough estimate. Three hundred words to the page, and my books were running around 200 pages. When I was turning in a book a month for Bill Hamling at Nightstand, I turned in a couple at 195 pages, which seemed right to me, but someone in Evanston determined that my manuscripts needed to be a little bit longer. I was advised that an extra ten pages ought to do it, so from then on I made sure every book ended on Page 205.

Ten chapters to a book, five of them at twenty pages, the other five at twenty-one. I look at the sentence I just wrote, and the whole regimen seems as formal as a sonnet and as formulaic as a haiku, and perhaps it was. But the system made it easier to know where I stood and if I'd done a full day's work. I wanted to give the publisher and the putative reader a full book; I did not want to give either of them a single extra page.

Or an extra word.

AND HOW LONG were the books I turned in?

Back then I'd have told you they probably ran around 55,000 words. I'd have been giving myself the benefit of the doubt. I've republished most of those early books, in ebook and paperback form, and I've produced audiobook editions of some of them—*21 Gay Street, Of Shame and Joy,*

The Adulterers. To do all this I've had to turn printed books into MS Word files, and if I open the file I can see the number of words at the bottom edge of the window.

And so I can tell you that *Carla*, my first book for Harry Shorten, ran to 47,800 words. (And that includes the legendary chapter-to-be-inserted-anywhere-in-the-book. No wonder he asked for that extra chapter. Even with it, the book was shorter than it really ought to have been.)

Campus Tramp, my first book for Bill Hamling, tips the scales at 46,900 words. *College for Sinners*, a later Nightstand title, runs to 45,500.

My very first novel, *Strange are the Ways of Love*, is back in print, and in audio as well, narrated by PJ Morgan. In the course of republishing it, I changed its title back to *Shadows,* and assigned the book to my long-standing female pen name, Jill Emerson. And just now I opened the Word file and confirmed that the book is a mere 43,000 words.

And that gives me the opportunity to apply 2020 hindsight to an error I made a few chapters ago, when I railed against Crest's excision of a chapter recounting the rape of one Peggy Corcoran. I retold the story of the Peggy Corcoran chapter in 2011, when I wrote about that early novel in *Afterthoughts.*

Five years later, I self-published the book under my original title, *Shadows,* with an open pen name: "Lawrence Block writing as Jill Emerson." That seemed only appropriate, as the book grew out of the same sensibility that would lead to subsequent Jill Emerson titles.

And then, reading through the book, I learned to my astonishment that the Peggy Corcoran chapter had been there all along. I know an editor at Crest wanted me to remove it, and I know I argued for its retention, but for all these years I'd thought I'd lost the argument, and it was now clear that I hadn't.

And so I've interrupted my younger self to set the record straight.

Never mind. The fact remains that *Shadows,* at 43,000 words, was and is a short book. So it's good they kept the chapter; it would have been even shorter without it.

ONE EXPLANATION FOR the brevity of those early books, as shown in their word count, is a matter of style. As both writer and reader, I've always been partial to books with an abundance of dialogue. I always had trouble reading books that consisted of page after page with nothing but uninterrupted narrative prose. Reading them was like listening to some disembodied narrator run off at the mouth, while reading extended dialogue exchanges was guilt-free eavesdropping.

A good writer could reveal character and advance storyline in dialogue. And even a bad writer could fill up pages.

So it was natural for me to let my characters talk to one another.

"See what I'm getting at?"

"You know, I think I do."

"One line just leads to another, and—"

"And you get a sense of the characters, even as their chitchat keeps the story moving."

"Right."

"Writing dialogue's easy, too."

"It is."

"You just let 'em talk and write down what they say."

"Exactly."

"And the pages fill up, and the reader's fine with it."

"And Bob's your uncle."

"Right. What does that mean, exactly?"

"What?"

" 'And Bob's your uncle.' Who's Bob, and how does he get to be your uncle?"

"I dunno. By marrying my mother's sister? Its just an expression, for the love of Mike."

"Back up, will you? Who's Mike?"

AH, THE MAGIC of dialogue. It's easy to write and even easier to read. It does fill the page, and you can see for yourself how much shorter the lines are than in passages of pure exposition. It comes to way more in printer's measure than it does in actual count-em-with-a-pencil-tip words.

Nor was dialogue the only way I found to run a manuscript to the requisite 205 pages while expending as few words as possible.

One rather obvious trick was never to end a chapter at or near the bottom of the page. Nowadays, writing on a computer and fitting an entire novel into a single document, I don't know where I am on a page when I decide it's time for a chapter to end. I don't even insert a page break. I skip a few lines, insert a trio of hashtags like this:

# # #

and get on with it.

But when I used a typewriter, whenever a chapter ended I would remove that sheet of paper from the typewriter, and the next chapter would begin on its own page. (And it would begin, let me add, halfway down that new page, even as the preceding chapter ended very near the top of its final page. Not on the first line of that page, because one did not want to be too obvious about this sort of thing, but perhaps five or six lines down.)

Ten chapters, five of twenty pages, five of twenty-one. Well, yes, but one occasionally broke ranks. If I was on, say, the twenty-first page of a particular chapter, and if the natural course of things had me more than halfway down the page, I'd take a deep breath and keep on going, finding enough to say to get me, oh, five or six lines down from the top of page 22.

Which meant the next day's chapter could be one page shorter.

THE OBJECT, SEE, was to deliver an acceptable manuscript with as little effort as possible. I think that may have been a goal from the beginning, but I wasn't consciously aware of it early on. My books for Harry Shorten, and my first books for Bill Hamling, were as good as I could make them within the confines of the form. Of course I wanted to complete each book as rapidly as possible—because writing was hard work, even for one who came relatively naturally to it, and because the sooner a day's work was done the sooner I could pursue other interests, and because once a book was completed I could get paid, and see my body of work extended by another volume.

And write something else.

The next sex novel, perhaps—but not necessarily.

See, I was always trying to do better work as well.

A short story, say.

Maybe a crime novel.

Something more ambitious than the books for Shorten and Hamling.

See what I did there?

What I'm still doing?

Short paragraphs. One-line paragraphs. They're easy to read, they break up pages of text nicely, and you can write like that for half a page or so without getting on the reader's nerves. And it gets that chapter written with fewer words than you'd otherwise be delivering.

Often enough, I'd incorporate this particular ploy in a sex scene. Let's say the participants are having at it—in a manner which is never entirely specified, even if designed to leave as little as possible to the imagination. And something like this appears:

He drove deeper.

And deeper.

And deeper still . . .

Oh, God help us. That's awfully deep, isn't it? If the birds eat the bread crumbs, the poor bastard will never find his way back again.

BUT I DIGRESS.

And, you know, that strikes me as a fine alternative title. *But I Digress*—with or without a trio of dots after it.

Not that I've lost enthusiasm for the original title, the one that came to me at Ragdale, not long after I began writing like a man with his hair on fire. *A Writer Prepares* is of course a phrase that echoes *An Actor Prepares,* Konstantin Stanislavski's book which explains his acting method by chronicling the first year of a fictional student being schooled in the method.

I know that now, because of the good offices of Google and Wikipedia, but when I picked it for the present volume all I knew was that Stanislavski had written a book with that title. And that its three words seemed suited to what I seemed to be writing.

And now I've embarked on another digression. What I wrote at Ragdale was propelled by a strong narrative drive. It flowed in a stream, the sort that comes cascading down the side of a mountain.

A quarter of a century later, it has aged into an old river. It takes its sweet time, it meanders, and if it maintains any kind of a pace at all it is surely an unhurried one. It traces a circuitous course, it silts up here and there, and its digressions and asides are oxbows.

Try to imagine 1994's memoirist writing the foregoing paragraph.

NO, I THINK what's called for here is a return to the form of the 1994 narrative, if not to its passion and energy. It may be no less self-indulgent, as self-indulgence seems to be an inevitable component of great age, but perhaps it can be more on topic.

What was I last writing about? Charles Heckelmann, and Monarch Books, and a couple of fictitious doctors. That was in Chapter Twelve.

So if I'm going to get on with it, what's needed is page break and a chapter title:

14

HECKELMANN DIDN'T LACK for imagination, and the world he lived in never failed to provide inspiration. I've mentioned how Elizabeth Taylor's poor health had led him to commission a quick biography from Don Westlake, even as the success another publisher had with one book (*The Power of Sexual Surrender* by Marie Robinson) had prompted him to order up another (*Sexual Surrender in Women,* by Benjamin Morse, M.D.)

Early in the papacy of John XXIII, Heckelmann decided a biography of the new pope would serve Monarch well, and he somehow enlisted Randall Garrett to write it. I haven't mentioned Randy before, but we crossed paths with some frequency. Don and I probably met him initially through Larry Janifer, who frequently wrote in collaboration with him, as did Robert Silverberg. Once met, Randy was not soon forgotten. He lived somewhere north of 96th Street and west of Broadway, and if he wasn't at home he was apt to be in the pub around the corner. I think it was Don who described him as a man who drank bar whiskey by choice.

And I don't think that was an exaggeration. At the time I knew him, you could not get a legal drink in the state of New York on Election Day. While the polls were open, bars were closed. That was true of every bar in the state.

Except for one. Which is why you could find Randy Garrett on any and every Election Day in the bar at the United Nations, which was not subject to the laws of New York.

Randy was unquestionably eccentric, not least of all in spiritual matters. He was a High Church Anglican, occasionally went on religious re-treats, and met regularly with a canon who served as his spiritual advisor. When he received the assignment to write Pope John's biography, he discussed the matter with the canon, and after he'd written the book he got the man to sign off on it. Then he submitted the book to the Vatican to obtain a *Nihil Obstat* and an *Imprimatur*. I guess he got what he needed, because the book did in fact appear in 1962, and copies still turn up now and then in the aftermarket.

In fact the book has a five-star review on Amazon, by Mike DePue, a Member of the Secular Franciscan Order, and I don't care if this is an ox-bow in my narrative river; I can't in good conscience fail to quote it to you:

> *This book's author is far more interesting than the book itself.*
> *There are a number of fine biographies of John XXIII and this one*
> *definitely is a journalistic, early-pontificate also-ran . . . . The author*
> *admits (p. 157) that he is not competent to assess the recent encyclical*
> *Mater et Magistra and must only describe Vatican Council II as*
> *forthcoming.*
>
> *As far as I can tell, no biography of the author, Randall Garrett*
> *(1927–1987), has yet been written. Given the known details of*
> *his life, this is surprising. Gordon Randall Phillip David Garrett*
> *is commonly described as a pioneering American science fiction and*
> *fantasy author and is notable as the mentor of Robert Silverberg.*
> *Best remembered at this point for his alternate world, 20th century*
> *Plantagenet dynasty Lord Darcy character, Garrett wrote an*
> *astonishing number of short stories under a plethora of pseudonyms.*
> *Despite a lifestyle that can euphemistically be described as turbulent,*
> *Garrett's devout side briefly appeared when he stopped writing*
> *and was ordained in the Old Catholic Church in the Seventies.*
> *Recidivism kicked in however; he abandoned the priesthood, took*

up writing once more, and married his third wife, who became his
collaborator during the last part of his life.

As a sign of the times, this book, inconsequential as it is, displays
a bishop's authorization to be published; rarely, if ever, would that
be found even in a major biography today. Since I must assign stars,
I'll go with five stars for background interest. The book's content, be it
said, is in the two-to-three star range.

I don't know of any biography of Randy, either, although there's probably been a fair amount written about him in science fiction fanzines and
such. If one should appear, you may put me down for a copy.

And whoever's mad enough to undertake the project might want to
include the following:

Randy was verbally skillful to an astonishing degree, and quick to arise
to a challenge. Confronted with the information that nothing rhymes
with either *orange* or *silver*, he produced in due course this artful quatrain:

> *"Though my hair has turned to silver,"*
> *said George Washington with pride,*
> *"Everybody knows I'm still ver–*
> *Acity personified."*

and followed it with this one:

> *Oh, I ate a poisoned orange*
> *And I know I'll soon be dead*
> *For I keep on seeing more ang–*
> *Elic forms about my bed.*

Randy's wordplay was dazzling, and apparently effortless. Just a few months ago I cited an example in "Ham For Breakfast," an introduction I wrote for Ken Wishnia's anthology, *Jewish Noir II*, and collected in *Hunting Buffalo With Bent Nails*:

> *A late friend of mine, the science fiction writer Randall P. Garrett, was a high church Anglican who took the whole business seriously, though not without humor. He met regularly with his spiritual adviser, an Episcopalian canon, and their long conversations were occasionally marked by jokes which Randy told, and told well. Some of these were, if not precisely off-color, a few degrees removed from lily white, and Randy thought to ask the man if it was inappropriate to tell such jokes in that particular setting.*
>
> *"Oh, not at all," the clergyman replied. "They're fine jokes. Besides, I can always use them as fodder for one of my sermons."*
>
> *"It's a wise canon," said Randy, "that knows its own fodder.*

I DON'T KNOW who it was in Scott Meredith's office who looked at Heckelmann's idea and picked Randy for the assignment, but it was an inspired choice. He'd selected a writer whose spiritual orientation made the project appealing, and one who could wrap it up and bring it in at the appointed hour without an undue expenditure of time and energy. I don't know what Monarch paid for the book, but I can't imagine it was more than $1500. There was no budget for travel, for interviews, for anything much beyond the kind of research one could conduct in the reading room of the New York Public Library. So of course it was a cut-and-paste job, but no one involved could have expected more. (And it's not every cut-and-paste job that can boast a *nihil obstat* and an *imprimatur*.)

By the same token, Don Westlake was a good choice to produce a cut-and-paste biography of Elizabeth Taylor—not because he had any particular interest in the woman, but because his competent professionalism was more than equal to the task, and because he could bring to it as well the enthusiasm of a neophyte. He had never written a pop biography before, so he could rise to the challenge of a new kind of task; afterward, having done what he'd set out to do, he could live and write for another forty-five years without ever again undertaking anything similar.

I suspect it was Henry Morrison who selected Randy and Don for these projects. He was wise to do so, and wiser still to leave me out of the picture. I might well have accepted either assignment, as I didn't have the sense to say no to anything that was actually offered to me, but in either instance I'd have made a dog's breakfast of the job.

With Ms. Taylor, I'd have felt that there was an unbridgeable distance between us—and I'd have been quite right. And I'd have been handcuffed as her biographer because writing about her life would have felt to me like an unpardonable invasion of privacy. (I was comfortable invading the privacy of Reinhard Heydrich in the space of 2500 words or so, but a full book about a living film star—no, I think not.)

And let's not even imagine my writing about Pope John—or any pope, really, or any gentleman of the cloth. I'd been raised as a Reform Jew, and my religious observance had ended with my bar mitzvah, while any spiritual dimension to my life had ceased a couple of years earlier, when I looked around my Sunday School classroom and decided that nobody really believed any of this crap, but that there was no harm in pretending.

So nobody chose me to write about either John or Elizabeth. But I got my own wacky assignment for Monarch Books.

I got to kill Fidel Castro.

IT WAS HENRY who gave me the assignment. "*Fidel Castro Assassinated,*" he said.

Really? When had this happened?

"It hasn't happened," Henry said, "but who's to say it won't? If it does, I don't know that Heckelmann will send flowers to the funeral, but you can bet he'll be congratulating himself for coming up with this one."

I said it seemed different from Don's Elizabeth Taylor project, where if she lived it was fine and if she died it was even better—better for Monarch Books, that is, if for nobody else.

"Of course it is," Henry said. "Don's writing a biography. You'll be writing a novel. Did you ever read *Rogue Male*? By Geoffrey Household? About the British sportsman who assassinates Hitler?"

Except, of course, that the assassination wasn't successful, and the intended target wasn't specifically Hitler, nor was the country of which he was the dictator identified as Germany.

"Well, in your book the country's Cuba," Henry said, "and the target is Fidel, and the attempt is successful. By the time the book is over, Señor Castro is dead. That's what makes your book special."

It was what would make it ridiculous—but if the thought crossed my mind, I didn't let myself entertain it.

Instead I got busy. I read what I could find on the subject, which wasn't much. And I began work on *Fidel Castro Assassinated*, by Lee Duncan.

It was Heckelmann who came up with the title, but Henry who supplied my pen name. Lee Duncan would be the pen name of a journalist whose actual identity would have to remain a secret—from the world, and also from Charles Heckelmann. That was evidently okay with Heckelmann, and it was certainly fine with me.

I had enough on my hands writing the book.

And it was a valuable one for me to write. Not in terms of dollars; my advance was $1500, at a time when I was getting $1200 for batting out 205 pages of dialogue and one-sentence paragraphs for Bill Hamling. And, while I'd have been in line for royalties if the book had earned them, it never even came close.

Indeed, it pretty much sank without a trace, so it had no direct impact on my career. But what it did do was impel me to develop new writing skills. Rather than dispatch a single trained assassin to draw a bead on Fidel, I posited some covert group—perhaps Cuban exiles, perhaps commercial interests—who hired five individuals and gave them the mission.

So I was writing a reasonably complicated multiple-viewpoint novel of adventure, and one that would require action scenes. The scenes ought to be exciting, and it would be a good idea to maintain a certain level of suspense.

I wrote the book without ever knowing very much about Cuba, or about Cubans on either side of the political divide. Nor did I have any idea what was about to happen in the world.

See, it must have been in the first months of 1961 that I got that initial telephone call from Henry. Sometime in February would be my guess, and while I can't tell you exactly when I began actually writing the thing, I know the precise date on which I skipped two lines and typed THE END. It was March 29.

I can tell you that with assurance because the next thing I did was roll a fresh sheet of paper into the typewriter, type FIDEL CASTRO AS-SASSINATED / by Lee Duncan / Dedication at the top, skip another half-dozen lines, and type this:

This is for AMY JO, who was born yesterday

My eldest daughter was indeed born on March 28. I'd spent the day at Flower Fifth Avenue Hospital, directly across the park from our apartment at 444 Central Park West. The following morning I finished the book for Monarch, and didn't have to work hard to come up with a dedication.

March 29, 1961. The disastrous Bay of Pigs invasion of Cuba took place April 17–21, less than a month later.

Coincidence?

I think not, or at least not entirely. I have to figure Heckelmann knew something, or thought he knew something. There were enough rumors flying around at the time for one or more of them to have reached his ear. He presumably was happy with the book I delivered, but I imagine time considerations would have predisposed him to take whatever I gave him and rush it into print.

Where it proved as disappointing as the invasion itself.

Fidel Castro Assassinated disappeared essentially without a trace. Then, half a century later, Hard Case Crime published it anew, with a much better title (*Killing Castro*), a far more inviting cover (hot-looking girl with bare midriff and cartridge belt), and my own name as author.

The Hard Case edition, as it happens, was published on March 29, 2011. That, you may note, is precisely fifty years after I finished writing the book.

Coincidence?

I think so.

By then Charles Heckelmann had been dead for six years, having reached the age of 91. I'll leave it to you and Google to find death dates for John XXIII and Elizabeth Taylor, but they were both gone by then, as alas were Randall Garrett and Donald Westlake.

But not Fidel Castro, who outlived damn near everybody and died—finally!—in November 2016 at the age of 90.

15

WHEN AMY WAS born—on March 28,1961, as you'll recall—we soon brought her home to a spacious two-bedroom apartment at 444 Central Park West. A year earlier, when we'd married and moved to New York, we'd taken a furnished one-bedroom apartment at 110 West 69th Street, between Columbus and Amsterdam; it suited us, but with a baby on the way we'd felt a need for more space.

The new apartment was quite luxurious, and reasonable enough at $202 a month, utilities included. The location, on the west side of the park between 104th and 105th Streets, was good and bad. The park access was a plus (although our apartment was at the rear of the building, and instead of a park view we got a good look at a housing project). There was a subway entrance—the Eighth Avenue local—just a block away. But shopping was three blocks away on Broadway, and one of those blocks—West 104th Street between Columbus and Amsterdam—was allegedly the most crime-ridden block in Manhattan outside of Harlem.

We liked the apartment, and settled into it. The formal dining room became my office, with a wall of bookcases and a desk sharing space with the dining table. Amy had her own bedroom, and we had ours, and each bedroom had its own bathroom. The living room was huge, and there was even a foyer. And I seem to remember a terrace, although we rarely set foot on it; it was narrow, as I recall, but you could go out there if you wanted to check out the housing project without having to look through a window.

By the time Amy was a year old we had moved four hundred miles away.

YOU MAY RECALL that I set out writing this whatever-it-is with Erskine Caldwell as my role model. His *Call It Experience* dealt only with his life as a writer, and it was my intention to follow his example and leave the rest of my life unexamined.

(Which, according to Socrates, would make it not worth living. But never mind.)

What I'm finding out, sitting at my desk here in Newberry, is that I seem to be more interested in examining my life in full than in trying to recall and recount the details of every book I wrote. If I was once reluctant to let anyone know anything much about me, I seem to have been utterly transformed into an old man desperate to tell all.

Well, not quite. But I've always found my life to be worth living, and in the years since that stay at Ragdale, I've become increasingly inclined to examine it.

SO WHY DID a young married couple, very comfortably settled into a very suitable apartment in the city of their dreams, pick up and go back where they came from?

Because that's what we did. We bought a postwar ranch house at 48 Ebling Avenue, in the Township of Tonawanda, a close-by suburb of Buffalo. As for why we did it, there were a few reasons.

One was that we were parents now, and that meant we were supposed to live in a one-family house, with a lawn and a back yard and, I suppose, a basement and an attic. A white picket fence was optional.

Now we wouldn't have had to move to the other end of the state to have these things. The house on Ebling cost us $27,500, and for that price we could almost certainly have found a decent house in Brooklyn or Queens where we'd have been just a subway ride away from Times Square. And back in 1962 we wouldn't have had to pay a lot more than that to buy a brownstone in the Village.

Nothing like that ever occurred to us. Nor, when Don Westlake moved even farther away than Canarsie, to a house in Englishtown, New Jersey, did we think of following him there, or looking for another New York City suburb.

No, we were going to move back to Buffalo, and for a simple if not terribly sensible reason:

A little over three months before Amy's birth, on December 17, 1960, the day before his 52nd birthday, my father died, suddenly and unexpectedly, of an aortic aneurysm.

I'VE WRITTEN ABOUT this. I had my own 52nd birthday on June 24, 1990, and not long after that date I wrote an essay, "Outliving a Father." At the time, the *New York Times Sunday Magazine* had a back-page feature consisting of a personal essay by a male writer, perhaps designed to demonstrate that men were sentient beings, that some of them actually had feelings. I wrote about my father's death and about the experience of reaching the age at which his life ended, and I sent it off, and they sent it back, and a couple of years later, when Ernie Bulow wanted some extra content for *After Hours: Conversations with Lawrence Block,* I dusted it off and gave it to him.

Since hardly anybody ever had a look at *After Hours,* I don't imagine "Outliving a Father" had many readers. I forgot about it myself until Terry Zobeck called it to my attention while compiling my bibliography. "Oh, right," I said. "That's where it went." And I probably should have included it in *Hunting Buffalo With Bent Nails,* but that book was already longer than it needed to me, and I told myself the essay had already been collected in Ernie Bulow's book.

Loretta and I had signed a lease for the Central Park West apartment, but we were still living at 110 West 69th Street when the telephone woke us in the middle of the night. It was my mother, calling to tell us my father had been rushed to the hospital. A couple of hours later here was another phone call, this from Moe Cheplove, a close friend of my parents and our family physician.

Game over.

We went home for the funeral, then returned to New York to move into our new apartment. Life went on, as it does, and we awaited the birth of our first child.

It's almost hard to remember that at the time a child's sex remained unknown until birth, and so we'd picked out names to cover both contingencies, Andrew Jonathan and Amy Jo. Boy or girl, the monogram would memorialize my father, Arthur Jerome Block.

Amy turned up on schedule. She was about a year old when we moved to the house in Tonawanda.

The reason for the move seems so clear to me now. I had not been there when my father died. That was an error, a sin of omission on my part, and I could best rectify it by returning.

I don't need to delve more deeply into this, and you don't need to read it. Sometime in the spring of 1962 we made our move.

I FIGURED I COULD write there as well as anywhere else. I'd grown up knowing that New York was where you went if you wanted to be a writer, and I'd acted accordingly, but I'd written as effectively in Buffalo and in Yellow Springs, Ohio, and wherever I lived I could be represented as effectively (or ineffectively) by the Scott Meredith agency.

The house on Ebling had three bedrooms, and I took one for an office; eventually I shifted operations to an alcove in the finished basement, where I was less aware of ringing phones and household conversations.

(And, after we'd been living there for perhaps a year, I took an office a few blocks away, in a small commercial building. I seem always to have had the impulse to get away to sequester myself with my work, and during our last months at 444 Central Park West, I'd taken a hotel room to work in—back once again at the Hotel Rio on West 47th Street.)

I was very productive in Tonawanda. I wrote a book a month for Bill Hamling, I wrote short stories and made my first sales to *Alfred Hitchcock's Mystery Magazine,* and I wrote, as the good Doctor Morse, more fictional non-fiction for Monarch, and for Lancer Books as well.

It was, as Robert Silverberg has spoken of his own early years, good hackwork.

Bob and I have had somewhat parallel careers, he in science fiction and I in crime, although it wasn't until fairly recently that we actually met and became friends. But I was certainly well aware of him, and knew that he was writing and selling close to a quarter of a million words a month—three books, that is to say, and the equivalent of a book's worth of magazine fiction.

I was never as systematic or as organized, nor did I get as much written and published. But years down the line, when each of us had long outgrown the world of Bill Hamling and Harry Shorten, and had in fact achieved Grand Master recognition in our respective genres, it was Bob's example that helped move me to acknowledge that early work.

He was quite candid, very much up-front about his beginnings. "It was good hackwork," he declared, and didn't deny authorship of the various works of Don Elliott and Loren Beauchamp and L. T. Woodward, M.D.

Now, of course, I've moved about as far from denial as one can. I've not only acknowledged and embraced that pseudonymous early work, but I've done everything I can to foist it anew upon the reading public. I've changed my label for the work from *sex novels* (which we all called them) and *soft-core pornography* (which everybody else called them) to *classic midcentury erotica*—which I may well be alone in calling them, but that's my story and I'm sticking with it.

IF ANYONE HAD suggested at the time that those early efforts might still find readers sixty years later, I'd have thought he was out of his mind. I certainly didn't expect or even hope that they might have a long life. I wanted them to earn immediate income for me—royalties were never a possibility, but they brought me a better living than I could have earned otherwise, and that was as much as I asked of them.

I also saw them as a way to grow and improve as a writer. They were on-the-job training, and this is not something I only realized after the fact. I saw it that way at the time. I was serving an apprenticeship, although I was not apprenticed to any particular master.

I think it's probably useful to remember how very young I was. In the spring of 1962, when Loretta and Amy and I moved from New York back to Buffalo, I was not yet twenty-four years old.

I remember—vividly—a thought I had a little later, on June 24, 1963. That was the day I turned twenty-five, and I recall looking at myself in the bathroom mirror and saying (perhaps out loud, perhaps in silence), "Well, I guess the boy wonder bit is over."

And that's really what it was. Like Samuel Johnson's observation of a woman's preaching, which he so memorably likened to a dog's walking on its hind legs, one really shouldn't ask if it were done well or not; the wonder was that it was done at all.

"Can you believe it? It's Larry Block, Lenore and Artie's son, and he's writing books and they're being published and he's actually making a living that way. Isn't that remarkable?"

Remarkable.

*   *   *

BACK IN BUFFALO, it was rather more remarkable than it had been in New York, where I'd had a batch of writers as friends and acquaintances. Other friends were doing other things in the arts, painting or playing music or singing, and if they were not yet successful they were on a path that could be expected to lead to success.

But I'd moved away from all that, and while the hours I put in at my desk, tapping away at my typewriter, were the part of my quotidian life that most defined me, the people with whom I spent time in Buffalo inhabited a vastly different universe.

We made some friends. Before we left New York, a visit to Buffalo and an evening spent with Ron and Doris Benice sparked an interest in coin collecting. Ron had been a friend and classmate of mine at Bennett High, and Doris had been a friend and classmate and sorority sister of Loretta's, and while I don't recall that we were to see that much of them socially, that one evening made an impact.

When I got back to our apartment on Central Park West, I took to going to the bank and coming home with rolls of coins, which I searched for dates and mint marks that matched spaces I hadn't yet filled in my Whitman Coin Folders. I embraced this hobby as I embraced so many pastimes, becoming quite obsessed with it. I subscribed to two newspapers, *Coin World* and *Numismatic News*, and by the time we moved back to Buffalo and into the house on Ebling Avenue, I was an ardent numismatist.

I'd collected stamps as a boy, and indeed while a high school student had purchased some from Ron Benice, who had briefly set himself up as a teenage stamp dealer. But now he was collecting coins, and so indeed was I.

When I was much younger, perhaps ten or twelve years old, my father had given me a handful of old coins he'd accumulated over the years—a few Indian Head pennies, a Barber dime, coins that had predated his own birth in 1908. One, I remember, was a Liberty Seated Dime issued in 1891, the last year coins of that design were produced. My specimen was good enough to grade somewhere between Extremely Fine and Almost Uncirculated, and while it was only worth a couple of dollars, having it led me to specialize in that particular series of coins. I collected other US coins as well, but Liberty Seated Dimes became my particular area of interest. I bought a Library of Coins album in which to house them, and I set about buying such examples as I encountered and could afford.

I didn't know anybody in New York who collected coins. But in Buffalo I found out about a coin club that met once a week, and I began going to it and found some fellows whose company was enjoyable enough.

Coins were not my only pastime. Not long after we settled in at 48 Ebling Avenue, I went to a pet shop and came home with an aquarium. I'd kept tropical fish in my parents' house on Starin Avenue, and it wasn't long before I had several tanks set up, with interesting and attractive fish in them. I was as passionate an aquarist as I was a numismatist, learning everything I could about the subject. Was there a magazine to which I subscribed? I don't recall that there was, but I remember a large and abundantly illustrated book, *Exotic Aquarium Fishes*, by a gentleman named William T. Innes; I read every word of it so many times I must have very nearly committed it to memory.

I'm pretty sure it was the fish that led to my friendship with Richie Brownstein. But it may have been the coins. I know he was an enthusiastic aquarist, and it seems to me he had a passing interest in coins as well. (Neither of these interests began to approach the scope and intensity of his interest in birds. More than anything else, he was always a passionate ornithologist.)

I don't suppose it matters what supplied the initial spark of the friendship. Richie was, by any imaginable standard, a character. I largely lost touch with him when we moved in mid-1964 from Buffalo to Racine,

Wisconsin, and fifteen years later someone shot him dead in his mother's living room, and I've never written about him. I think it's time I did.

Richie was two years older than I, the son of a prominent and successful Buffalo attorney. He'd graduated from Bennett, and he'd been destined to go through the University of Buffalo and UB Law School, but somehow that didn't happen. I believe he did earn a bachelor's degree and somehow didn't get anywhere in law school, but I'm not sure just when it was that his education stopped, and there's no one to ask. When I knew him, the presumption was that he'd eventually return to law school long enough to get through it.

Did he do any work during the two years of our friendship? I don't believe he did. I think his father cut him a check every month, and supplied whatever was needed. Richie was married—to Marilyn Applebaum, who had been one year behind me at Bennett. They had two girls, Robin and Dina, and lived in a rented house a ten-minute drive from us.

Richie was a hustler. He was a good bridge player, a better-than-good gin rummy player, and it would have suited him to spend much of his life downtown at the Montefiore Club, say, playing cards for hours on end and making sure he won more often than he lost.

A lifelong friend of mine, Jerry Carp, once told me a story about Richie, who had somehow managed to inveigle Jerry into a pushup contest, with a cash bet as to who could do the most pushups. Richie was short and slight, and not at all athletic, and while he may have had a kind of wiry muscularity, it certainly didn't show. As I recall, he'd had a bout of rheumatic fever in childhood, and as a result had never participated in sports. Jerry was a natural athlete, a star tennis player at Bennett, and an obvious clear favorite in any athletic competition with Richie.

I don't know how Richie managed to set Jerry up, but I can imagine. And he'd have known it was a set-up, because he'd have done enough pushups in private to be confident of his ability to win the day. The only thing he failed to do was keep Jerry from realizing after the fact that he'd been suckered; in an ideal con game, the mark never does know the score.

From then on, Jerry never liked or respected Richie. But I'm not sure that's something Richie would have cared about.

He hustled me once, but in a very small way. One night he and I were at loose ends, and he came over to my house and suggested we play gun rummy. I grew up knowing the game, although I can't say I cared for it much, and I let him coax me into playing, and that we make it interesting by playing for money. The stakes we set were very small, and we played, and at one point I noticed that Richie had been jotting something down on a pad, and I asked him what it was.

"Oh, it's nothing," he said, clearly embarrassed, and he tore off the top sheet and crumpled it up and stuffed it in his pocket. "Just notes to myself," he said. "Nothing important."

And we went on, but the thing was I'd managed to read the note he'd written to himself. *Win slow,* it said.

One might call that an interesting tell. The dollar or two he took from me that night—we didn't play for long, or raise the stakes—was a small price to pay to learn who the fellow was.

Now I might have taken it personally, or simply been judgmental, and let go of my friendship (if that's what it was) with Richie. But I enjoyed his company, and while I wouldn't want to play cards with him again, or trust the little weasel any farther than I could throw him, I kind of liked him.

One time the two of us took a trip, driving east on the Thruway to a coin show in Cobleskill, New York. We went first to Saratoga Springs, where a horse named Su Mac Lad, a trotter, was running in some presumably important race. (And I just Googled Su Mac Lad, and I'll be damned if I didn't remember the animal's name, and even spell it correctly. It is just astonishing what sticks in one mind, especially in view of all that doesn't.)

Richie bet a few dollars on Su Mac Lad, but the horse was the favorite, and Richie had dragged us there not for the opportunity to win a couple of bucks but because he wanted to watch this great horse compete. We did, and he won. Then we went on to Cobleskill, in Schoharie County, where I suppose I bought some coins, though I can't remember any of that.

I may have introduced Richie to Les Zeller, my closest numismatic friend then and for many years thereafter. Les lived nearby in Troy—well, in Watervliet, actually—and when he was about 35 he began an affair with an eleven-year-old girl. The two conducted a monogamous relationship that lasted seven years, and I never had a judgment on that, either.

But back to Richie. I don't remember a great deal about that weekend, except that one night he and I both participated in a poker game held in another numismatist's motel room. And all I remember about that is that the room was too smoky for me to stay in the game. At the time I smoked upwards of two packs a day of unfiltered cigarettes—Camels, generally, but sometimes Luckies, and occasionally English Ovals. And even so I couldn't stay in that room.

Another odd thing to remember.

But the most memorable incident of the trip came early on, when we were racing east on the Thruway. We'd taken Richie's car, and he was driving. "Steer for me," he said abruptly, and took his hands off the steering wheel and began removing his jacket, which he'd evidently found uncomfortably warm. He got the jacket off, he turned around and placed it in the backseat, all without letting up on the gas pedal. He seemed unutterably confident in my ability to reach over and take hold of the wheel and keep us from running off the road or into someone.

And indeed within not too many seconds he was facing forward and once again gripping the steering wheel. We stayed on the road. We didn't hit anybody, nor did anybody hit us.

Jesus.

There were a couple of other times when the business of driving didn't have one hundred percent of his attention. At least once he caught sight of a bird and was interested enough to respond by picking up the pair of binoculars he kept at hand and driving with one hand while he used the other to hold the binoculars to his eyes. He kept the car going forward at high speed even as he gave all of his attention to the creature flying off somewhere ahead of us. "A yellow-bellied sapsucker," he then said with satisfaction (or whatever fucking species it may have been). Binoculars down, both hands on wheel, and on we went.

Jesus.

THROUGH RICHIE I MET another fellow, his next door neighbor, Earl Dworkin. Earl and his wife Ellie also had two daughters, Joy and Leslie; they later would have a son, John. Earl was a sales rep, selling books to college bookstores, while he put himself through graduate school in clinical psychology at the University of Buffalo.

And the story of how he got into the field strikes me as worth telling. He'd gone to college—Cornell, I think it was—and had been keeping company with Ellie, and the relationship was getting more serious than he wanted, so he decided to extricate himself from it while getting his military obligation out of the way.

So Earl went down and enlisted, and Ellie discovered she was pregnant, and the next thing he knew he was (a) married and (b) in the service for the next two years.

That's probably a good enough story by itself, but it got better. Right after basic training, the base psychiatrist wherever Earl was stationed spotted him as a bright and personable and perceptive young fellow, and recruited him for special duty as his assistant. Earl's duty would consist of screening every GI who showed up for a psychiatric consultation. Almost every case, the doctor told him, would fall into one of three categories: "I miss my mom," "I want to kill my sergeant," and "I can't stand guys looking at me in the shower." There were certain appropriate responses in each category, and Earl could furnish them; if this didn't do the trick, he could pass them on to the shrink.

Earl learned the responses, and practiced with his boss, and soon sat down at the desk they'd given him and waited for his first client. Guy walked in, sat down, looked around furtively, frowned, and was clearly unhappy. Earl asked him to state the nature of his problem, and waited to find out whether it was Mom or Sarge or the guys in the shower that would turn out to be the cause of his misery.

Guy motioned him in close, dropped his voice. "Part of my head is missing," he said.

Bingo! His very first consultation, and there he was sitting across the desk from a man in the grip of a full-blown psychotic delusion.

"I'll be right back," Earl told him, and he went and got hold of the shrink, and the poor bastard with part of his head missing was out of there on a Section Eight—and Earl was hooked. From that point on, most of the servicemen on the other side of his desk were basic Mom / Sarge / Shower cases, and he found he was pretty good at sorting them out and dispensing emotional Band-Aids and aspirin; moreover, he realized he'd discovered his métier, and knew what he wanted to do with his life.

He did work his way through graduate school, did support his family while picking up his doctorate, and wound up in private practice as a child psychologist in Schenectady, New York. Somewhere along the way he became a nationally ranked squash player.

It was while he was pursuing his

16

September 21, 2020
New York City

AND HERE I am again.

After what I'm comfortable calling an extended absence. Six months ago, almost to the day, I left Newberry abruptly. I'd planned an Amtrak return to New York around the end of the month, but Covid-19 considerations led me to fly home on March 20.

New York was not yet under official lockdown, but you could see it coming. As a writer, and an essentially antisocial one in the bargain, I figured I was better off than most when it came to social distancing. I'd been socially distanced in the apartment in Newberry, and I could easily lead pretty much the same life in New York, settling in at my desk and—unable to duck out for lunch with a friend, or drop in at a bookshop, or catch an AA meeting—I'd get tons of work done.

Right.

I did in fact continue working on this book, at least for a few days. I believe "Chapter Fourteen" was written in New York, and perhaps part of the chapter before it as well. But I can't be certain, and what does it matter? It was still March when I wrote "It was while he was pursuing his" and stopped right there.

Intending to finish the sentence, and say more about my friend Earl, when I returned to my desk the following morning.

Now someone—it may have been Hemingway—advised ending a day's work in the middle of a sentence, so that one would be able to pick it up knowing how to continue. Since I never opened the file from that day to this, I don't know that it would have made any difference if I'd finished the sentence, or stopped at the end of the one preceding it.

Now, six months later, I don't know what Earl was pursuing, and I don't care any more than you do. He wound up as a clinical psychologist in Schenectady, New York, and we stayed in loose contact over the years.

He's an interesting fellow, and his friendship certainly brightened my stay in Buffalo, but I'm not sure why I found myself writing about him and Richie Brownstein. Garrulity, I suspect, has a lot to do with it; the aging mind travels backward in time and feels the urge to report on everything it encounters back there. And I suppose certain incidents are interesting enough in and of themselves to justify the detour.

At this point I don't see how I can go on without telling you that, while I lost touch with Richie when I moved on to Racine, Wisconsin, in mid-1964, his life went on.

At least until it didn't.

He was never quite able to get through law school, and finally found a way to become an attorney without a law degree. At the time it was still possible for a law clerk to take the state bar exam and qualify in that fashion; it didn't happen often, but Richie served as a clerk in his father's office, studied diligently (or not) for the exam, took it and passed it, and after a certain amount of time working for his father, set up his own practice with a partner.

He became a criminal lawyer, and—as sometimes happens—went on to become a criminal in the bargain. A drug dealer, specifically, and he made money at it, as one can, and he ran risks and cut corners, because that's the sort of fellow he was. And he evidently reached a point where he owed money he couldn't pay, and one day in 1979 he was in his mother's living room, alone in the house except for whoever it may have been who shot him in the forehead.

Richie, we hardly knew ye . . .

If the cops knew who did it, they were never able to make a case. It remains unsolved.

17

I'M NOT SURE what I wrote in our first year in Tonawanda. More of the same, as I recall. There were short stories, and four of them sold to *Alfred Hitchcock's Mystery Magazine,* a market I'd been previously unable to crack. There were a few books by Dr. Benjamin Morse, for Heckelmann at Monarch and for Larry T. Shaw at Lancer. And every month there was the usual Andrew Shaw title for Bill Hamling's Nightstand Books.

It's hard to recall just what I wrote when, and as far as the Nightstand titles are concerned, there's not that much that remains in memory. The books for Midwood and Nightstand constituted a wonderful apprenticeship; I can't think of a better way for me to have learned how to write fiction.

But I suspect I may have stayed too long at the fair. My monthly novel was a monthly chore, and taught me less and less as I put less and less of myself into it. And sometimes I was barely aware of what I was writing even as I was writing it.

A case in point: My daughter Jill was born in 1963 on Memorial Day. We didn't have any medical insurance at the time, and the enormity of that lapse was somewhat offset by the fact that medical costs were a fraction of what they are now, and a very small fraction at that. As I recall, the obstetrician's fee and the hospital bill together came to a little less than $2500.

Still, it was more than I had on hand. I called Henry and asked if there was a way I could earn some money quickly. "I'm pretty sure Bill would take an extra book from you this month," he said.

I'd built myself a serviceable office in the pine-paneled basement of the house on Ebling, but found I was more comfortable with a place to write outside the house. I'd rented one a quarter of a mile away, at the corner of Brighton and Eggert, and the day after I spoke with Henry I went there first thing in the morning and typed furiously for eight hours. I did the same thing the following day. The third day was more of the same, except that I quit work three hours earlier, at 2:00 pm.

Because I'd completed the book.

I've no idea what that particular book was called, or what it was about—and I can't even blame this lack on an old man's memory. I had forgotten virtually everything about the book within a day or two after I'd finished it. I forgot some of it *while* I was writing it, and the one thing that slowed my typing was the occasional need to flip through the stack of finished papers to find out what name I'd given to a character.

Never mind. The book did what it was supposed to. Hamling's editor didn't find anything to object to, and the $1200 Nightstand paid for it—$1080 after commission—helped me clear my medical debt.

A good thing, too. We'd already grown quite fond of Jill, and the last thing I wanted was for them to send some fucking Repo Man to take her away from us.

A WRITER CAN do his work anywhere. All I needed, really, was a chair and a table and a typewriter and paper. (And, back in the day, carbon paper. When I got to the end of the page, I took it from the platen, put the sheet of bond paper on one pile and the carbon copy on another, and sandwiched the sheet of carbon paper between two new pieces of paper and returned the result to the typewriter. Yes, it was a lot to go through. And yes, nostalgia requires a willful suspension of memory.)

My basement nook on Ebling Avenue and my second-floor office at Brighton and Eggert were both at least as comfortable as any room I'd had at my disposal in Manhattan. And I was in fact quite capable of writing there, and did get a considerable amount of work done.

But, if the move back to Buffalo didn't reduce my productivity, it did undercut my growth as a writer. The closest writer of my acquaintance was four hundred miles away, and while I exchanged no end of letters with Don Westlake and Hal Dresner, it wasn't the same as devoting idle afternoons and evenings to a mix of banter and shoptalk. Richie Brownstein and Earl Dworkin were interesting company, as were some of the fellows I met in numismatic circles, but they weren't writers—and, in fact, I was the only writer any of them knew.

When I finished a book or story, I mailed it to Henry; previously I'd go to his office and hand it to him, and have a long or short conversation, very likely about writing or publishing. And back then I'd see him every Tuesday evening at the weekly low-stakes poker game, where half or more of the players would be writers.

I did get to New York periodically, for a few days at a time. And we did have a visit from Don and Nedra Westlake and another from Hal and Marcia Dresner—and, when Hal's marriage had failed and Don's was on shaky legs, a visit from the two of them at the start of a buddy trip of theirs to Mexico. (While they were staying with us, one of them put a load of clothes in our washing machine, and his blue jeans dyed the other's shirts an unfortunate blue. I think it was Hal's jeans and Don's shirts, but I can't be sure—and it's pretty much the same story either way, isn't it?)

The point is that I was very much out of the loop, and that the interaction with other writers had been important to me, and by moving back to Buffalo I had deprived myself of it.

*   *   *

THE WORLD OF soft-core erotica was itself an inspiration for fiction. Hal, before he ditched that world entirely and the East Coast along with it for a screenwriting career in Hollywood, wrote a comic novel called *The Man Who Wrote Dirty Books*. Henry sold it to Simon and Schuster, and Hal tells of the time his editor, Peter Schwed, took him down the hall to meet the firm's surviving partner, M. Lincoln Schuster, who was essentially retired but retained an office.

"Max," Schwed said, "I'd like you to meet Hal Dresner. He's written a marvelous first novel and we're excited to be publishing it."

Schuster looked off into the middle distance. "Writers," he said. "They keep writing books. They never learn!"

A few years down the line, Don would address the same topic in *Adios, Scheherazade*, published in 1970.

For my part, not long after we settled in at the house on Ebling, I wrote my own novel about a couple of fellows turning out paperback erotica. I hung a cryptic title on it—*No Deposit No Return*—and sent it off to Henry. He didn't like it at all, and wrote a note to Don expressing his concern, and wondering how to tell me how utterly it missed the mark. I guess he found a way, because I put the book aside and never sent it anywhere.

And now, more than fifty years later, I remember next to nothing about the book, and am unable to put my hands on it. There was a time in the early 1970s when I donated a box of manuscripts to the University of Oregon, and I included the unpublished manuscript of *No Deposit No Return*—or at least I think I did. I've asked the good people in Eugene to look for it, and they've been unable to turn it up, or any evidence that I ever sent it to them.

That's a pity, because I'd welcome a look at it. I suspect Henry was quite right and the book is embarrassingly unpublishable, but I wouldn't mind seeing how it looks from the perspective of half a century. I'm pretty sure I'd wince at the glimpse it would give me of the callow lad who wrote it, but all these years later perhaps I could cut him some slack.

And I have to say I don't believe it would embarrass me enough to keep me from publishing it.

But never mind. *NDNR* is, alas, gone forever, and its disappearance is surely no great loss either to literature or to me. Still, things do turn up, don't they? If you, Dear Reader, should ever stumble upon a manuscript thus entitled, or any evidence of the existence of such a manuscript, I trust you'll let me know.

[*NB: In 1976, thirteen or fourteen years after I wrote and shelved my novel, Walt Disney Productions released a family comedy starring David Niven, Darren McGavin, Don Knotts, and Herschel Bernardi; the title was* No Deposit No Return. *I've never seen it, and indeed was entirely unaware of it until a few minutes ago when I Googled the title. The film very obviously has nothing in common with what I wrote beyond the title—and that it too, according to the critics, was Not Very Good. I mention it now to forestall any thoughtful reader who might otherwise send me the script thereof.*]

I DID WRITE a crime novel during the first of those years in Buffalo.

The idea was Don Westlake's. He told it to me one night at his house in Canarsie, probably in 1960. A couple on their honeymoon witness a gang killing at the resort where they're about to consummate their marriage; the hoodlums beat up the groom and rape the bride and go back where they came from. Whereupon the newlyweds do *not* report the crime to the police but seek revenge on their own.

He had a title, he said. He'd call it *Deadly Honeymoon.*

I said it was a terrific idea, and he said he couldn't wait to get to work on it, and time passed. He and Nedra and their sons relocated to Englishtown, New Jersey. Loretta and I and Amy moved to Tonawanda. And at one point I found myself thinking about *Deadly Honeymoon.*

I mean, really thinking about it.

And eventually I picked up the phone. "That idea you had," I said. "*Deadly Honeymoon.* Did you ever do anything with it?"

He hadn't.

"Are you planning to? Because I can't get it out of my head, and if you're not planning to write it—"

"It's yours," he said.

I WROTE IT. I sent it off to Henry. I guess he liked it well enough, and I believe he sent it to Knox Burger at Gold Medal, and that Knox sent it back. And Henry may have sent it somewhere else, or maybe not, but before long he sent it back to me.

Right after he'd sent me a letter informing me that the Scott Meredith Literary Agency no longer wanted to represent me.

18

I STILL DON'T know exactly what brought this about.

I'm not sure of the date but it would have been in the summer or fall of 1963. I think I'd turned down some assignment Henry had given me, and I may have displayed a soupçon of attitude, but if so I can't remember anything about it. Out of the blue, and quite to my astonishment, I got a note from Henry explaining that they had counted on me to take what was offered, or words to that effect, and that they were dropping me as a client.

Period.

Henry and I have had a long subsequent history, and are friends today, and when I look back on it, it strikes me as surpassingly odd that I've never asked him what all of that was about. I believe at the time he announced the decision as Scott's, and I suppose ultimately it would have to have been, but I'm fairly sure Scott did nothing more than rubber-stamp Henry's decision; he almost certainly heard about it after the fact.

As to what prompted it, I've been told in recent years that Henry had some sort of emotional meltdown around that time. I couldn't guess what personal issues he may have brought to the table, but I do know that the ethical miasma that was the Meredith agency weighed heavily upon him.

(You may recall Henry's plan to write a novel on the subject; he chose *We Lie Like Hell* as its title. The pervasive dishonesty that clung to the place never did sit well with him. on the one hand, he disapproved of it and recoiled from it; on the other, he proved to be disconcertingly good at it. He was born, it might be instructive to mention, under the sign of Gemini.)

I've heard that Henry began behaving oddly around the time he dropped me. He neglected to return signed contracts, let inquiries of all manner go unanswered, and in a variety of ways was remiss in taking care of business. While it was a couple of writer friends who told me as much, their ultimate source was Scott himself, hardly an impartial observer and an accomplished liar in his own right.

According to Scott, he returned from a vacation to find that Henry had screwed things up royally, leaving him with no recourse but to fire him.

According to Henry, he left of his own accord because he just couldn't bear working there anymore.

I don't know which of the two comes closer to the truth, nor do I much care. However their little drama played out, it did so some months after I ceased to be a client of the agency.

I was 24 years old, with a wife and two kids and a mortgage and, suddenly, no source of income.

I don't know why the hell I wasn't terrified.

NOR DO I KNOW why I didn't make an effort to do something about it. I could have caught the next train to New York and tried to work things out face to face. At the very least, I could have picked up the phone and called Henry and asked him what I could do to make things right. I could have eaten a little dirt, if that was required. But I didn't even write a letter with the aim of ameliorating the situation.

I just flat accepted it:

"You're fired."

"Oh. Well, okay, I guess."

Was it pride? That's an obvious explanation, but I don't really think that was it. It seems more likely that I saw this new state of affairs as a new reality, and took it for granted that there was nothing I could do to change things.

All I could do was accept it.

And, you know, it was damn well unacceptable. It's not that I was stranded without an agent some four hundred miles away from the publishing industry's seat of government. I was also instantly and permanently exiled from the market from which I drew the greater portion of my income.

Bill Hamling's operation—Nightstand Books, Midnight Readers, Greenleaf Publications, whatever—was a closed shop. Scott supplied Hamling with a certain number of titles every month, and Hamling didn't accept outside submissions. (Scott, I was to learn later, had a very good thing here. He took a 10% commission from each writer's earnings, which was standard; he also pocketed a finder's or expediter's fee from Hamling which more or less doubled his earnings from the enterprise. The writers, of course, knew only about the 10% commission. It should be noted, however, that Scott figured the forces of censorship would descend sooner or later, and wanted to make sure he wasn't standing in front of the fan when the shit hit it. He accordingly set up a blind corporation to handle transactions with Blake Pharmaceutical, the blind corporation that Hamling set up. All this so I could learn to write novels by producing books for the sort of reader who turned the pages with one hand.)

For a couple of years I'd been writing a book a month for Hamling, and now that market was closed to me. Other publishers, while they might not be closed shops, would be tricky for me to deal with. Monarch, for instance—while I didn't particularly want to continues Benjamin Morse's career with Charles Heckelmann, I couldn't see that I had the option. Heckelmann didn't know who Lawrence Block was, and thought Ben Morse was the pen name of a Chicago doctor, one Morton A. Benjamin.

It all looked pretty bleak.

In fact, looking back at it all these years later, I wonder what kept me from putting my typewriter on a shelf and looking for a job. As far as I can remember, I never once considered so doing, and I wonder why.

One explanation lies in the fact that, aside from writing fee reports at SMLA and working in the mailroom at Pines Publications, I had nothing at all to put on a résumé. But there must have been something I could have done. I was living in the city I'd grown up in, and my parents' social circle included any number of people who could have given me a job, or told me where to look for one. My two great-aunts, Sal and Nettie Nathan, had spent decades holding important positions at Trico Corporation, purveyor of windshield wipers to the world. Sal was head of payroll, Nettie assistant to the president. I suspect they could have found something for me, or pointed me in a useful direction.

I could have found some sort of entrée to the world of real estate, or insurance, or investments. I didn't have a college degree, but that needn't have mattered, and as far as that goes I could have picked up a BA at the University of Buffalo without too much difficulty. Hell, I could have hung on for a couple of additional years and added a law degree to my collection.

None of this occurred to me, any more than it had occurred to me to talk my way back into Henry's good graces, and it all has me shaking my head in wonder. My work as a fictioneer demanded more than anything else a supple and versatile imagination. And yet, when I examine my own life, I appear to have had no imagination to speak of.

I was a writer. I had written my way into this mess. I would have to write my way out of it.

FIRST, THOUGH, I HAD one pretty clear-cut problem. At the time when Henry's *Dear John* letter landed in my mailbox, I was well into that month's manuscript for Bill Hamling. I didn't know any other publisher for whom it might prove suitable, and I hated to waste all the work that had gone into it.

So I wrote a letter to Bill Hamling. I'd never met the man, and had no real sense of who he might be, but I knew he was the man at Nightstand who could say yea or nay, and at least he'd know who I was. I'd been writing books for him since I knocked out *Campus Tramp* in the summer of 1959, and his list of Andrew Shaw titles included not only all the books I'd written for him, but also all the books Bill Coons had ghosted on my behalf.

I told him that, as he'd probably heard, Scott Meredith was no longer my agent, and thus I was unable to continue writing books for him. But, I explained, I'd had a work in progress at the time the agency terminated our relationship, and I wondered if I could at least finish that book and send it to him.

Days later, I got a phone call from Hamling. "What shit is this?" he demanded. (This, I've been given to understand, was a phrase that came frequently to his lips.) He went on to say that I was a favorite writer, that I'd been with him from the beginning, and that he certainly wanted me to go on writing for him. He'd call Scott and make sure this all worked out.

Either that night or the next night I got a call from Scott himself.

I have a physical memory of taking the call in the bedroom of the Ebling house. It was the first time I'd ever spoken to Scott on the phone, and only the third or fourth time I'd ever talked with him at all. He said he'd spoken with Bill Hamling, and that Hamling wanted to publish my work in progress, but that of course I knew their arrangement was such that Hamling could only accept manuscripts submitted by Scott.

"But we'll make an exception here," he said. "If you complete the book, we're willing for you to send it to us, and we'll submit it to Nightstand, and forward their payment to you."

I said I'd appreciate that.

"But I have a better idea," Scott continued. "Why don't you come back as a client? We'll let bygones be bygones, and you can continue writing and we'll continue to represent you."

"No," I said. "I don't want to do that."

I must have been out of my fucking mind.

19

REALLY. WHAT THE hell was I thinking?

I realize there's a human tendency to regard as irreversible actions which are actually nothing of the sort. As a case in point, I'm reminded of a late friend of mine named John McCarthy, a positively mesmerizing storyteller who bore a strong physical resemblance to Ulysses S. Grant. John, whom I knew from AA, was once invited to audition for the job of hosting a radio talk show, an unlikely direction for a man whose work was building maintenance. The audition went poorly and the radio people wound up going with somebody else; a pity, as John would have been a natural.

At a meeting one evening he shared that he'd lost it at work that morning and had thrown a fit, culminating in his announcing that he quit, that they could take this job and shove it. He'd stormed out, and that was that.

The following evening he reported that he'd had second thoughts, and that he'd accordingly gone to work at the usual hour that morning. The conversation at the job site went something like this:

"What are you doing here?"

"I work here."

"But you quit."

"I know, but that was yesterday. I've changed my mind."

"But . . . Can you do that?"

"I don't see why not. Could you pass me that wrench?"

John developed liver cancer some years ago, and died the hard death that illness gives you. I'm sorry he's gone but glad I knew him for a time, and grateful for what he taught me—that I could change my mind.

It would have been a useful lesson to have learned earlier.

WHILE I MAY not have known I could change my mind, you'd think at the very least I'd have wanted to. But it wasn't until very recently that I ever thought of the decision as a bad one, let alone one I might have undone. For whatever reason—probably youth or pride or stupidity, three elements that tend to march in lockstep—I'd taken what I thought was the only proper course, and I really didn't look back.

It's not uncommon, a while after an apparent reversal of fortune, to proclaim the occurrence "the best thing that could have happened to me." If I hadn't lost that job, I'd never made millions selling widgets to midgets. If that partner hadn't jilted me, I wouldn't have met the love of my life. If that birth control device hadn't failed, I'd miss the joy of grandfatherhood.

And so on.

All of this is of a piece with the notion that everything that happens is always for the best, in Voltaire's best of all possible worlds. Because I myself am very happy with the life I lead now, it's not difficult for me to regard all of the past as the indispensable prelude to the present. If today is a consummation devoutly to be wished, how can I regret anything that helped bring it into being?

Now we can embrace that as a great spiritual truth, or dismiss it out of hand as a load of happy horseshit. Alternatively, we can label it axiomatic, and not subject to judgment.

Like, you know, whatever.

In this particular instance, Henry's curious decision to drop me from the SMLA roster, and my own even more curious decision to stay dropped, stand almost sixty years later as something for which I am profoundly grateful.

NECESSITY, THE PROVERBIAL mother of invention, plays that role as well in reinvention. My writing career, which had brought me surprising success at an early age, had suddenly run out of road. I was the head and sole supporter of a family of four, and if I was going to keep all our heads above water, I had to find some way to generate income. And, since I was evidently unable to see any other career in my future, that meant I would have to find something new to write and someone new to publish it.

The first thing I did, of course, was finish up that month's book for Nightstand. I sent it to Henry who sent it to Hamling, and in due course I got paid. That was good, but it was a dead end. There would be no more books by Andrew Shaw.

Nor would there be more books by Benjamin Morse, MD. I'd become increasingly uncomfortable wearing the good doctor's white coat, but I'd have donned it again if I could have figured out how to carry it off without an agent.

Enter John Warren Wells.

JOHN WARREN WELLS got his first gig via a phone conversation with Larry T. Shaw, then editor at Lancer Books. I'd met Larry once or twice back in 1957, when I was just starting working for Scott. At the time he was married to Lee Hoffman, and my friend Dave Van Ronk spent many evenings in their company and quite a few nights sleeping on their living-room couch.

Lee was a science fiction fan, and that's how she and Larry got together; he edited a couple of science fiction magazines before he wound up at Lancer. She was also a folk music enthusiast, and adapted the SF-ish concept of a fanzine to folk music, editing and publishing a 'zine called

Caravan. (I wrote songs or song parodies now and then, and Lee found a home in *Caravan* for a couple of them. As I've mentioned earlier, *The Bosses' Songbook* had its beginnings one evening when Dave and Lee and I waxed creative.)

By the time I called Larry Shaw, he and Lee had gone their separate ways, and Larry left the editorship of a science fiction magazine and went to work for Irwin Stein at Lancer Books. And, when he'd settled in at Lancer, Henry had sold him three Benjamin Morse titles, *The Sexual Deviate,* *A Modern Marriage Manual,* and *The Sexual Behavior of the American College Girl.* (I'd be hard put to argue that the permanent retirement of Dr. Morse was any great loss to the world.)

When I called Larry, I confided that I'd been the writer who worked with Dr. Morse, and wondered if there was something I might write for Lancer. We did some brainstorming, and I'm not sure which of us came up with the idea for a book on comparative sex techniques. I suspect it was his idea, although I know the title was mine: *Eros and Capricorn: a cross-cultural survey of sex techniques.* The title, as far as I could make out, didn't mean anything at all, but I have to say I liked the sound of it.

I pointed out that the book would emerge more from the library than from Morse's voluminous case files, and that perhaps I could write it myself and leave the doctor out of it. Larry thought about it and agreed it was simpler that way. Did I have a name I'd want to use on it?

"John Warren Wells," I said.

He thought the name, like the title, had a nice ring to it. And did I suppose Dr. Morse might be inclined to furnish an introduction?

I said I figured I could talk him into it.

SO I WROTE *Eros and Capricorn* and I got paid for it—probably $1500. That's what I'd received for the Morse books, and this time around I didn't have to pay an agent's commission. And I must have received something—$100? $200?—for Morse's introduction.

More important, although I didn't know it at the time, was that I'd launched another aspect of self on what would prove to be an extensive career. By the time he elected to hang it up in 1974, John Warren Wells had published 19 books, along with a monthly column in *Swank Magazine*.

While the first JWW title, *Eros and Capricorn*, was essentially a product of library research, the rest of the books were structured more like the Morse titles, with each chapter consisting of a case history. The *Swank* column started out under the title "Group Grope" but soon morphed into "Letters to John Warren Wells."

I made up the case histories, and wrote the letters myself.

Well, mostly. Over time, JWW's work began to evolve into legitimacy. Take the *Swank* column, for instance. The first several entries consisted almost entirely of letters I composed myself, and I would contend that's the case with the initial installments of all letters-to-the-editor columns. How could anyone be expected to contribute to a column before having been given a chance to know it existed?

Of course, now and then the books would draw a letter from a reader, and when I got one that felt like a good fit I'd include it in the *Swank* column. And, once the column began to reach readers, my correspondence increased. I never stopped writing fictional letters, but an ever-increasing portion of the column's contents was comprised of actual letters I received.

(Of course, that didn't mean that all of my correspondents adhered strictly to the truth. While I occasionally sensed that a letter was largely exhibitionism and invention, that didn't necessarily disqualify it from appearing in print. If I could make up letters out of the whole cloth, why shouldn't my readers have the same right?)

I did respond to letters, and occasionally met in person with readers who'd written to me. And, gradually, case histories based on these people enriched and enlivened future books.

I'll skip ahead, if I may, to JWW's greatest triumph. This would have been toward the end of the 1960s, by which time I was living in New Brunswick, New Jersey, and represented once again by Henry Morrison, by that time in business on his own.

Henry had an office on East 38th Street, and one afternoon I walked into it. "I have a million-dollar idea," I announced, "and all I'm going to tell you is the title and the subtitle. *Tricks of the Trade: A Hooker's Handbook of Sexual Technique.*"

Henry thought for a moment, and not a terribly long moment at that. Then he picked up the phone and called Nina Finkelstein at New American Library. Within ten minutes I had a deal, and a $7500 advance.

Now by this time John Warren Wells had followed *Eros and Capricorn* with three more books for Lancer, and another, *The Wife-Swap Report*, for Dell. I'd received $1500 advances from Lancer, but Henry got me $3000 from Dell—and for a little while the book had proved almost impossible to write.

It took me a while to figure it out. Dell had contracted to pay me twice as much for *The Wife-Swap Report* as I regularly received from Lancer, and that meant they'd be expecting a book that was twice as good as the books I'd been writing for Lancer, and how on earth was I going to manage that? It's not as though I'd been holding back. John Warren Wells was doing his very best for Lancer, so how could he be expected to produce something twice as good for Dell?

Well, as soon as I became aware of the nature of my problem, it ceased to exist. Dell didn't want me to write something twice as good as what I was giving Lancer. They wanted me to write essentially what I was already writing, but to write it for them.

And, once I'd achieved that *Duh* moment, I wrote the book, to the evident satisfaction of all concerned.

So I was prepared for *Tricks of the Trade*, and while I was delighted by the high price I was to get for it, I knew that I could credit it to the great commercial potential of the idea I'd come up with, and not worry that Nina and NAL expected me to up my game.

Still, in order to deliver the best possible book, didn't it stand to reason that I ought to do more than settle in at my desk and conjure ten or a dozen prostitutes out of my imagination? Shouldn't the book be at least to some extent what it would purport to be, the transcription of actual interviews with actual sex workers?

I should say (or perhaps shouldn't say) that this was an area in which I was not entirely without hands-on experience. While I'd never called it research or deducted it as a business expense, I'd acquired a certain familiarity with the profession and its practitioners. But I hadn't lugged along a tape recorder, or asked a lot of personal questions.

A friend from Antioch, Peter Hochstein, was at the time a an advertising copywriter at Ogilvy & Mather, and when I talked about *Tricks of the Trade* he told me I ought to consult his friend and colleague, Dick Watson, then well established at Benton & Bowles. Dick, I was told, had learned to walk the straight and narrow path between monogamy and adultery, and did so by availing himself of the services of call girls. No messy relationships, no chance of either party inconveniently falling in love with the other, and a bottom-line figure almost certainly lower than even the most modest wining and dining.

"Watson keeps a file," Peter told me. "He rates them by a batch of variables, of which *attitude* is the most important. If you really want a hooker with the gift of gab, and with a decent attitude in the bargain, he can probably point one out to you."

And so it wasn't long before I borrowed an eight-track tape recorder from another writer friend and schlepped it over to the Murray Hill apartment where Elizabeth lived. (I remember her last name, but you really don't need to know it.) I explained the premise of the book, managed to get the tape recorder running, and talked with her for an hour or so. I don't remember what fee we'd arranged, but whatever it was I paid it, and lugged the tape recorder back home.

And wrote the chapter. It seems to me I then dug another two or three chapters out of my imagination so that Henry could run them all by Nina Finkelstein and get her to greenlight my writing the rest of the book. She thought they were fine, but he did tell me that she felt one of the sample chapters was just not as good as the others. It wasn't as interesting, and you didn't get as vivid or convincing a sense of the woman at its core.

You can guess which chapter she had in mind.

A lesson there. Truth may or may not be stranger than fiction, but, by God, it's less entertaining, and nowhere near as realistic.

BUT I'VE GOTTEN ahead of myself. Let's return where we were, to a brick ranch house in a northern suburb of Buffalo. My association with Henry had shifted abruptly into the past, and it would be a couple of years before we came again into one another's lives.

Looking for a way to pay the mortgage and put food on the table, I'd created a new self in the persona of John Warren Wells. And, right around the same time, I added another self to the family.

Jill Emerson.

20

861 Brighton Road
Tonawanda, New York 14151
4 April 1964

Mr. John J. Plunkett, Editor
Midwood Books
505 Eighth Avenue
New York 18, New York

Dear Mr. Plunkett:

I am enclosing herewith a novel, SHADOWS AND
TWILIGHT, for your consideration. I hope you enjoy it,
and look forward to hearing from you.

My best wishes,
Sincerely,
Jill Emerson

TOWER PUBLICATIONS, INC.
505 EIGHTH AVENUE
NEW YORK 18, N.Y.
Bryant 9-6070

April 8, 1964
Miss Jill Emerson
861 Brighton Road
Tonawanda, N.Y. 14151

Dear Miss Emerson:

We are enclosing contracts for your original
manuscript entitled SHADOWS AND TWILIGHT which
we are happy to accept for publication. We would
appreciate the prompt return of all three signed
copies so that we can initiate payment and schedule
this novel for future production. Please note that the
advance payment has been divided due to the necessity
for a limited amount of re-write.

Before we go into the areas for re-write, may I
personally congratulate you for having written a
particularly fine novel on this sensitive theme. I read it
myself and enjoyed it immensely. I have no doubt that
this novel will rank with those Midwood-Tower Books
written by such established authors as Valerie Taylor,
Laura Duchamp, etc.

We would appreciate a small summary of your
background, both personal and professional, for our
files since we sometimes do brief biographies of our
better authors on back covers. I am also curious as to
how you happened to submit this manuscript to us,
and in particular, to me by name . . .

. . . Once again, may I say that we are most happy
to add your name to our growing list of talented
contributors. We hope that SHADOWS AND TWILIGHT
is but the first of many such novels we shall publish.

Very truly yours,
John J. Plunkett,
Editor-in-Chief

AND SO, IN APRIL of 1964, Jill Emerson was loosed upon the world.

It must have been sometime in March when I began writing the book
I submitted to John Plunkett. It couldn't have taken very long to write.
It's a short book, the published version runs to just over 45,000 words,
and I doubt it took me more than two weeks start to finish. All I recall
of the writing of it is that I was eager to write the book, eager to see how
it went.

I don't know that I saw it as a new beginning, but there's no getting
around the fact that I was going back to my roots. The first novel I wrote,
which I had in fact called *Shadows* until Crest changed it to *Strange Are
the Ways of Love*, was a sensitive novel of the lesbian experience. Now, half
a dozen years and dozens of books later, I was once again getting in touch
with my inner lesbian.

Well, why not? While I had precious little hands-on experience as a lesbian, I had plenty of experience writing lesbian fiction. It made perfect sense for me to write such a book, and to submit it to Midwood; I had, after all, been one of their original writers. (The first numbered title on their list was #7—*Love Nest*, by Robert Silverberg writing as Loren Beauchamp. Two Sheldon Lord titles, *Carla* and *A Strange Kind of Love*, were #8 and #9.)

I hadn't written anything for Harry Shorten's company in a few years, but not because we'd had any sort of a falling-out. Hamling was paying significantly more, and a monthly book for him was as much erotica as I'd wanted to turn out. Now, though, there was no reason not to pick up the phone and call Harry, or write him a letter. His was not a closed shop, and my break with Scott wouldn't make him disinclined to resume publishing Sheldon Lord.

But here's what I did instead: I wrote an entire book on speculation, and mailed it to a complete stranger, one whose name I'd never encountered until I read it in *Writer's Market*. And I'd fabricated a brand-new name for the enterprise, so that I was attempting an over-the-transom submission of a first novel by an entirely unestablished writer.

I'll say this for Jill Emerson. She did not lack for nerve.

BUT WHY?

Didn't I know better? I'd been making a living as a writer for what, six years? And before that I'd spent most of a year working for an agent. I knew what happened to over-the-transom submissions. Nobody ever sold anything that way. If you were lucky after a couple of months someone actually looked at what you'd submitted and sent it back to you.

Well, look at the dates on those letters, will you? On April 4, I put *Shadows and Twilight* in the mail. Once I'd done so, I lost no time in adding Jill's name to my office mailbox, and I didn't have long to wait. Four days later, essentially by return mail, John Plunkett got back to me with a detailed letter of acceptance and, *mirabile dictu*, a contract.

Just like that.

I WAS, AS you might imagine, overjoyed. I'd succeeded against all odds, and the odds had been considerable. To keep things in proportion, let's acknowledge that Midwood-Tower Publications wasn't up there with Alfred Knopf and Random House. It was a second-tier paperback publisher seeking always to offer reading material hot enough to satisfy their customers' prurient interest while sufficiently circumspect to keep its purveyors out of jail.

Even so, it felt like a triumph, and all these years it still strikes me as remarkable.

And it seemed to prove something. I'd made the sale without an agent, or indeed without anyone to open a door for me. The manuscript I'd submitted had no one to run interference for it; it could only speak for itself.

I can't pretend it was an act of monumental courage to submit the book the way I did, because what was I risking? If someone at 505 Eighth Avenue sent it back, all I'd be out was postage.

And the reward justified the risk, because that acceptance letter bolstered my sense of my own worth beyond measure.

It was over twenty years later, in 1987, when Joyce Carol Oates published a novel under the name Rosamond Smith. She was not just using a pen name; she kept the whole affair a secret from her longtime agent and enlisted another agent, a personal friend, to submit the manuscript. Her hope was that readers could come to the work with none of the preconceptions that would attend a novel with her own name on it, but in fact by the time the book was to be published the cat was out of the bag.

Still, she'd shown herself that she could do it. Her book could speak for itself.

Even as I had done back in 1964.

I KEPT ALL of Jill's Midwood-Tower correspondence—with John J. Plunkett and, later, with Sanford Levine. Miraculously, it survived.

I'm tempted to include the entire file—something like twenty of them, the last dated 21 May 1965. But that strikes me as over the top in self-indulgence, even for this book. Surely a sampling of excerpts will suffice.

JE to JJP, 10 April 64:

. . . SHADOWS AND TWILIGHT is my first novel, although I've done some poetry and short stories, all of which aroused a monumental groundswell of editorial apathy. I'm 26 years old. Born in John O'Hara country—Bethel, Pa. Moved here with family about twenty years ago. Two years at the University of Illinois, two more at Northwestern. Moved to New York and made the Village scene for longer than I care to remember, alternating some unimpressive clerical jobs with some happy periods of unemployment. I moved back home about eight months ago, bound and determined to bat my head against the wall until I produced a salable book. The result of that was S & T. An unexciting life I suppose, but it's had its moments.

How did I happen to submit the book to you? Because of the Midwood Books I've read, I guess. And as for my writing to you by name, I'm afraid the explanation is prosaic in the extreme. Just looked up Midwood in Writer's Market . . .

JE to JJP, 14 April 64:

I've managed to come up with about thirty pages of revisions for SHADOWS AND TWILIGHT. I've tried to work toward the two ends you mentioned—cutting out dull wordage and sharpening the erotic material. I'm not sure whether or not I've succeeded, but hope you'll be happy with what I've done . . .

JJP to JE, 16 April 64:

Dear Jill,

Please forgive the informality but I can't help feeling as though I have the right. This occurs every time I discover a new writer of promise . . . paternal instinct, I suppose. Well, twenty-six is young.

We received the revised manuscript pages and you seem to have done a fine job . . .

After years of putting out trash, prior to my joining the firm, we are now attracting the top writers in this field and plan to continue doing so. You have added your name to those of Valerie Taylor and Laura Duchamp, two acknowledged top sellers, who now

write exclusively and regularly for us. I haven't any
doubts but that, with one or to more novels, you'll
rank with them . . . I want you to continue submitting
to us at regular intervals so that we can promote JILL
EMERSON into a familiar and highly successful name.

21

October 19, 2020
New York City

IT'S REMARKABLE, AND more than a little dismaying, how long it's taking me to wrap this up. Four weeks ago I picked up what I hesitate to call a work-in-progress, and wrote the preceding eight thousand words in fits and starts. That's only a little more than what I wrote in a day back in 1994, when the beginnings of this book gushed out of me in Lake Forest. Still, I was getting the work done, and then a week or two ago I wasn't. I'd worked every day for a week, and then I took a day off, and by the time I looked up, I discovered I'd Van Winkeled my way to the present moment.

I wonder why.

Some of it can be blamed on circumstance. The Covid-19 pandemic rages on, in what's either a second or third wave, depending who's counting. There's a critical national election two weeks away, with its outcome and the future of American democracy by no means certain. I've been spending almost every hour of almost every day in my apartment, and while it's a stretch to compare my life to that of a prisoner in solitary confinement, the metaphor does come readily to mind.

Why, under these conditions, would I rush to my desk each morning? Why would I struggle to recall and record essentially trivial thoughts and actions from 1964?

Along with circumstance, there's age. There will always be people eager to tell you that age is just a number, but the number of the young man in Tonawanda was 25, and the number of the old man in Greenwich Village is 82, and, as I've taken to remarking, if you insist on telling me age is just a number, well, *Go fuck yourself* is just a suggestion.

I'm very much aware of age these days. The virus which rages around us all is particularly effective at thinning the ranks of the elderly. I've lost close friends to it, and can only expect to lose more. My age, in and of itself, makes me vulnerable, and the coronary bypass surgery I had a couple of years ago certainly constitutes a co-morbidity. If I get the virus, I'll very likely die of it; if I don't get it, it's only a question of time before I die of something else.

Of course that last is true of everybody. We're all of us mortal, and it's always a question of time before mortality has its way with us. But that thought, and the words it's couched in, resonate very differently for a man of 25 and a man of 82.

And age does other things besides bringing one within sight of a finish line. It diminishes energy, clouds focus, and blurs memory. I suspect that's generally true, and I know it's specifically the case for me.

I'm an old man writing about a young man, and about that young man's world. Who knows what I remember of either the man or the world? For years I prided myself in a memory that I could trust, but I can no longer trust the memory I have, and I'm not sure but that my earlier trust may have been misplaced. In addition to a good memory, I also had a fiction writer's imagination—and I can't say with absolute assurance that there were no gaps in that memory, gaps plugged by my imagination without my being aware of it.

That's a little abstract, and I can't see that contemplating it can lead to anything more rewarding than a headache.

But what's a memory, and what's merely the recognition of a memory?

The earliest childhood memory I have would have been when I was two or three years old. At the time I lived with my parents in the lower flat of a two-family house at 2155 Delaware Avenue, in Buffalo. A family named Gugino lived above us, and the son, a year older than I, was named Charles. And my first memory is of our visiting the Guginos, and being outside on their upstairs porch, and playing with Charlie.

Except that I don't remember it. I remember *that* I remember it, that I once cited it as my earliest memory. I'm not sure I can even say that I recall remembering it. I know that I did once remember it, or did at least identify it as a memory, or—

Never mind.

IT WASN'T LONG after Charlie Gugino and I did or did not play together on his upstairs porch that my parents and I moved from 2155 Delaware to 673 Parkside Avenue, where we lived until shortly before my sister, Betsy, was born in May of 1943. By then my father had bought a house at 422 Starin Avenue.

I remember all those house numbers. I can't think why they should linger in the mind the way they do. I remember telephone numbers I haven't dialed in over sixty years. I remember the year of the defeat of the Spanish Armada because my father once observed that it was the same as my grandmother's phone number, PArkside 1588. Our phone number on Starin was PArkside 0527. My friend Dick Lederman lived at 82 North Drive, and his phone number was PArkside 0396. Jerry Carp's was VIctoria 8296.

I'm still friends with both Dick and Jerry, though I have no idea what their current phone numbers might be. I'm still in touch with Larry Levy, who lived at 66 Dana Road. Larry's phone number started with RI for Riverside, but I forget the four digits that followed. Of course there's a chance they'll come to me.

Memory.

Sooner or later, I suppose, those addresses and phone numbers will follow Charlie Gugino's porch into the void. While it's a small satisfaction to know that I no longer have to worry about early-onset dementia, what mind I've got left could slip away—and very likely will, unless I beat it to the punch by dying first. And if I do in fact outlive my mind, I won't know it at first. And then I will. And then I won't . . .

You know what? I'm not going to think about that. Long ago some journalist was kind enough to point out that every marriage ends in either divorce or death, and I'm not going to think about that, either.

You might want to do the same. And, while you're at it, it might profit you to spend the next ten minutes not thinking of a white rhinoceros.

22

SO.

Jill Emerson.

I'd thought to write more about Jill, and could easily have done so at length. She and I have had a good run together, with her complete works running to eight novels. What began with two sensitive lesbian romances for John Plunkett at Midwood (*Warm and Willing* and *Enough of Sorrow*) continued with three erotic paperback originals for Berkley (*Thirty*, *Threesome*, and *A Madwoman's Diary*), a Berkley hardcover novel that was equal parts of Grace Metalious and John O'Hara (*The Trouble With Eden*), and a mainstream novel (*A Week as Andrea Benstock*) published by Arbor House in hardcover and serialized in *Redbook*.

Andrea Benstock was published in 1975, eleven years after *Warm and Willing*, and for years those seven books constituted Jill's complete works. Then in 2011 what had started as a series of short stories with an unnamed homicidal heroine grew into an episodic novel. I called it *Getting Off* and gave it the subtitle *A Novel of Sex and Violence*. Hard Case Crime published it with an open pen name: "Lawrence Block writing as Jill Emerson."

It's hard to defend from a commercial standpoint. Jill's name on *Getting Off* couldn't have gained me any sales, and very likely cost me a few. It led some readers to figure it was an old book in sheep's clothing, while others figured it bore a pen name because I didn't think highly of it. But adding it to Jill's opus was something I somehow knew I wanted to do, and I guess I felt quite strongly about it, and nine years later it's impossible for me to tell you why.

When I had a look recently at my correspondence with John Plunkett, a batch of letters I'd cherished enough to hang on to for so many years, I couldn't avoid seeing an unflattering aspect of myself. Those over-the-transom sales to Midwood delighted me not only because they validated my talent and showed I could stay afloat without Scott or Henry's hands on the helm. That was a comfort, certainly, but what added a bit of dark delight to the mix was the feeling that I was getting over, that I was making a fool of an editor who thought he was discovering me and helping me develop as a writer.

Seeing it in that light, after so many years, has served to drain the joy from the whole business. I don't think any less of the books, or of the important steps involved in writing and publishing them. But I do think a bit less of myself.

THERE ARE, AS I mentioned, nine Jill Emerson titles, and I've only mentioned eight. The ninth brings things full circle; it's my very first novel, *Shadows*, which originally appeared as *Strange Are the Ways of Love* by "Lesley Evans." In 2010 I allowed Open Road to reissue it as an ebook with my name replacing Lesley's, and eight years later I brought it out myself, as an ebook and paperback, as *Shadows* by Lawrence Block as Jill Emerson. Which seems only right.

I thought I might write about each of Jill's titles, but I've already done so; *Afterthoughts*, which collects some four dozen essays about various backlist titles, covers her career in as much detail as anyone could want. The book's out of print as I write these lines, but should be available again in both printed and electronic form by the time you read them.

I should add, though, that I did write that second book for Midwood. I called it *Enough of Sorrow*, the title drawn from a short poem by Mary

Carolyn Davies. Remarkably, Plunkett kept my title, and filled the back cover with lavish praise— "Seldom has any writer so dramatically ripped away the veils of mystery that obscure the emotional and physical aspects of lesbianism. Seldom has any writer so completely reflected an understanding and appreciation of the kind of relationship that exists between women. Seldom has so difficult and elusive a subject been handled with such startling candor and poignant sensitivity."—and going on to proclaim it the winner of the 1965 Midwood Award for Literary Excellence.

Wow.

My very first award, and it came at a time when I had every reason to assume it would be my last. I only learned of the award when I saw a copy of the book, and although there's an impressive-looking gold seal on the front cover to go with the high praise on the back, I'm not sure it's accurate to designate it an award. There was no statuette to put on the shelf, no medallion to brandish, and certainly no cash prize. Indeed, it was an award which was never to be given again, however many equally worthy titles Midwood may have gone onto publish.

So I suspect it might better be described as a blurb.

Still, you take what you can get. You can say it's spinach, and you can say the hell with it, but I say my book won the 1965 Midwood Award for Literary Excellence, and yours didn't.

So there.

YOU WOULD THINK, wouldn't you, that I'd have found the blurb and the packaging and the award encouraging. You would expect one book after another to follow in the wake of *Enough of Sorrow*. You would foresee Jill Emerson's emergence as a major name in lesbian fiction, fulfilling John Plunkett's dream by standing alongside Valerie Taylor and Laura Duchamp in that particular pantheon.

Well, go know. That was the last book I was ever to write for Midwood, the last contact I would ever have with John J. Plunkett.

I can't explain this, to you or to myself. I don't believe I ever considered writing a third book, and it's not until now, recalling those days, that it ever occurred to me to that my failure to do so was in any way remarkable.

If I can't explain it, I can at least put it into context. I was in Tonawanda, living on Ebling Avenue and working in my office on Brighton Road, when I wrote and sold *Warm and Willing*. But by the time I wrote *Enough of Sorrow*, I was many miles away in Racine, Wisconsin, living in the eastern half of a two-family house at 4051 Marquette Drive, and leading another life altogether.

23

WHEN I GOT that letter of dismissal from Henry Morrison, it effectively dropped me in the deep end of the pool. To keep from drowning, I'd had to learn to swim.

I don't know that I took to it like a fish to water, but I'll hang on to the metaphor long enough to point out that I'd spawned two new selves in the personae of Jill Emerson and John Warren Wells. I reached out as well to Bernie Williams at Beacon Books, for whom I'd written a handful of books as Sheldon Lord; I wound up having lunch with him on a visit to New York, and sold him a crime novel with a card cheat background. (Beacon published it as *The Sex Shuffle;* many years later Hard Case Crime reissued the book as *Lucky at Cards.*)

Around the same time, a new publisher in Buffalo got in touch with me and wanted me to write a Nightstand-type book for him. If I ever knew who steered him in my direction, I've long since forgotten—nor do I remember the name of the fellow I dealt with, or if I ever knew it in the first place.

We settled on a price of $500. I wrote one, and I put a title on it, which I don't begin to recall, and a pen name, which I do. See, I looked down at the box of typing paper I'd used, and I chose the name Howard Bond.

(You know what I think I did? I think I plagiarized myself. If I re-member correctly—and that's a very tentative hypothesis—one of the fellow writers of the narrator of that lost novel of mine, *No Deposit No*

Return, used as a pen name the brand of paper on which he'd typed the book. It may in fact have been Howard Bond.)

Because neither of us had any reason to trust the other, we met downtown and I gave him the manuscript and he gave me the money.

I went home. A few days later I got a phone call from him. He thought the book I gave him was too short. Was I sure it was long enough?

I suspect it was in fact shorter than what I'd been in the habit of delivering to Hamling, but I certainly wasn't inclined to do anything about it. Just as Abraham Lincoln's legs were long enough to reach from his body to the ground, so was my manuscript long enough to reach from the first page to the last.

So I assured him it was the right length, and he may or may not have been convinced, but that was the last I ever heard from him. I never gave the book another thought, and when I recalled the incident years later I assumed the book had never been published.

When Terry Zobeck was working away at my bibliography, *A Trawl Among the Shelves*, I kept recalling books and stories and articles of mine that had slipped my mind, and reporting what I could recall; Terry, apparently indefatigable, would scour the internet until he came up with a copy of the new discovery, add it to his collection, and write it up for the bibliography.

Until finally Howard Bond's effort came to mind, and I wrote about it in the afterword I'd agreed to supply for *ATATS*. I rather doubted it had ever seen print, and even if it had, how could he possibly turn it up? I couldn't say what I'd called it, or what imprint the publisher might have devised for his venture. All I remembered was my pen name.

And that was evidently enough. Item A66 in *A Trawl Among the Shelves* reads like so: [*Sex Takes a Holiday*, 1964. Connoisseur Publications (FN 112); Cleveland, OH; ($0.75); 159 pp.; no statement of printing. As Howard Bond. (PBO; novel)]

Terry has a copy, and so do I. I've flipped through it, and while nothing I've read rings any kind of a bell, I can recognize it as my work. Will ego and avarice render me shameless enough to reissue the thing in my Collection of Classic Erotica?

Maybe.

THE SCRAMBLE TO make a living and the search for fresh markets for my work led me in a variety of new directions. Numismatics had been playing an increasing role in my life, and the diversion it provided during our last months in Manhattan had grown considerably in Buffalo, where I had no writers for company but a good number of coin collectors. It's not uncommon for collectors to transform their hobby into a business, and I leaned a little in that direction, going to far as to take a bourse table at a local coin show and do a bit of buying and selling.

That didn't really lead anywhere. But what I also thought to do was write an article that hitched crime writing and numismatics, and it changed my life.

I'd read, not for the first time, Raymond Chandler's *The High Window,* a key element of which is the history of a notable early American coin, the Brasher Doubloon. The novel is of course a classic of hardboiled crime fiction, and I thought I might write about it for a numismatic audience. I did so, and called what I wrote "Raymond Chandler and the Brasher Doubloon," and sent it off to the *Whitman Numismatic Journal,* in Racine.

I knew the Whitman name, as the company produced the coin folders and albums I'd been endeavoring to fill. I didn't know the firm was a division of Western Printing and Lithographing, and all I knew about Racine was that it was somewhere in Wisconsin. As for the magazine, I knew that it was new, and I may or may not have seen a copy at the time;

the first issue came out in January, 1964, and it couldn't have been very long after that when I wrote and mailed in my effort.

Ken Bressett was the magazine's editor, and I got his letter of acceptance by return mail. I can't recall what I was paid for it, but it couldn't have been more than twenty-five or thirty dollars. I know he wrote that my piece was exactly the sort of thing he wanted for the *Journal*, and that he hoped I'd write more.

That was encouraging, and I was grateful for the encouragement. I followed Chandler with Maria Theresa, the Austrian empress whose likeness graced a silver thaler for generations; the dollar-sized coin was recognized and accepted throughout the Middle East, and thus neither the woman's likeness nor the 1780 date was ever changed. My set of the Encyclopedia Britannica supplied me with enough historical information about the good woman to fill an article aimed at a numismatic audience, and I wrote it up and sent it off, and Ken was happy to have it.

Well, what the hell. My own greatest collecting interest was a set of Liberty Seated Dimes. The series was a long one, coined at various US mints from 1837 to 1891, and for some reason I found it fascinating to seek out an example in choice condition of each date and mint. I wrote about it in some detail, and sent it off not to Whitman but to *Numismatic Scrapbook*, where it was promptly accepted.

The first of these pieces to see print was the Raymond Chandler article in the *Whitman Numismatic Journal*. They published it in July, and by then I was getting up every morning at six, putting on a tie and a jacket, and sitting down two hours later at my desk in Racine.

AND HOW DID that happen? Well, sometime that spring, after I'd sold those two articles to the *Whitman Numismatic Journal*, Ken Bressett called to tell me a business trip was going to put him in Buffalo the following evening. Could he take me to dinner? We met at a downtown restaurant and spent a couple of hours, and by the end of the meal he'd suggested there might be a place for me at Whitman. Some weeks later Loretta and I visited Racine, visited the company's offices, met a variety of people, and got a look at the town.

I was offered a job as an assistant or associate editor. The company would pay for our relocation to Racine, and my annual starting salary would be $6000.

Now that's not very much money now, but it wasn't much money then, either. A figure that sticks in my mind is my gross writing income for 1962; as I recall, the total amount I received from Scott Meredith, after commission, came to $32,000. Now that was in fact a lot of money at the time, and substantially more than our lifestyle required. We didn't live high, and even after the break with Scott Meredith cut my income to the bone, I was finding ways to support myself and my family.

So why would such a small salary lure me off to Wisconsin? We'd have to sell our house, we'd have to pack up and move, and we'd wind up with considerably less money to live on.

If things worked out, of course, that salary would grow over time. If I proved to be suited to corporate life, I could have a career in Racine, working for the next forty years or so for a rather paternalistic company that rewarded loyalty. There was, I must say, some appeal in that, notwithstanding the fact that it was a life for which I'd never longed, and one in fact I'd never even considered.

Nor did I have any reason to believe I would like it, or even tolerate it. I'd never structured my life around an alarm clock and a calendar. I was in the habit of staying up as long as I wanted and sleeping as late as I wanted, and deciding for myself what I would do with each day as it came along. I put on a necktie once or twice a month when an occasion demanded it, but otherwise I lived in jeans and khakis and shirts with the collars unbuttoned. I'd had facial hair in one form or another over the years, and while I had shaved my most recent beard a year or so before that dinner with Ken, I tended to go a few days between shaves.

When I visited the coin supply division's offices in Racine, every man I saw was wearing a white shirt and a tie. They'd all worn jackets to the office that morning, and many were still wearing them.

Was that the life I wanted? It certainly wasn't one I had sought, and what made me think it was even one I could tolerate?

AS A MATTER of fact, I think my expectations were pretty modest. I figured there would be things I'd enjoy about living in Racine and working at Whitman, and others I wouldn't like. But there was one thing I knew the move would do.

It would get us out of Buffalo.

Our life on Ebling Avenue was not unpleasant. But it was certainly not what we'd had in mind when we got married and moved to New York. We'd returned to Buffalo because of an obligation I had seemed to feel when I wasn't around for my father's death.

My mother was not unhappy to have us around, but neither did she require our presence; for all that my father's death had been a blow, she had adjusted to her new reality, had created a career for herself as a librarian, and had a new man in her life. It was essential to her that she not make her new status as a grandmother the focal point of her life—and, if we wanted a baby sitter, we picked up the phone and called a teenager.

I don't think I'd have had a problem telling her that we'd decided to move back to New York, that social and professional reasons made such a move compelling. If I were to write her dialogue, I imagine it would be something like this: "Well, I'll miss you. But I could never understand why you moved back here in the first place."

Loretta's mother was a different story. She didn't have much of a life, and what she did have centered on her grandchildren.

Which is not to say that I minded miring the poor woman in disappointment. I just had to make to look as though I had a good reason. If all I wanted was to be a writer, well, I could stay in Buffalo, couldn't I? But if I wanted to take advantage of this great career opportunity, then I had to move north and west.

And later, after a couple of years in Wisconsin, we could all move back to New York where we belonged, and I wouldn't look like the bad guy.

AND SO WE listed the house, and somebody bought it. And in July I went out to Racine and stayed at a motel while I settled into the job, and Loretta followed a few weeks later, once the movers had packed up our stuff.

Here's something I'd forgotten: My first day on the job, I confounded everybody by requesting a typewriter. I'd taken it for granted that there'd be one on my desk, for use in correspondence and for the articles I'd be writing for the *Journal*. Ken, and everyone else in the office, had taken it just as completely for granted that I'd do what every other man in the place did, which was dictate whatever had to be written to one of the secretaries.

Ah, sweet culture shock. I got the typewriter.

24

IT WAS SOMETIME in July of 1964 when I started work at Whitman. It must have been February or March of 1966, a little over a year and a half later, when I cleared out my desk and went home.

The move, as I've noted, was in large part a neurotic and unquestionably passive-aggressive way to get out of Buffalo and back to New York. Wherever I was going with my life, Racine was never a destination.

What would you call it? A side trip? A detour?

Something like that. But I've never felt it was a mistake, or regretted the time I spent on that stretch of road.

HERE'S ONE THING that surprised me about my job. I turned out to be good at it.

Oh, I'd expected to be at least equal to the task of writing articles for the *Journal* and editing the work of other contributors. But I found marketing and advertising at least as interesting as editorial, and nobody in the coin supply division was paying them much attention. There was a vacuum there, and nobody was anything but grateful when I moved to fill it. I wrote ads, I planned and carried out direct-mail campaigns, I wrote catalog copy and worked with the corporate art department to create the coin division's sales catalog.

The coin supply division's sales manager was an amiable fellow named Pete; he was good at most aspects of his job, but he hated writing sales letters and was hopeless at it. He got me to draft letters for him, basked in the good response they got, and I'm sure he thought he was exploiting me in the process; I enjoyed the task, and others throughout the company knew why Pete's letters showed so much improvement.

I got to know Werner, the advertising agency executive who serviced our account. I read books on advertising and marketing, and got the company to spring for a subscription to *Advertising Age,* and read each weekly issue all the way through. Not because I felt it was something I was supposed to do, or in the hope that any higher-ups would notice, but because it was genuinely interesting.

I don't want to spend too much time on this. I had a job and I did it, and the job expanded as I found new areas in which to extend myself, and by the end of 1965 it was becoming clear that what had begun as a detour, a diverting side trip, had almost without my awareness transformed itself into A Job With A Future.

My starting salary, as I've noted, was $6000. At the earliest appropriate interval, I'd been given the maximum raise to $7200. That still wasn't much money, but it was a step in the right direction.

And my co-workers liked me. There were a batch of low-key feuds and resentments in the office, but as far as I could tell I was getting along just fine with everybody. I could have that job as long as I wanted it. Western Printing, just a generation removed from the basement print shop established by two brothers, was very much a paternalistic corporation, and not given to a lot of hiring and firing. If you did your job reasonably well and got along with your colleagues, you were set until it was time to retire—and, with your participation in profit-sharing and various benefits, that retirement would be a comfortable one.

The world has changed since then, and the idea of working for a single corporate employer for forty or fifty years seems incomprehensible to anyone entering the work force in the 21st century. Back in 1965, it was eminently possible and made perfect sense.

It was, after all, the American Dream. That phrase has been around a long time, but it has acquired different meanings over the years. Nowadays it seems to suggest not the mere possibility of a comfortable middle-class life but the opportunity—almost the God-given right—to grow rich. I don't know how it happened, but the American Dream would now seem to consist of wealth beyond the dreams of avarice.

And, of course, for most people it's quite unattainable.

Sixty years ago, the American Dream was there for the taking. If you were white and native-born, if you were willing to work forty hours a week and stay out of trouble, you could hold a corporate job, buy a comfortable suburban home, drive a well-engineered American car, raise a family, put your kids through college . . .

And so on.

This had never been my particular dream, but I was not incapable of seeing its appeal. And as the months passed it became clear that it was mine for the dreaming.

I couldn't expect much personal advancement within the coin supply division, as it was essentially a corporate backwater, turning a decent profit but with no real opportunity for growth and expansion. But my own future would lie outside the coin division. It became evident that another division of Whitman, the marketing department, had its corporate eye on me. That department had long been something of an afterthought, but now it was destined for growth, and I'd received hints that I was being groomed to grow along with it.

A Job With A Future. That's not at all what I had expected to find in Racine, but there it was. I didn't even have to reach out and take it. All I had to do was wait for it to come to me.

And that's all it took, really, for me to realize that wasn't what I wanted. Once I could see what was available to me, it was time to go back to New York.

Time to go back to being a writer.

BUT OF COURSE I had never stopped being a writer.

I hadn't even considered stopping. One good thing about my low salary was that I knew from the beginning I would have to supplement it with writing income. Our duplex had three bedrooms on the second floor, and we let Amy and Jill share one and set up the smallest as a home office.

I arrived in Racine with a couple of works in progress. I'd been working on a novel about a couple of confidence men, and had even squeezed in a couple of trips to scout locations in Toronto and Olean. I finished it in Racine, and Knox Burger bought it for Gold Medal, and published it in 1965.

By then I had an agent, although I never met the fellow, and I can't be sure what he did or didn't handle for me. He was Gerald Kelly, a principal in the firm of Kelly, Bramhall & Ford, and he got in touch with me via Bill Coons, that friend of Don Westlake's who'd been my original ghostwriter with Nightstand. When Scott Meredith dropped me from the client list, they dropped Bill as well, and he hooked up with Jerry Kelly, whom he'd either recently met or knew from school. All I know is that Bill called to tell me he had a new agent, and was I looking for an agent? Because if I was, his friend would like to represent me.

Well, no one else in the profession had expressed interest, and I was stuck in Buffalo with no idea how to go about finding an agent. So I agreed to be represented by KBF, but not exclusively; I'd continue to work directly with such markets as Midwood and Beacon and Lancer.

It seems to me I sent Kelly a couple of stories, and he sold at least one of them to *Alfred Hitchcock's Mystery Magazine.* And I'm pretty sure it was he who handled the sale of *The Girl With the Long Green Heart* to Gold Medal.

But I never did meet Jerry Kelly, and we didn't do a lot of business together. Thirty years later I found myself in a small English-language AA meeting in Madrid, and one of the attendees turned out to be Tom Ford, once the partner of Gerald Kelly and Dave Bramhall. That gave us something to talk about, but not for more than a paragraph or two.

And a paragraph or two is as much as my connection with KBF requires here. But if I'm going to digress, I think a more appropriate topic might be ghostwriters in general, and Bill Coons in particular.

BEFORE I FOUND myself in a room at Ragdale, with the original fifty thousand words of *A Writer Prepares* rushing out of me in a verbal flood, I was committed to keeping my beginnings in the world of erotica not merely at arm's length, but out of sight altogether. When a collector turned up at a signing with something by Sheldon Lord or Andrew Shaw, I refused to sign it, or even to confirm or deny its authorship.

More than once, I remarked that the best thing about that early work was that it had not been printed on acid-free paper. "God speed the acid," I would say.

Well, that's changed, obviously. I've devoted no end of words to the subject in this present volume, and I've spent a good amount of time and energy in recent years resuscitating virtually all of my early titles, giving them a second life as ebooks and paperbacks.

But of all the reasons I gave myself for disavowing that early work, one argument still seems to make some sense.

Not all of it was mine.

I've always been grateful for my apprenticeship in the world of erotica. It served me well. But there's a danger in settling too comfortably into an apprenticeship. Sometime in 1961, I felt it was time to stop writing a monthly Andrew Shaw novel for Bill Hamling's operation.

But the deal was a difficult one to walk away from. I talked it over with Don Westlake, and together we hatched an idea. There was this fellow named Bill Coons he'd known for a few years, either in college or in the service; Bill had done some writing in college, and had always wanted to be a writer, but now he was married and living in Syracuse with a kid on the way and a minimum-wage job unloading trucks in a warehouse. It was hardly the life he'd dreamed of, but it seemed to be the one he was stuck with.

There's this story about two wise guys with an interest in a young singer. They persuade an agent to catch the young man's act, and he gives them the bad news—the fellow just doesn't have what it takes. They're disappointed, because they like the kid and they've invested a lot of money in him, paying his rent and springing for singing and dancing lessons and wardrobe and such. So where do they go from here?

Finally an inspiration. "Let's see," one of them says. "What's the kid weigh? Maybe one-fifty-five, one-sixty?"

"So?"

"Well, fuck it. We'll make a middleweight out of him."

Don and I took Bill Coons and made a writer out of him.

I look back on it, and I realize how remarkable it is that it worked. I don't know how much writing Bill had done, and there's no one alive to ask, so it's possible that he had once begun work on a novel, and possibly even completed a draft. But I don't think he'd ever published a word of anything, and here we were bringing him to New York and offering him a job turning out a novel every thirty days.

The two of us sat down with Bill in my apartment in New York. We gave him books of mine to read, and pointed out ways he could mimic my style. And there were certain tells he could incorporate.

The name *Schwerner*, for example. Steve Schwerner, my freshman roommate at Antioch, had once mentioned that his surname was unique to members of his family; there were, he assured me, no other Schwerners in the world.

Well, it struck me that the least I could do was spread the name around, and for a couple of years I made a point of including one character named Schwerner in every book I wrote.

Similarly, Don and I had both taken to using *A Sound of Distant Drums*—or some word play derived from that phrase—whenever the title of a book or play was called for.

Bill accordingly was instructed to have some minor character named Schwerner in the books he ghosted, and to make similar use of those distant drums. I don't know that anyone at Nightstand paid any attention to any of this, but it paid off in unexpected fashion decades later, when aficionados of the genre pored over the books looking for textual evidence of their actual authorship. "This must be Block's," one would write, "because there's a character named Dave Schwerner, and a wino is described as being passed out in 'a mound of wistful bums.'"

Right.

IT DIDN'T TAKE Don long to recruit ghosts of his own. He'd done a book or two for Hamling as Alan Marshall, the name he'd used for Midwood, and Hamling wanted a book a month from him, and Don agreed; almost all of the Alan Marshall books for Nightstand were the work of hands other than Don's. Hal Dresner joined in, enlisting others to supply a monthly Don Holliday novel.

I don't know what arrangements Don and Hal had with their various ghostwriters, but I know that mine with Bill and subsequent ghosts gave me an off-the-top payment of $200, with the remaining $1000 going to the writer. There were, alas, no royalties for either of us. The $1200 was a flat fee, irrespective of copies printed or copies sold.

Financially speaking, it wasn't a bad deal for the ghosts. The $1000 was at least as much as a new writer could get selling books under his own name, and this way the sale was guaranteed. Bill Coons could walk into a sure income of $12,000 a year—well, $10,800 after Scott took his commission. He was learning a trade, and his was a well-paying apprenticeship.

Still, I'm not sure we did him a favor. Like everyone, he hoped his ghostwriting would lead to something better. It did for some; Dave Case, a friend of Bill's who became Hal's most spirited ghost, wound up making a name for himself as a horror writer, and there were others who went on to self-sustaining writing careers.

Bill died in 2001, and I'd lost track of him decades ago and don't know what his last years were like. But I can't imagine they were much fun. I'll pass along two stories about the man, at the risk of speaking ill of the dead; they're good stories, and I suspect I'm the only person around who can tell them.

The first would have taken place fairly early in Bill's ghosting career, when he was living with his wife and daughter in Washington Heights— but not too early, because it was after Nightstand had upped their order to two Andrew Shaw titles a month. I'd let myself be lured back into the game. So we were each writing a monthly book, and you'd think one of Hamling's editors would have to have suspected something, but if so he kept it to himself. Bill and I wrote our books and the checks kept coming.

And one day I gave him a call. "I wrote three chapters of a book," I said, "and I just went dead on it, and I hate it, and I don't want to write any more of it but I hate to let sixty pages go to waste. Why don't you read what I've done, and if you can see a way to go on you can write the next three chapters, and then we'll alternate until we've got a book. And Henry can submit it as our collaboration."

"By Andrew Shaw and Dell Holland?"

Dell Holland was the pen name Bill had chosen for his own non-Shaw work.

"Sure," I said. "And we'll each write half the book and take half the money."

That sounded fine to him, so I got on the A train and took the three chapters uptown. "A sow's ear," I said. "Make some kind of a purse out of it. It doesn't have to be silk."

Then the two of us went out for a beer. Maybe two beers, or even three, and then I got back on the subway and headed home.

And he returned to his apartment. His wife had come home in the interim, and saw the stack of sow's-ear manuscript on the table where Bill had left it, and she was just finishing the last page when he walked in the door.

"This is really good," she told him. "You're really improving, honey. This is far and away the best thing you've ever written."

ONE OF THE best things about the story—and one of the worst things as well—is that Bill chose to tell it on himself. The fellow was not without a sense of irony. And he did in fact write the next three chapters, and we shuttled the manuscript back and forth until it was done, and Henry sent it to Nightstand and in due course it was published. Not by Andrew Shaw & Dell Holland, Nightstand never used dual bylines, but as *Man For Rent*, by John Dexter. (That was a house name, fastened at the editor's whim on odd books and extra books, and this was both.)

Bill did publish at least two titles as Dell Holland, *Sin Town* (Bedside Books) and *Illusion of Lust* (Playtime). But turning out the monthly Andrew Shaw title took up most of his time.

And in fact it was often a struggle for him to meet his deadlines, a frequent source of irritation to Henry. At some point prior to the birth of a second child, Bill and Cammy moved to Patchogue, a good ways out of town in Long Island's Suffolk County. There were presumably fewer distractions out there, but Bill made do with what distractions the place offered, and timely delivery became increasingly problematic.

Eventually one book was close to two weeks late. He finally got it done and hopped into his car to deliver it, drove through the Queens-Midtown Tunnel, and managed to find a parking spot on West 47th Street not a block from the Scott Meredith offices.

Well, didn't that call for a beer? He walked away from the car and ducked around the corner to a hospitable tavern on Sixth Avenue, and he had a beer, and, well, maybe he had a second beer.

Then he headed for his car, and wouldn't you know it? Someone had broken into it, and stole whatever was loose, and that included a shopping bag with the overdue manuscript.

Of course he kept a carbon copy. And of course the copy was in the same shopping bag with the original, and both were gone, never to be seen again.

OR AT LEAST that's the story he told.

Do you figure it's true? For years on end, it never once occurred to me to wonder. Who would be fool enough to make up a story that reflected so poorly upon the teller? *Yeah, I suppose I should have gone straight upstairs and turned the thing over to Henry, but, you know, it was a long dry drive and I'd feel a whole lot better with a beer in me. And yeah, I suppose I should have taken the manuscript with me, but why chance leaving it in some ginmill? And yeah, I guess it was a bonehead move to bring the carbon copy along, since I had no use for it in New York, but it was in the bag with the original, and I guess I wasn't thinking . . .*

When you make yourself the butt of such a buttheaded story, how could it be anything other than the truth?

But maybe he made it up. Maybe he never wrote that month's book, or at least never got to the end of it, and he was way past deadline, so why not tell Henry that the dog ate his homework? The story made him look like an asshole, but he already looked like an asshole, so what difference did it make? And this way nobody could yell at him, because he was the victim here, his hard work stolen and never to be seen again.

And he could drive back to Patchogue and finish however much he'd actually already written, and turn it in as the following month's book. He could even turn it in on time. Hell, he'd be back on schedule.

AFTER I PARTED company with Scott Meredith, Bill's ghosting gig vanished. A few years down the line he got a teaching position at Skidmore College, and I think that's what he was doing when he got arrested for selling a couple of tabs of LSD to an undercover narcotics agent. With the outstanding luck and great talent for self-preservation he'd displayed all his life, the poor son of a bitch wound up in Attica Prison. After the Attica riot in 1971, he squeezed that particular lemon into a lead article for the *New York Times Sunday Magazine*, then expanded the narrative into a book, *Attica Diary*. As far as I can tell, that was the last thing he wrote.

I think it was Don who likened Bill to that character in Al Capp's *Li'l Abner* who went through life with a dark cloud forever suspended above his head. He had rotten luck all his life, and a generally frail constitution in the bargain. Someone speculated that, in spite of it all, Bill was destined to live an exceedingly long life.

"No," Don said, "but it will *seem* exceedingly long."

25

November 25, 2020
New York City

WELL, THAT WAS an extended digression, wasn't it? Bill Coons deserved inclusion here, I think, along with the whole phenomenon of new writers hitching a ride on the pen names of their more seasoned fellows, but it's yanked me away from Racine and sent me down another tributary of Memory Lane.

I think it's time to wrap this up.

The problem, of course, is determining a natural end point for this narrative. I've heard it remarked that God created orgasm so that people would know when to stop fucking, and a proper climax plays much the same role in a book.

But *A Writer Prepares* is meant to be my own imperfect recollection of my own early years in the profession, and who's to say just how long those early years lasted?

In some respects I suppose they're still going on. I'm still learning things, even if what I most often discover is the extent of my own ignorance.

A memory, if you will. I was fourteen years old, and this thought came to me: "Oh to be eleven again, knowing what I know now."

Whatever did I think I knew?

Never mind. The words come back, over and over again, with only the numbers updated. And as long as I'm around I trust I'll offer up a silent apology every year for the fool I was the year before.

> *There was this brilliantly talented albeit unpublished writer, I'd been given to understand, who would write one novel after another, each building up to the brink of a conclusion, and then ending abruptly with a one-sentence chapter: "And then the boiler blew up and killed them all." They could be out in the middle of the desert, a hundred miles from the nearest boiler. It didn't matter. That's what he wrote, at least according to this tale told in publishing circles, and one can very likely infer what might have been the seminal event in his own unhappy life.*

I seem to have told this story more than once. It's to be found in the book description I supplied when I republished an old Andrew Shaw title as an entry in my Collection of Classic Erotica. (One with a real eye-roller of a title: *High School Sex Club*.) A Google search shows that I supplied a slightly different version for an Authors Guild Newsletter interview. I'm not sure who I heard it from—Don Westlake? Larry Janifer? Nor have I ever been entirely convinced that it's other than apocryphal.

Really, though, what difference does it make? Whether or not it ever happened, the lesson is there for all time. Sick of what you're writing? Itching to be done with it?

Take a breath. Skip a space:

"And then the boiler blew up and killed them all."

I'M TEMPTED. BUT there's a better note to end on, to wrap up my stint in Racine and, arguably, mark the end of my apprenticeship. And it started well before we made the move to Tonawanda.

At about the same time, two otherwise unrelated facts came to my notice. The first was tucked almost invisibly into an extended *Time Magazine* feature article on the phenomenon of sleep. I don't remember the points covered, but the material must have been interesting enough to keep me reading. Eventually the author, who'd made the point that scientists differed on the precise function of sleep and how it achieved its ends, allowed almost as an aside that there were a handful of cases of individuals who lived their lives without sleeping at all.

I thought that was pretty interesting. What could a person do with an extra eight hours in every day? All those things you told yourself you wanted to do if only you had the time—well, you'd have that time, wouldn't you? You want to learn Portuguese? Want to play the bassoon? Dude, you've been sleeping away close to 3000 hours a year. That's all the time in the world. Why stop at Portuguese? Why limit yourself to a single woodwind? Before you know it, you could be a one-man band and an interpreter at the UN.

You get the point. My imagination latched on to the notion of a protagonist who'd lost the ability to sleep. Someone in the *Time* article had posited the existence of a sleep center in the brain, possibly hidden away in the hypothalamus, so why couldn't my hero have had his sleep center destroyed? He could have served in Korea, he could have been wounded by a shard of shrapnel, and who was to say it might not have left him in a state of permanent insomnia?

So that was one fact, and where it led.

The other turned up in an encyclopedia, the 1948 edition of the Britannica some enterprising salesmen had palmed off on my parents. Something, very possibly a numismatic matter, had led me to look up the royal House of Stuart. I already knew that James I was the first Stuart on the English throne, and that Anne was the last, and I was dimly aware of the Old Pretender—James III, in the eyes of his supporters—and the Young Pretender, whom we know as Bonnie Prince Charlie. I read how a

British force under the Duke of Cumberland routed the Jacobite army at Culloden in 1745, and put paid to Charlie's efforts for all time.

That was, at the very least, interesting. But what I never expected and found truly remarkable was the fact that the House of Stuart had *not* disappeared, and that there was in fact still a Stuart Pretender to the English throne. He was, you'll be pleased to know, one Albrecht Luitpold Ferdinand Michael, Duke of Bavaria; his eldest son Franz, born in 1933, is his heir and the current Pretender, and if the House of Stuart were to be restored, he and his wife and kids would have Buckingham Palace all to themselves.

Gosh.

Now that issue of *Time* must have had extensive readership, and I couldn't begin to guess how many readers had access to the Britannica. But both factoids—about sleep, about the Stuarts—came to me one upon the heels of the other. And all at once I combined them, and now my Sleepless Knight had something to do with all those extra hours. He could hatch a plot to depose that usurper, Elizabeth Battenberg, and restore the House of Stuart to the British throne.

That would have been in 1962 or 1963, while I was still a Scott Meredith client, because I remember telling Henry my idea. He was encouraging, but I needed more than encouragement. I needed a story, and all I had were a hero and a quest. I thought about it some, and it didn't go anywhere, and I put it aside and forgot about it.

Sometime in 1965, when I was a year or so into my sojourn in Racine, a fellow I knew by reputation turned up at the office. His name was Lincoln W. Higgie III, but my colleagues in the coin division knew him as Bill; in 1962, Whitman had published his book, *The Colonial Coinage of the U.S. Virgin Islands.* He was back in the States after a few years in Istanbul, where he'd risked life and liberty spiriting ancient coins and antiquities out of the country.

We hit it off, Bill and I, and I invited him home for dinner. He showed up at the appointed hour with a bottle of Bushmill's Irish whiskey. Loretta put dinner on the table, and Bill and I wound up in the living room, draining the bottle and talking the night away.

He did most of the talking, because he had far more interesting stories to recount. What he'd spent his time doing had been a violation of Turkish law, and to commit such a violation was to take one's life in one's hands, and Bill had had a few close shaves and talked eloquently about them. Once, he recalled, he'd boarded a plane bound from Istanbul to Zurich, and his carry-on bag held a package of ancient artifacts to which he held no clear title and the export of which was strictly forbidden.

He found himself seated alongside a grandmotherly Englishwoman with a pleasant if distant manner. Some impulse led him to take his package from his carry-on and ask her if she could perhaps tuck it into her purse. She did so, and stowed her purse in the overhead compartment.

The plane closed its doors in preparation for takeoff. But it didn't go anywhere, and after a few minutes the doors opened and some uniformed officers boarded and walked directly to Bill Higgie. They hauled him off the plane, they strip-searched him, they went through his carry-on bag as if sifting a haystack for needles, and at length they returned him to the plane with an apology that by no means struck him as heartfelt.

When they landed in Zurich, Bill's seatmate retrieved her purse and handed over the small package. "I don't know what you have in here," she said, "and believe me, young man, I don't want to know. But what a marvelous adventure!"

I'm sure I enjoyed hearing that story as much as the English lady enjoyed playing a part in it, and there were others equally compelling. But the one that had the most impact was long and rambling, with an inconclusive ending. I'm a little vague on its details, the bottle of Bushmill's was mostly empty by then, but it concerned a group of men, several of them employees of the Arabian-American Oil Company, who'd learned that the Armenian community of what was then Smyrna and has since become Izmir, preparing to flee what would become the 1915 Genocide, gathered together all the gold in their possession and interred the hoard in the concrete porch of a house in Balikesir.

Against all odds, they managed to identify the house in question, and locate it. They went there and broke into the porch, only to find that someone had got there before them. Evidence indicated that the Armenian gold had been there once, but it was there no longer.

Oh well. We finished the whiskey. Bill went home. I went to bed.

I woke up the next morning in time to shower and shave and get to my desk on time. And, wonder of wonders, I had something to keep my hangover company; I remembered the conversation. Most of it, anyway—including the story of the Armenian gold in Balikesir.

And I remembered as well the hero I'd caught a glimpse of a couple of years before, the fellow with a shard of shrapnel in his hypothalamus, the permanently wide-eyed chap with plenty of time to learn languages and scratch out a living writing term papers and theses for college students.

You remember him, don't you? That wide-awake fellow who dreamed of restoring the House of Stuart? I may have already come up with a name for him back in Tonawanda, before I had a tale for him to tell. In any event, I certainly knew his name now. It was Evan Michael Tanner, and I was now able to see him as a devotee of not a single lost cause but a few dozen of them. He'd be a diehard Jacobite, to be sure, but he'd also be a fellow of the Flat Earth Society and an officer in the Latvian Army in Exile—and, by God, a devoted member of the League for the Restoration of Cilician Armenia.

And that's how he'd learn about that house in Balikesir. And, calling for support upon all the nuts and cranks who were his boon companions in various far-flung fringe groups and irredentist movements, he'd find that house and break into the vault where the treasure of Smyrna had spent the past half century. And, unlike those hapless schlubs from Aramco, he'd damn well find it.

AND SO HE did. In the early weeks of 1966, I told that story in some fifty-five thousand words. I sent it off to Henry Morrison, and he sold it to Knox Burger at Gold Medal.

Yes, Henry Morrison. A year or two previously, Henry had left Scott Meredith (of his own volition or not, depending whose version you believe) and set up on his own as a literary agent. Some months earlier, while Henry was still Scott's henchman, Don Westlake had gone through an acrimonious and indeed litigious break with the agency, and to the surprise of all parties, not least of all himself, he became the first client of the new Henry Morrison agency.

Henry reached out to ask if I'd done anything with *Deadly Honeymoon*, which he'd returned to me back when the shit hit the fan. Because, he said, he thought he might be able to sell it. I reclaimed it from Kelly, Bramhall & Ford, who'd been unable to do anything with it; then I sent it to Henry, and indeed some months later he went on to place it with Mary Heathcote at Macmillan, where it would become my first hardcover novel.

And so, when I'd finished my thriller about Evan Michael Tanner, I mailed it off to Henry. He sent it to Knox, and the next thing I knew I had a contract, and the book had a new title: *The Thief Who Couldn't Sleep*. (I'd called it something else, but have no idea what that might have been.)

But even before I'd finished writing the book, I knew I wasn't ready to say goodbye to its narrator. It was my first book about Evan Tanner.

There would be others.

*   *   *

EIGHT IN ALL. Before *The Thief Who Couldn't Sleep* was set in type, and probably before it got past the copy editor's desk, I was busy writing *The Canceled Czech,* and for the next several years the series grew as I managed to keep Tanner busy with two or three adventures a year. The first six books appeared as paperback originals from Gold Medal, the seventh (*Me Tanner, You Jane*) as a Macmillan hardcover.

I'd managed to become the author of a series, and that had been a goal of mine almost from the beginning. As a reader, I'd always particularly enjoyed renewing my acquaintance with a character I'd already found appealing; if Nero Wolfe or Miss Jane Marple or Lew Archer or Ed and Am Hunter had charmed me once, why wouldn't I want to spend another couple of hundred pages in their company?

If this was true for a reader, wouldn't it be that much more the case for a writer? On the creative side, you didn't have to reinvent the wheel every time you sat down in front of a blank page. Your character and his world were already there, waiting for you to come with things for him to do. And, from a commercial standpoint, the readers of one book were a natural core audience for the next. As the series grew, you'd be building a following.

None of this would seem to need saying now, with the publishing industry so committed to the idea of series in genre fiction that the decision to accept or reject a first novel often hinges upon whether the writer plans more books about the character. You'd need a memory almost as long as my own to know that such was not always the case.

Series characters have always been popular with readers—generations of children grew up with an unquenchable thirst for more stories about Nancy Drew and the Bobbsey Twins and the Hardy Boys, along with Tarzan and the Lone Ranger and all those oddballs in the Land of Oz. And one need only recall that Shakespeare wrote *The Merry Wives of Windsor* because Queen Elizabeth wanted to see another play about Falstaff.

At the same time, a book in a series was tacitly regarded as limited, both artistically and commercially. A successful novel, one was given to understand, ought to use up its lead character, leaving him changed at the end of it and hardly a good choice for further installments. To go on writing book after book about an unchanging protagonist was to spend one's life repeating oneself, putting in endless hours on a literary assembly line.

And, while your core readership might stay with you over the course of a series, the whole enterprise had a ceiling as well as a floor. A series, you see, was undeniably genre fiction. A recurring detective made it very clear that what you had written was a mystery, and the publishing industry of the day knew how to define a mystery. It was a book-length work of fiction in which a crime was central to the plot, and one with a maximum sale of six thousand hardcover copies.

There were exceptions, of course. Once in a blue moon a work of crime fiction hit the bestseller lists, in which case it was recognized by all concerned to be something else. It brought off its escape from the ghetto by somehow transcending the genre.

What changed this? I'd point first to Agatha Christie, who wrote two novels to be published after her death. In 1975 *Curtain* constituted the final appearance of Hercule Poirot, and Miss Marple took her own last bow a year later in *Sleeping Murder.*

Both were bestsellers. Both were undeniably mysteries, and in fact entries in longstanding series.

The industry raised a collective eyebrow. And adjusted to a new reality.

FOR MY PART, I'd always wanted to write a series. *Coward's Kiss*, my first private eye novel, had starred one Ed London, who struck me even then as a fairly colorless chap.

The book was my second sale to Gold Medal, and I'm sure it's not coincidental that, like *Grifter's Game*, I wrote it with lower expectations. I'd received an assignment to write a TV tie-in novel based on *Markham*, a weekly series which starred Ray Milland as one Roy Markham. Belmont Books, a third-tier paperback house, had acquired the rights, and I'd get $1000 for a novel in which Mr. Markham would set about solving a case of my own devising.

By the time I was halfway through the book, I decided it might have greater possibilities. I finished it and gave it to Henry, who agreed, and he sent it to Knox, who liked it enough to buy it. He had a couple of editorial suggestions; the one I recall was that I change not only the protagonist's surname but his first name as well; *Roy*, Knox said, had been the name of his sergeant in basic training, and it wasn't a name he wanted to encounter attached to a Gold Medal hero.

So I changed his name to Ed London. And I traded in the less than heroic Renault Dauphine I'd had him driving, a requirement I'd been lumbered with as that French automaker had been one of the show's sponsors.

Knox took the book, and I then had to return to Roy Markham and wrap up the assignment for Belmont. Meanwhile the series got canceled, and Ray Milland went on to other things, but his picture graced the cover of *Markham: The Case of the Pornographic Photos*, which is a notably clunky title and subtitle.

Ed London's title wasn't a whole lot better. I'd called it *Coward's Kiss*, a reference to the quatrain from Oscar Wilde's *Ballad of Reading Gaol* about each man killing the thing he loves: "The coward does it with a kiss / The brave man with a sword." It appeared as *Death Pulls a Doublecross*.

I never liked that title, and Ed London had struck me even then as a fairly colorless chap. Still, he was a private eye, and he'd emerged alive at the end of a published novel, so another book about him seemed the natural next step. But I couldn't get it written. (I did turn out a trio of lackluster novellas about him, all published in 1962–3 in *Man's Magazine* and subsequently appearing as *The Lost Cases of Ed London*; you can find them now in a collection of my earliest crime fiction, *One Night Stands and Lost Weekends*. And you can find both novels available, one as *Coward's Kiss*, the other as *You Could Call It Murder*.)

And there were other occasions when, as I wrapped up a novel, I found myself laying the groundwork for a sequel. I did so in *The Girl with the Long Green Heart*; the two con men, having betrayed one another over the titular Jezebel, follow a knock-down drag-out fistfight with the grudging admission that they had indeed worked well together. Would they resume their partnership in some future caper?

They never did, nor did I spend much time contemplating the possibility. But I'd clearly left the door open, and I've had a few correspondents over the years wondering if there might be more in store for John Hayden and Doug Rance.

That could have made sense, if I'd put my mind to it and found the right sort of story for them. What made less sense was the wrap-up of *Deadly Honeymoon*, which found the bride and groom, having exacted their revenge and at long last consummated their marriage, musing that their successful joint quest might have spoiled them for the white-picket-fence existence they'd been headed for. But what other career might they consider?

Don Westlake saw right away where I was going. "By God," he said, "you've set it up for a sequel. The two of them would constitute the least likely detective partnership since Bertha Cool and Donald Lam."

Well, of course I never gave a moment's real thought to the Deadly

Honeymoon Detective Agency (although it does have a ring to it, doesn't it?) Nor did the green-hearted girl ever develop any other colorful body parts. (I did, half a century later, echo that title with *The Girl With the Deep Blue Eyes*, but the two books had nothing in common but their titles.)

Tanner was different. He changed my life.

BUT NOT DRAMATICALLY. *The Thief Who Couldn't Sleep* didn't get me out of Racine; I'd already left my job and set in motion a return to the New York area before I wrote a single word in Tanner's voice. Nor did he make me rich and famous. Gold Medal took on those first six books and seemed happy enough to publish them, but none went back for a second printing. It was their flat sales that led me to move *Me Tanner, You Jane* to Macmillan, where its hardcover edition got a little more critical attention than its predecessors while reaching fewer readers. (It wasn't reprinted in paperback. In those days, hardcover publishers sold reprint rights to paperback houses. Or, as in the case of *MTYJ*, didn't.)

So how did Tanner change my life?

I think I can credit him with marking the end of my apprenticeship. While I'd made my career choice in Miss Jepson's eleventh-grade English class, and while I'd been quick to mail poems and stories to otherwise blameless magazines and tape their rejection slips to my wall, I became an apprentice writer the moment I walked off the job at Mildred's Chowderhouse and set about writing a daily short story upstairs of that barbershop in Hyannis.

That phase ended when I began writing about Tanner. Because his first appearance was a novel only I could have written, from the point of view of a character no one else could have created, an imaginary chap who told his story in a voice that was uniquely mine.

I don't want to overstate this. I'm reluctant to denigrate the body of work that preceded *Thief* as derivative and meretricious; some of my ten-day wonders for Bill Hamling were both those things to one degree or another, but a number of those early books and stories did a good enough job of being what they'd set out to be.

There are in fact readers today who would contend that some of my earliest crime novels—*Grifter's Game* and *Borderline*, for instance—have a drive and an energy and a verbal economy that make them more satisfying than the more ambitious novels that have followed them. I don't agree, not at all, but I'm able to see their point. And who's to say my judgment of the work is any more valid than anyone else's?

Never mind. The point is that my earlier work, whatever its strengths and weaknesses, was at bottom derivative and generic; it was the work of an imaginative and talented young man determined to make his mark as a writer.

By the time I'd written that first book about Tanner, that mark, let us be clear, was still unmade.

But I had found my voice and was on my way. Writing Tanner was an exhilarating experience, and it spoiled me. I'd written a book I was born to write, and that's how I wanted to spend the rest of my life.

26

SO I THINK IT'S time to bring this book to a close. It's early 1966 in the narrative, and I'm almost twenty-eight years old, with a wife and two daughters and enough published books and stories to fill a shelf. I've written a novel I can regard as the end of my apprenticeship, and not coincidentally I've wrapped up a successful experiment with corporate life and will return to freelance writing in and around New York City.

A Writer Prepares. Indeed—and I've spewed out an abundance of words chronicling that preparation, and I can't be alone in thinking what I've written is more than enough.

And yet there's a sense in which my apprenticeship has never ended, for how could it? *A Trawl Among the Shelves*, Terry Zobeck's comprehensive bibliography of my work, begins with a section of books published as individual volumes. *The Thief Who Couldn't Sleep* is A71; the most recent, *Dead Girl Blues*, is A209. Once Tanner helped me find my voice, I've apparently found it impossible to shut up.

That's 128 books since the putative end of my apprenticeship, and not a few of them were written with no higher goal than to keep the pot boiling. But the humblest of them were the work of a writer who was at least maturing if not altogether mature. One could question the worth of John Warren Wells's books, but they were a healthy cut above those of Benjamin Morse, MD. Jill Emerson's three paperback originals for Berkley—*Thirty, Threesome*, and *A Madwoman's Diary*—were as erotically purposed as any of the Lord/Shaw titles, but they played the game at a much higher level.

AND HERE I AM, so many years later, sitting in front of a computer and trying to come up with the requisite words. I don't know how much time I have left, but I have that in common with the rest of the human race. I'm grateful for the time I've had, and that I've been privileged to spend it making things out of words.

I think I've written my last work of fiction, but I would have told you as much several books ago. Like Rick Blaine, who came to Casablanca for the waters, I was misinformed.

A few years ago my friend Oto Penzler, a bookseller and independent publisher, told me a story. Some years earlier he'd had dinner with Leon Uris, whose bestselling novels *Battle Cry* and *Exodus* he'd much admired. Uris confided that he'd recently completed a new novel and hadn't found a publisher for it. His regular house had passed on it, and no one else who'd seen it had leapt at the opportunity to take it on. Otto expressed interest and Uris promised to send it over.

Otto was elated—until he read the book. He found a way to return the manuscript diplomatically, and walked away shaking his head.

I found the story chilling. I felt for Otto and the awkwardness of the position in which he'd found himself, and I also felt for Leon Uris, whose work I too had enjoyed and admired. I envisioned myself in his position, an old man who'd rounded out a distinguished career by writing a genuinely bad book.

It's way too easy to stay too long at the fair.

*   *   *

URIS DID EVENTUALLY find someone to publish his book, and while it wasn't well received, I don't suppose it did his reputation any great harm.

And I don't worry too much about my own reputation; if I did, I'd probably retire many of those early pseudonymous works I've been so pleased to republish. Those chips can fall where they may.

None of the work's going to last very long, anyway. A writer sounds even sillier than a politician when he goes on and on about his legacy. Some of the books will be around longer than I, but only by a few years, and why should that matter to me? If there is indeed life after life, I doubt I'll squander much of it caring whether somebody's having a good time reading *Ronald Rabbit is a Dirty Old Man.*

A Last Word

January 24, 2021
New York City

AND THAT'S THAT.

In the past month, I've come to the conclusion that I'll be happiest self-publishing this memoir. I've explored some other possibilities and am grateful to several publishers who've expressed varying degrees of interest. But publishing *A Writer Prepares* myself has two undeniable advantages.

The first is that the text won't be filtered by any editorial sensibilities other than my own. This, I hasten to admit, is not always a Good Thing. A more objective eye than the author's can lead to a considerably improved book.

And that might well be the case here. But this is such a thoroughly personal book that I'd really prefer to dispense its content directly from my lips to your ears. Nor do I have either the energy or the patience for the to-and-fro process of working with an editor, toward what always is but rarely appears to be a common goal.

Or the time.

And time, let me say, is the second advantage of self-publication. It's my intention to bring out this volume just five months from now as I write these lines. June 24, 2021, will be my 83rd birthday, and it will also be publication day for *A Writer Prepares*, even as that date in 2020 was pub day for my novel, *Dead Girl Blues*.

I like the synchronicity. Even more, I like the fact that the book will be published sooner rather than later—indeed, a good deal sooner rather than a whole lot later.

That's always been my inclination.

Don Westlake told me of an acquaintance with an unqualified passion for fast driving; the fellow's ideal, Don said, would be to have a car that would get from Point A to Point B in zero seconds. (In various guises, the chap found his way into Don's fiction, not least of all in the person of Stan Murch, designated driver for the Dortmunder Gang. Of course there was also a lot of Don himself in Murch, as far as that goes, but never mind.)

I've been that way about publication. When I finish a book, I want things to happen ASAP. Once I'd skipped two spaces and typed "THE END" I wanted nothing so much as to get up from my desk, go outside, walk around the corner, and see that very book on a bookstore shelf.

Point A to Point B.

Zero seconds.

OVER THE YEARS, of course, I've learned patience. Time takes time.

Even as it flies.

And, as it does that, it teaches impatience.

Sometimes by example. It was around the start of 2020 that I decided to return to work on this book, and since that date I've marked the passing of the following writer friends and acquaintances:

Mary Higgins Clark.

Clive Cussler.

Jerrold Mundis.

Patrick Trese.

Patricia Bosworth.

Bruce Jay Friedman.

Pete Hamill.

Parnell Hall.

John Lutz.

And Walter Bernstein. I didn't know him well, but relished his company the handful of times our paths crossed. I really thought Walter might live forever, but nobody lives forever, and just yesterday, at the age of 101, he too joined the majority.

EVERYBODY DIES.

That's the title of the fourteenth Matthew Scudder novel, and when it came out I was sometimes asked if it was intended to be philosophical or descriptive. Why, I wondered, couldn't it be both?

And it was for the epigraph of *A Long Line of Dead Men* that I quoted a few quatrains of William Dunbar's "Lament for the Makers," a posthumous roll call of Scottish poets, each stanza ending with *Timor mortis conturbat me.*

"Fear of death disturbs me."

That's Google Translate's helpful suggestion. But an online Latin-English dictionary declines to supply *to disturb*, offering instead "to confuse, to disquiet, to confound, to derange, to dismay, to upset, to mix up."

Indeed. All those things.

A WEEK AGO, Lynne and I went over to a public high school on Stanton Street and received our first doses of Moderna's vaccine. For close to a year I've been as socially distanced as Simeon Stylites, and all that time I've taken it for granted that somewhere along the way I'll come down with the virus. And, with a medical history that includes atrial fibrillation and bypass surgery, I could realistically expect to die of it.

Well, maybe not. Perhaps the city will replenish its now-exhausted supply of vaccine, and perhaps we'll get our second round of shots, and perhaps they'll truly keep the virus at bay.

Perhaps the time remaining to me might be measured not in weeks or months but in actual years.

I certainly hope that's the case. When I had my bypass just three years ago, it was almost exhilarating to realize just how much I wanted to live, not so much for fear of the darkness as out of a desire to remain a little longer in the light.

I had things I wanted to do—and, indeed, I've had the luck to do some of them. Even more than that, I wanted to know what would happen next.

See, I've *always* wanted to know what happens next.

MEANWHILE, I'LL HURRY this book into print. On my birthday, as I've proposed—and by that time I'll have witnessed the publication of *Afterthoughts: Version 2.0,* a consideration of some of my backlist titles. And *Collectibles,* my latest effort to demonstrate that anthologism is the last refuge of the used-up writer.

And, God help me, there a story I sort of want to write, probably a novella. I'm not desperate to write it, and I certainly don't feel that it needs to be written, but each time I push the idea aside it manages to come back. Even if I begin writing it, I may very well lose interest along the way, or find it impossible to summon up the energy to see it through.

Before it's written, I may have added my own name to that list.

A Writer Prepares.

LAWRENCE BLOCK is a Mystery Writers of America Grand Master. His work over the past half century has earned him multiple Edgar Allan Poe and Shamus awards, the U.K. Diamond Dagger for lifetime achievement, and recognition in Germany, France, Taiwan, and Japan. His latest novel is *Dead Girl Blues*; other recent fiction includes *A Time to Scatter Stones, Keller's Fedora*, and *The Burglar in Short Order*. In addition to novels and short fiction, he has written episodic television (*Tilt!*) and the Wong Kar-wai film, *My Blueberry Nights*.

Block contributed a fiction column in Writer's Digest for fourteen years, and has published several books for writers, including the classic *Telling Lies for Fun & Profit* and the updated and expanded *Writing the Novel from Plot to Print to Pixel*. His nonfiction has been collected in *The Crime of Our Lives* (about mystery fiction) and *Hunting Buffalo with Bent Nails* (about everything else). Most recently, his collection of columns about stamp collecting, *Generally Speaking*, has found a substantial audience throughout and far beyond the philatelic community.

Lawrence Block has lately found a new career as an anthologist (*At Home in the Dark*; *From Sea to Stormy Sea*) and served as writer-in-residence at South Carolina's Newberry College. He is a modest and humble fellow, although you would never guess as much from this biographical note.

Email: lawbloc@gmail.com
Twitter: @LawrenceBlock
Facebook: lawrence.block
Website: lawrenceblock.com

MY NEWSLETTER: I get out an email newsletter at unpredictable intervals, but rarely more often than every other week. I'll be happy to add you to the distribution list. A blank email to lawbloc@gmail. com with "newsletter" in the subject line will get you on the list, and a click of the "Unsubscribe" link will get you off it, should you ultimately decide you're happier without it.